"McCurry breaks new ground by ap'   nt
therapy to the treatment of anxiety di   is
based on solid principles and offers unc   s
to help parents treat this common but (

—James T. Grimm, MD,   , child psychiatrist
    in Eugene, OR

"This book is a tremendous contribution to parents who want to help their children with the spectrum of anxieties that can hinder optimal development. McCurry provides a whole range of techniques that parents can use to help their children accept and handle anxious feelings that can cripple them in their daily lives. He is a stellar guide to this new and exciting approach. Without a doubt, this book will be valuable to parents and therapists alike who want to help build children's social and emotional competence through effective management of anxiety."

—Laura Kastner, Ph.D., clinical associate professor of
    psychiatry and behavioral sciences at the University
    of Washington

"*Parenting Your Anxious Child with Mindfulness and Acceptance* is a funny, warm, and wise resource for parents. This book is full of very useful specific suggestions, ideas, and how-tos for parenting an anxious child. What makes it special is Christopher McCurry's very compassionate guidance through the process of dealing with all the intense emotions and questions that parents have as they work to best help their anxious children. This book will be incredibly helpful to many kids and families."

—Stacy Shaw Welch, Ph.D., director of the Anxiety and
    Stress Reduction Center in Seattle, WA

"For years I've looked in vain for books on acceptance-based strategies for anxious children and their parents. McCurry's book was well worth the wait. His crystal clear writing, sprinkled with humor and touching self-disclosure, makes techniques such as validation and mindfulness immediately understandable and accessible. As a scientist-practitioner, I'm impressed with McCurry's thoughtful consideration of current developmental research in the formulation of his clinical model and recommendations. The book contains many useful and concrete strategies for helping parents to regulate their own thoughts and feelings in order to help their child stand up to anxiety."

—Matthew L. Speltz, Ph.D., professor of psychiatry and behavioral sciences at the University of Washington School of Medicine and chief of outpatient psychiatry services at Children's Hospital and Regional Medical Center in Seattle, WA

"This book is an awesome and timely parent resource for those seeking to help their anxious child be positive, strong, and happy in this age of economic and social uncertainty. McCurry's extensive professional background clearly shines through as he helps parents understand and intervene when their anxious child is in need."

—Steve Curtis, Ph.D., NCSP, child clinical psychologist, nationally certified school psychologist, and author of *Understanding Your Child's Puzzling Behavior*

Parenting Your Anxious Child with Mindfulness and Acceptance

a powerful new approach to overcoming fear, panic, and worry using acceptance and commitment therapy

Christopher McCurry, Ph.D.

New Harbinger Publications, Inc.

Publisher's Note

This publication is designed to provide accurate and authoritative information in regard to the subject matter covered. It is sold with the understanding that the publisher is not engaged in rendering psychological, financial, legal, or other professional services. If expert assistance or counseling is needed, the services of a competent professional should be sought.

Distributed in Canada by Raincoast Books

Copyright © 2009 by Christopher McCurry
New Harbinger Publications, Inc.
5674 Shattuck Avenue
Oakland, CA 94609
www.newharbinger.com

All Rights Reserved
Printed in the United States of America
Acquired by Tesilya Hanauer; Cover design by Amy Shoup;
Edited by Jean Blomquist

Library of Congress Cataloging-in-Publication Data

McCurry, Christopher.
 Parenting your anxious child with mindfulness and acceptance : a powerful new approach to overcoming fear, panic, and worry using acceptance and commitment therapy / Christopher McCurry.
    p. cm.
Includes bibliographical references.
ISBN-13: 978-1-57224-579-2 (pbk. : alk. paper)
ISBN-10: 1-57224-579-4 (pbk. : alk. paper)
1. Parenting. 2. Acceptance and commitment therapy. I. Title.
HQ755.8.M423 2009
649'.154--dc22

                                        2008052208

15 14 13

10 9 8 7 6 5 4 3

To my parents, Joan and James E. McCurry

The road that stretches before us is a challenge to the heart long before it tests the strength of our legs. Our destiny is to run to the edge of the world and beyond, off into the darkness: sure, for all our blindness; secure, for all our helplessness; strong, for all our weakness; gaily in love, for all the pressure on our hearts.

—Thomas Aquinas
Summa Theologica

Contents

Dear reader,

Welcome to New Harbinger Publications. New Harbinger is dedicated to publishing books based on acceptance and commitment therapy (ACT, said as one word) and its application to specific areas of mental health. New Harbinger has a long-standing reputation as a publisher of quality, well-researched books for general and professional audiences.

All parents wish their children to be free from suffering, and yet they must face the inevitable truth that their best efforts cannot entirely protect their children from various forms of suffering. Anxiety and fear are two of those unwelcome emotional pains of life that cannot be avoided. When our children suffer, we as parents also suffer. It is natural for parents to react in some way to alleviate their child's anxious suffering—and their own, too. The tricky part is knowing how to be responsive in a way that is helpful for your child, you as a parent, and your family. This book, *Parenting Your Anxious Child with Acceptance and Commitment: How Responsive Parenting Can Help You and Your Child Feel Better*, will show you how to do just that using ACT.

The author of this book is a father with extensive professional experience working with anxious children and their parents using ACT. You will find that he has packed this book with a wealth of practical techniques and know-how that will help empower you and your anxious child to be more responsive and less reactive when anxiety flares up. And, a good deal of what you'll find in this book will be new to you. Doing something new is exactly what is called for when doing more of the same is not working. Learning new and more skillful ways of responding to your anxious child will help defuse anxiety and make room for other more vital and meaningful possibilities.

Here, it is important to be mindful that anxiety is not a choice. Nobody asks for anxiety, and most people don't like it either. The choice is not about whether to have anxiety and fear. The choice is whether to live a meaningful life with the joys, pains, and sorrows that will show up along the way. It is here, in the realm of choices and actions, that we have lots of control even when feeling anxious or afraid. This book builds on this insight. It will show you how to respond to your child's anxiety in a way that will weaken its power to keep your child and you stuck. The book itself is filled with a rich set of ideas and practical strategies and exercises for you and for your child, too. We think you'll find that the book will enrich your life as a parent and help move you and your child forward in ways that uphold your best intentions.

As part of New Harbinger's commitment to publishing books based on sound, scientific, clinical research, Steven C. Hayes, Ph.D., Georg Eifert, Ph.D., and I oversee all prospective books for the *Acceptance and Commitment Therapy Series*. As ACT series editors, we review all ACT books published by New Harbinger, comment on proposals and offer guidance as needed, and use a gentle hand in making suggestions regarding the content, depth, and scope of each book.

Books in the *Acceptance and Commitment Therapy Series*:

- Have an adequate database, appropriate to the strength of the claims being made.

- Are theoretically coherent. They will fit with the ACT model and underlying behavioral principles as they have evolved at the time of writing.

- Orient the reader toward unresolved empirical issues.

- Do not overlap needlessly with existing volumes.

- Avoid jargon and unnecessary entanglement with proprietary methods, leaving ACT work open and available.

- Keep the focus always on what is good for the reader.

- Support the further development of the field.

- Provide information in a way that is of practical use to readers.

These guidelines reflect the values of the broader ACT community. You'll see all of them brought to life in this book. They are meant to ensure that professionals and the general public get information that can truly be helpful, and that can further our ability to alleviate human suffering by inviting creative practitioners into the process of developing, applying, and refining this approach to meet the needs of the human condition. Consider this book such an invitation.

Sincerely,

John Forsyth, Ph.D.

Foreword

A few days ago I was drinking my morning coffee, idly reading the morning paper while the morning news played in the background. "What's that?" asked Stevie, my three-year-old. I looked up at the fifty-inch TV screen a few yards away. It showed scenes from the latest bombings in the Middle East. I saw (and with some sense of horror I saw that Stevie saw) a man, terribly wounded, being hauled quickly away from a burning building. I paused, trying to find words. "They are fighting" I said. "It's very sad. Been going on a long time." Stevie bowed his head for a moment as if in thought. Without another word he slowly squatted down and began to play with his Lightning McQueen car. In the background, the news had shifted from the Middle East to the latest economic news. It was grim.

The human mind did not evolve for the present day. Children have always been exposed to stories, both painful and joyful, and they have always experienced highs and terrible lows at least occasionally, but now our children are exposed to a daily diet of images and words about the most positive and most negative things the world has to offer. Children born today will be exposed to many million more words and images than you and I were as we grew up. Modern technology has unleashed a cacophony of symbols. Inside them is everything imaginable, but very often what is shown is what hurts. As they say in the media, "If it bleeds, it leads."

This massive exposure to words and images is changing the world of our children. It is not all negative. Despite the weaknesses of the educational system, worldwide the intellectual skills of children are increasing as a result. IQ tests have to have new norms every several years so that the average IQ scores do not rise above those of the bright children of yesteryear. The sense of wonder we have as parents is known to be partly correct. Our children *are* smarter in many ways; they *do* know so much more and think about so many more things than we did; and they *do* grow up so much faster. But they also face emotional challenges we never faced, and the challenges come earlier. That combination of busy, untrained minds and fearsome worries and concerns is difficult. Humans beings can fear not only the dangers we directly experience but also the dangers we imagine. We can want not only what is directly in front of us but also what we are told about. It is no wonder that childhood struggles are not decreasing. Modern children have a hard row to hoe.

Children need help to manage this. It is wonderful that they understand more about the world. But they also need to understand more about themselves. We need to create modern minds for the modern world.

That, in many ways, is a parent's ultimate task. And that, I believe, is what this wonderful and wise book is about.

Emotions evolved to elicit action—now. Anger prepares animals to fight; fear prepares them to flee; hunger prepares them to seek food. Composed of bodily changes and motivations to act, such emotions demand immediate action.

But when emotions become entangled in our more recently evolved capacity for symbolic, predictive, evaluative thought—especially when that capacity is in overdrive due to the age of chatter in which we live—we often experience emotions that do *not* require immediate action. In a simpler world, we could muddle through the difficulties this creates. But modern technology has made that strategy untenable. What are children to do with the fear they feel about events taking place elsewhere on the planet? What are they to do with the urges and wants they feel from commercials for sugar-loaded food or brand new toys? What is little Stevie to do with the emotions evoked by a bloodied body and by bread lines?

We need to teach our children more about how to deal with their own thoughts and feelings in a way that is healthy. In the modern world, emotional intelligence is just as important as the more traditional kind of intelligence. To do that we need to be wiser ourselves. Suppressive, avoidant, and mindless approaches to the experiences within simply will not cut it anymore. We can hardly ask our children to do what we ourselves cannot do.

This book argues that we, parents and children alike, need to learn to accept our feelings, without being driven by them and without rushing to remove ones we do not like. Trying to get rid of feelings only drives them underground while simultaneously giving them more capacity to control behavior without our awareness.

Acceptance of emotion requires another step, however. We also need to learn to watch our thoughts, without reflexively adopting the worldview dictated by them. Thoughts are easily programmed, and they are nothing to be right about—or wrong about. They are just thoughts. Some of those thoughts will not be attractive because they are constantly being programmed by sources we do not control. We will hear in our own minds the echoes of the fear, judgment, bias, or prejudice to which we are exposed nearly every day. The point is not to feel bad about the existence of such thoughts in our heads, nor to feel self-righteous about the thoughts we have that we agree with. The point is to be more conscious, open, and flexible in how we translate thoughts into action. Knowing how to do that requires a final step.

While being aware of our feelings and thoughts, we must make mindful choices about what to actually do, based on chosen values. Our emotions are a legacy of our entire development as a species, and our thoughts are an echo of our history. Fear, anger, and desire are part of the human condition. They can sensitize us to what is going on in the moment—but we have to learn how to have them without being had by them.

The emotional imperative of "now" is just too automatic and mindless to be trusted in the modern world. Modern minds need to learn to be guided by values and choices, not just by emotional and cognitive programming. Human beings are the only animals who can interpose mindful awareness and values-based choice between urges and actions. Now, more than ever, that is what we need, as parents. And now, more than ever, that is what our children need to learn from us. This book will walk you through the step-by-step process of doing exactly that.

I've known and respected Chris McCurry for more than twenty years. He's a good psychologist, a good man, and a good father. And he's written the kind of book I wish I had read when I was first a parent, nearly forty years ago. Yes, this book is about parenting your anxious child. But more than that, it is about how parents can create modern minds for a modern world, so that their children will grow and prosper. If you are a parent, you know there is nothing more precious than that.

Steven C. Hayes, Ph.D.
University of Nevada

Acknowledgments

There are many people whose ideas have informed this work and whose kind support I deeply appreciate. First I wish to acknowledge and thank my professors and colleagues from those many years in graduate school: Dorothy Piontkowski, Harmon Van Peeke, Shantilal Shaw, Ron Johnson, Al Salami, Kathy Dark, Steve Hayes, Steve Graybar, Kelly Wilson, Linda Hayes, Ted Young, Barbara Kohlenberg, Duane Varble, Gerald Patterson, Bob Peterson, Leigh Silverton, Don Jackson, and Marcia Bennett.

I want to thank my colleagues and supervisors at the University of Washington in Seattle for their role in my training and the beginning of my career, especially Matt Speltz, Jack McClellan, Eric Trupin, Elizabeth McCauley, Nancy Robinson, Alan Unis, Laura Kastner, and Andy Benjamin. And more recently I have been blessed with great mentors, friends, and colleagues who continue to teach, encourage, and inspire me: Steve Engelberg, Steve and Jane Curtis, Bill O'Hanlon, Rob Janes, Annie Stocker, and all the folks at Associates in Behavior and Child Development, Inc.

I want to gratefully acknowledge Stacy Shaw Welch and Maureen Maddox for their helpful comments on the manuscript. I also want to acknowledge the contribution of individuals I have not had the privilege of meeting but whose work has inspired me and informed this book: Laurie Greco, Georg Eifert, John Forsyth, Jean Dumas, and Robert Wahler.

To my editors—Tesilya Hanauer, Jess Beebe, John Forsyth, Jean M. Blomquist—and everyone at New Harbinger: I can't thank you enough for your faith, kindness, patience, and support.

Finally, to my family: I want to gratefully acknowledge their unfailing love and support through the years. To my wife, Sue, and my son, Ian: you are the heart of my life. Thank you for being there.

The road that stretches before us is a challenge to the heart long before it tests the strength of our legs. Our destiny is to run to the edge of the world and beyond, off into the darkness: sure, for all our blindness; secure, for all our helplessness; strong, for all our weakness; gaily in love, for all the pressure on our hearts.

Thomas Aquinas
Summa Theologica

Introduction

One evening, within days of my son coming home from the hospital as a newborn, I had my first visceral experience of the anxiety parenting had in store for me. I was in our basement watching the evening news. I don't remember the specifics of the story that set me off, but it was one of those "if it bleeds, it leads" news stories about harm coming to some child, a kidnapping or a hit-and-run accident most likely.

Now generally I'm not overwhelmed by emotion, and I tend to take bad news involving strangers with a certain detachment. But this time, perhaps because I was somewhat sleep deprived and fresh from the whole childbirth-miracle experience, it hit me hard. Into my mind flooded every image of every awful thing that could happen over the next twenty years to the tiny, precious, days-old baby upstairs. I lost it. Part of me felt a little alarmed by my reaction, but at the same time I was aware that I couldn't control it in the least.

I came upstairs in a state of semihysteria, weeping and blubbering. My mother was still with us, having come up to Seattle for the birth of her newest grandson. She was sitting on the couch in the living room, reading. She looked up when I came into the room, but said nothing as I sat down next to her and told her, between sobs, what I had plunged into. She didn't say anything for several minutes, just letting me talk. Then my mother quietly began to tell me about what it was like when my oldest sister, her firstborn, came into this world.

It was in the years just after the Second World War. Europe was in ruins. Millions of people were homeless or refugees. Many tens of thousands of children were orphaned and displaced from communities and families. All of this was presented to the American public through newspaper and magazine articles, radio programs, and newsreel footage. Pictures of huddled children in rags—wandering through bombed-out cities, lost and alone in the world—dominated our national psyche. This country, after all, had been spared these horrors.

My mother said those images had affected her deeply. As a new mother she had ached for the parents who were separated from their children or who had died not knowing what would become of them. To think that her little girl might be one of those lost and frightened children, that she might not be there for her child, had seemed unbearable.

That was the state of the world when my mother became a parent, filled with terror and anguish. But she did learn to bear that anxiety, she said, even through later fears of nuclear war with the Soviet Union or the first time one of her children went unescorted to play at a friend's house.

As it was for my mother, being a parent is the most wonderful and terrifying thing I will ever do. It has opened me up to a range and depth of emotional experience I wouldn't have thought possible. Parenting has brought out the best in me, and the worst in me. The anxiety I felt that night when my son was a few days old has never really left. But my mother's story, and even more so her calm and accepting stance toward my state, got me through that evening and through many difficult times since.

Anxiety is part of life. It is a part of your child's life as your child explores a world that is fraught with challenges, uncertainty, and real danger. It is part of your life as a parent as you guide your child on that journey of discovery with your heart in your throat. As a parent, I am on that same journey with you every day. This book is for us.

THE PROBLEM: ANXIETY IS CONTAGIOUS

Between four and fourteen million children in the United States could be, and perhaps are, diagnosed with an anxiety disorder. Many more experience transient fears or worries at some time (Connolly & Bernstein, 2007; U.S. Census Bureau, 2000). Anxiety can be provoked by countless situations or by seemingly nothing at all. Anxiety shows up in a host of forms: physical reactions such as nausea, trembling, and shortness of breath; worries and other troublesome thoughts; and behaviors—some that may be clearly related to anxiety or fear (such as clinging) and others that may be confusing or hard to connect to anxiety (such as anger outbursts or poor attention in school).

In this book, I will describe how *anxiety behavior*—the many outward manifestations of anxiety, such as crying, clinging, or even aggression—serves two purposes. First, it is your child's attempt to communicate these upsetting thoughts and feelings to you. Your child needs to communicate this distress to you so that, second, you will help solve this problem. From the standpoint of the upset child, solving the anxiety problem invariably means getting rid of the fear or anxiety. Somehow. Now.

This process is simple and straightforward, for example, in the case of a spider: "Mom, there's a spider on my bed!" You go into your child's bedroom, or you send in your spouse, and you remove the spider. The message your child conveyed was explicit and clear (and also implicit in some ways): "There's a spider on my bed, I'm scared [or grossed out], and I want you to get rid of it now!" The solution to the problem is straightforward: you remove the spider. The upset fades quickly, and you and your child return to what you were each doing.

Your child's fear, anxiety, and subsequent reactions to threat, or the appearance of threat, come from necessary and biologically based security systems deep within the brain. These systems came about (designed or evolved, as you prefer) to ensure your child's safety by motivating him or her to take action: "Mom!"

But the above situation does not describe an anxiety disorder. By definition, as we will see, a true *anxiety disorder* occurs when the behavior of the child (or adult), when anxious, is over-the-top in some way, and this behavior interferes with the child's or adult's development or day-to-day functioning. For example, your child has a panic attack (shaking, gasping for breath, dizzy, and so on) at the sight of the spider and refuses to go into the bedroom until you have inspected it carefully to make sure there are no spiders in there. Your child cries and pleads with you to wash the sheets that the spider has contaminated. These behaviors would suggest an anxiety disorder, and you would be motivated to address these feelings, thoughts, and behaviors.

But still, the situation with the spider and all the emotions and behaviors associated with it are fairly straightforward. Consider this situation: It's Monday morning and everyone is getting ready to leave the house for school and work. Your middle child, a son, slowly paces the floor near you, moaning and holding his stomach. What's the message? What are you expected to do? Given your history with Monday mornings and your familiarity with your middle child, the message may be readily apparent to you and you may know very well what this child wants you to do. He's feeling nervous and worried about school (there's a test today), and he's hoping you'll allow him to stay home because of his stomachache. It's your move.

Let me add one more complicating factor to the mix—that anxiety is contagious—and get to the heart of what this book is about. If you strike a tuning fork and place it close to a second but silent tuning fork, the second tuning fork will begin to vibrate and sing. This is called a *sympathetic vibration*. When your child feels frightened or is consumed with worry, when your child's behavior churns toward avoiding what he or she needs to do or toward attempts at getting you to rescue him or her, you will have your own characteristic reactions in the form of feelings, thoughts, and behaviors. Depending on the situation and your mood, you may react with calm, supportive parental behaviors that smoothly guide your child to a successful resolution of the problem. But if you're reading this book (and you are), then often these episodes are likely marked by your own "sympathetic anxiety," or perhaps frustration, discouragement, worry, impatience, memories from your own childhood, or any number of thoughts and feelings your child's anxiety and behavior typically provoke in you. Perhaps in those moments your behavior toward your child is less than helpful.

The Anxiety Dance

As a parent myself, I believe that, second only to your child not being able to breathe, seeing your child in an anxious state evokes the most distressing feelings you can experience. Your own reactions to the child's upset—your thoughts, feelings, and actions—are themselves a product of necessary and biologically based security systems deep within your brain. Your security system and the flood of emotions and thoughts it produces are there to ensure your child's safety by motivating you to act.

Of course, which actions you take in the midst of anxiety-provoking situations matters. This is an obvious fact to any parent, but it is a fact that is curiously absent from most definitions of child anxiety and sadly lacking in our standard treatment models.

If things are not going well when your child feels afraid or anxious, it seems obvious that these unpleasant thoughts and feelings are the culprit. You may think, "If my child weren't so upset, I wouldn't be so upset, and we'd both be more functional, not to mention happier." So, from the standpoint of the upset parent, solving the anxiety problem invariably means getting rid of the fear, anxiety, frustration, or discouragement somehow—your child's first so that you can be rid of yours.

If this is the solution to anxiety—to avoid it or get rid of it, or perhaps grit your teeth and get through it—then what often happens next is something I call the "anxiety dance": you and your child engage in a series of moves or steps that lead to a conclusion. Sometimes that conclusion is positive and growth enhancing, as when the child feels supported, is taught and encouraged to use appropriate coping strategies, and has an experience that gives the child new insight into himself or herself and confidence to face similar situations in the future. Unfortunately, the anxiety dance often leads instead to further upset for everyone and a lack of growth toward, or even regression from, the effective communication, self-regulation, and problem-solving skills you want for your child.

This book is about changing the dance you and your child are stuck in. It's likely that you and your child perform this dance with little awareness of how it works or even that you are doing it. As such, the dance is very difficult to change. But you both learned to do this dance together. Together you will learn a new dance, one that is more effective because it is a *response* rather than a *reaction* to the upset both you and your child experience.

THE PROMISE: SUPPLE AND RESPONSIVE PARENTING

Successfully treating an anxiety disorder means more than eliminating or even reducing the anxiety symptoms. A successful approach requires addressing both the inner world of your child's thoughts and feelings and the outer world of your child's anxious behaviors—as well as how these inner and outer worlds invite you to engage, for better or for worse, in the anxiety dance. This book will help you understand the nature of that dance: why you and your child must do it together, and how you can create a new dance to effectively solve problems and promote your child's growth when anxiety shows up.

The approach presented here is directed toward encouraging effective communication, cooperation, competence, and autonomy. In the long run, your child's increased sense of competence, and the increased security this brings, will reduce the anxiety and fear provoked by common situations. But more importantly, since anxiety is a fact of life, your child will learn to deal more effectively with those situations that invite feelings of fear and anxiety. Your child will learn to better communicate his or her feelings and needs to you and to ask for your help in less provocative ways. You will be less reactive and more responsive to these requests for help. Your child will be better able to utilize your help. You will feel more relaxed and effective as a parent. Your child will feel an increased sense of security, and so on. A new dance.

THE PROGRAM: ACCEPTANCE AND COMMITMENT

In the pages that follow, I describe a new approach to understanding and treating anxiety in children. It emphasizes the distinction between *anxiety*, the varied sets of thoughts and feelings related to real or imagined threats, and *anxious behaviors*, the many and varied outward actions your child engages in when anxious. Anxiety itself, the thoughts and feelings, is very difficult to change directly. Attempts at getting rid of anxious thoughts and feelings can, in fact, increase the frequency or strength of those physical and mental events.

The program I put forward does not seek to reduce or change your child's anxiety, at least not directly. Instead the program is centered on strategies for changing the anxious behaviors and replacing them with more effective, age-appropriate behaviors when the child is anxious. But to do this you first must understand why your child is producing anxious behaviors when he or she is anxious. We must ask, what are these anxious behaviors trying to accomplish?

This book will not teach you how to fill out fear thermometers or do exposure exercises or guide your anxious child to a happy place. I will not be talking about point charts or reward systems. The intention behind this book is not to turn you into your child's therapist or life coach. My intention is to show you how to be a responsive parent when your child is feeling fearful or anxious and needs your understanding and help. Together we will examine anxiety and fear from the standpoint of traditional diagnosis and from the standpoint of common factors and processes involved in anxiety disorders and in child behavior generally.

What I Am About

Let me take a moment to tell you about myself and the approach to understanding and treating anxiety found in this book. I am a clinical child psychologist in private practice in Seattle, Washington. I am the father of a now fourteen-year-old young man. My wife is also a psychologist, working on problems of aging. Over the past twenty-plus years, I have worked in a variety of treatment settings, from high-intensity residential centers and medical facilities to outpatient clinics. I have worked with a wide range of childhood psychological conditions and with parents from all walks of life. I have seen firsthand how common childhood anxiety is, how diverse its manifestations are, and how large an impact it can have on a child and a family.

After earning a master's degree in developmental psychology, I studied for my Ph.D. at the University of Nevada, Reno. The approach taken in this book is from the work of one of my teachers there, Steven C. Hayes. Over the last thirty years, Dr. Hayes has been developing a way of thinking about human suffering and alleviating that suffering that is both unique and powerfully effective. His approach, called acceptance and commitment therapy (shortened to ACT, and pronounced as the word "act" instead of "a-c-t"), is one of a number of new psychotherapies that take a somewhat different approach to understanding and treating the problems of living.

What makes ACT different is not so much the techniques: we still talk about troublesome thoughts and feelings, suggest metaphors and coping exercises, and set goals for treatment. What sets ACT and these new therapies apart, and in my experience makes them so effective, is how problems of living (such as anxiety) are understood and how the focus of therapy—acceptance and commitment—is informed by this understanding.

This therapy approach emphasizes an "acceptance" of one's problems and conditions, though not from the standpoint of resignation or having to like being anxious. The kind of acceptance I will talk about recognizes the reality of a situation, such as being anxious at that moment, and looks it squarely in the eye. It's only from really acknowledging and understanding your situation, or your child's, that truly helpful action can be taken.

That brings us to the "commitment" portion of ACT. I will show you how to think about what you really want for your child and yourself in those anxiety-provoking situations—and it may not be to simply make everyone feel better. Without committed goals we would get nowhere in life. And without some acceptance of effort and even discomfort, we would never achieve those goals. Think of childbirth, as an example. Goals provide the context in which effort and struggle make sense and help us grow.

As such, acceptance and commitment therapy is called a *contextual* approach to the problems of living. This means that symptoms and other troublesome behaviors cannot be taken out of context. Running away can be adaptive in some contexts, such as playing a game of tag or when a tree is falling. In other contexts, such as a birthday party or a parking lot, running away would be unusual and problematic.

This book will look at your child's anxiety in multiple contexts. I will discuss everyday situations that provoke fear and anxiety, as well as the biological, developmental, and social contexts of anxiety. And the most important social context of your child's life, and likely of yours, is the parent-child relationship. To not examine anxiety in this vital context is to miss important ways of understanding your child's anxiety. To not include the parent-child relationship in treatment is to miss opportunities and powerful tools for making a difference.

Why I Wrote This Book

Quite simply, I wrote this book because I have always been interested in how parents and their children interact with each other; how, through mutual influence, both are changed forever. I have seen the power of these interactions for good and for ill. I wanted to harness that power for good and use it to help families such as yours gain a measure of peace and a sense of effectiveness in parenting, this incredible job we get up and do every day. Along with others working in this field, I wanted to extend the power of the acceptance and commitment therapy approach into the arena of family functioning. I hope this book will accomplish these tasks.

Chapter Summaries

Two quick notes about how this book is organized. First, dealing with gender pronouns is always tricky. I will be describing several fictional children as case examples in this book, two boys and two girls. When I mention them, I will of course refer to them as "he" and "she" respectively. In talking more generally about children, or referring to "your child," I will be alternating gender by chapter, male for the odd chapters and female for the even chapters.

Second, I will be addressing my thoughts to "you," the reader. If I sometimes lapse into "we," this likely reflects an idea or situation we are all struggling with.

The first chapters—chapters 1 through 3—describe anxiety in children and the particular forms it can take. I will quickly pass through the standard diagnostic model with its emphasis on individual anxiety subtypes that are based on symptom type: separation anxiety disorder, obsessive-compulsive disorder, and the like. I will focus instead on an analysis of the common features of anxiety disorders and how anxiety functions in the life of a child, specifically as it involves you, the parent.

In chapters 4 and 5, I will introduce acceptance and commitment therapy and describe how this treatment approach provides a new way of thinking about and addressing problems of living, especially anxiety. I will go on to show you how to connect with your values as a parent and to articulate the goals you have for yourself and for your child. It is the commitment to these goals that will make it possible for you and your child to break free of the oppressive anxiety behaviors—the anxiety dance—that you are now experiencing.

Chapters 6 through 9 provide strategies and exercises for changing how you and your child view and approach anxiety-provoking situations. I will offer coping and life skills necessary to face a world in which anxiety can be a daily occurrence. I will show you how, as a parent, you can manage anxiety-provoking situations to get to the best possible goal-oriented outcome, while also using the situation as an opportunity to increase your child's skill, competence, and autonomy. I will talk about the most difficult situations—for example, when your child is both anxious and angry or defiant.

So, in the coming pages, I hope to give you some new ways of thinking about your child's anxiety. I will describe a new approach you can take toward anxiety and other troublesome thoughts and feelings when they show up. This approach, balancing acceptance and commitment, will allow you to be responsive to your child's needs and at the same time see anxiety-provoking situations as opportunities to help your child understand himself or herself, to solve real problems and achieve important goals, and to live life to the fullest. Let's begin.

CHAPTER 1

Clinical Diagnosis and the Form of Childhood Anxiety

If you are reading this book, perhaps you are anticipating, or have been through, a diagnostic assessment with a school counselor, psychologist, family physician, or psychiatrist. In this chapter, I address the world of child mental health diagnosis in order to help you to understand the standard diagnostic process and to appreciate its usefulness as well as its limitations. I'll spend some time talking about what anxiety is and describe its common features. I will also describe some of the more common subtypes of anxiety that children can experience. Finally, the impact of anxiety on the life a child and his family will be considered.

WHAT IS ANXIETY?

Anxiety is a complex reaction to a perceived threat. Many authors make a distinction between anxiety and fear. *Fear* is the intense reaction we experience in the face of immediate danger. It is natural, automatic, and necessary for our survival.

Consider this scenario: While walking with your child down the sidewalk near your home, a large dog in a neighbor's yard suddenly hits the fence beside you and starts barking fiercely. Both you and your child startle and withdraw quickly. Your arm may instinctively reach out to enclose your child and pull him away from the danger. You feel the blood pounding in your ears. Your child starts to cry. That is fear. The anxiety comes later.

Fear in the Moment: Fight, Flight, or Freeze

You may recall the *fight-or-flight response* from high school biology. This is a cascade of lightening-fast, automatic physiological events preparing us to fight or to flee whatever is threatening us. I add "freeze" in describing this response, since often fear results in a paralysis of mind and body. However, in the coming pages I will simply refer to this phenomenon using the standard term "fight-or-flight response."

Deep within our brains are collections of neural circuits responsible for monitoring the body and the environment for signs of trouble. When danger is perceived, the alarm is sounded, and what happens next is automatic and almost impossible to stop once it gets going. First, adrenaline is dumped into the bloodstream from the adrenal glands sitting on top of the kidneys. Adrenaline is a multipurpose hormone that causes over twenty immediate biological responses. I'll list just a few examples:

- Pupils dilate to let in more light and enhance vision.

- Heart rate increases to move oxygen-carrying blood cells quickly through the body.

- Breathing quickens to provide oxygen and expel carbon dioxide.

- Capillaries near the surface of the skin close off to minimize bleeding in case of injury (which is why we become pale when we're frightened).

- Palms become a bit sweaty, which improves grip.

Unfortunately, these bodily reactions show up suddenly (an alarming event in itself) and tend to be pretty unpleasant. There are, of course, "adrenaline junkies": people who seem to thrive on arousing their sense of danger through activities such as bungee jumping or auto theft. To a large extent, it's all in how you think about it, as I will describe later.

By and large, at least for young children, this fight-or-flight physiological roller-coaster ride is quite disturbing. But it would be a poor defense mechanism if it didn't get our attention and make us leery of going through *that* again. Imagine a pleasant and softly chiming home smoke detector. It would not be helpful in an emergency. As an adult, you can appreciate the need for a robust and even alarming mechanism for calling your attention to danger. But your child just knows he is in acute distress and wants it stopped—now.

False Alarms and Persistent Alarms

If the fight-or-flight response simply got us activated to escape real dangers in life, the way a smoke detector might rouse you from your sleep when your house in on fire, there would be no problem. Unfortunately, as I will describe below, the mind's alarm system can naturally be set at extremely sensitive levels or be programmed through experience to respond when there is in fact no danger present: a false alarm.

Similarly there are times when the fight-or-flight system keeps putting out adrenaline and other signals long after the danger has passed. A friend recently told me about a malfunctioning smoke detector in his house. It kept beeping over and over, as if the batteries needed to be replaced. He replaced the batteries and the beeping continued, disturbing his infant son's nap. Finally, in frustration, my friend pulled the detector from the ceiling, opened a window, and tossed it outside, where it shattered into a dozen pieces on the driveway. Satisfied, he started to close the window but stopped when he heard a faint but clear *beep-beep-beep* coming from the pile of debris in his driveway. It was as if the poor smoke detector were saying, "You can throw me out the window, but I'm still going to do my job!" In the same way your child's mind may be saying, "I don't care about rational arguments, I'm going to keep this child safe at any cost." Unfortunately, as we will see, the cost of overreacting to or getting stuck in false alarms can be quite high.

The Stomach: Innocent Victim of an Overzealous Mind

One especially important fight-or-flight reaction is the shifting of blood from the digestive system to the large muscle groups. The muscles' enriched blood supply is supposed to help in the fighting or fleeing that our mind thinks is necessary. Unfortunately, the stomach's sudden loss of blood supply can create nausea—sometimes low-grade, sometimes acute. Stomachaches of various kinds are a very common complaint in anxious children and can be quite debilitating.

When children tell me about their anxious stomachaches, I give them a description of the fight-or-flight response. I will describe this to a child by saying that his brain is thinking, "We don't have time to be digesting food. We're under attack! Send the blood to the muscles!" Then I will ask that child, "How do you think your stomach feels about having its blood taken away and given to the muscles?" All agree that this makes the stomach very unhappy. To their delight, I play the part of a stomach, all upset and contorted and complaining bitterly about the unfairness of it all.

I tell children that this is why their stomachs feel so unhappy when they're scared or anxious, like on Monday mornings when they have to go to school. Their overly concerned brain has given away the stomach's blood to the muscles, and this is why they feel like throwing up. Maybe they do throw up. But it is not because they are sick or in any real danger. In later chapters, I will describe strategies for soothing the fight-or-flight response and, importantly, for moving on from it as quickly as possible without setting off a lot of unhelpful anxious behaviors that only serve to keep your child stuck in his misery.

Anxiety: What Might Happen

Anxiety is closely related to fear, but it tends to be associated less with actual events in the present moment than with the *anticipation* of danger or discomfort. To return to our scenario, after your encounter with the barking dog, you or your child may begin thinking about that dog at some later time—say, prior to your next walk. You may even experience a degree of the same physical arousal you felt in that frightening moment; your breathing and heart rate quicken, for example. In your mind, you may replay the event. Your thoughts may run to anger or sorrow or annoyance. Your child may cry and state he doesn't want to go near that yard again or perhaps not even go on another walk. That is anxiety.

Anxiety can be more complex than fear because it involves many reactions—some automatic, and some conscious and purposeful. Among these reactions is a myriad of private or internal experiences, such as thoughts, feelings, memories, and physical sensations. Just thinking about or remembering a frightening event can evoke some echo of the fight-or-flight response in the body, which elicits judgmental thoughts ("It's happening again—this is bad"), which invites more intense feelings, and on and on.

In addition to these privately experienced thoughts and feelings, there are many ways anxiety can be observed by others. There can be intense, agitated, and distressed behaviors such as crying, shaking, clinging, running away, and even anger and aggression. At other times, anxious behaviors may take the form of silence, withdrawal, or inhibition. Anxiety in children is particularly complex because these behaviors so often are attempts at obtaining an adult's protection. In the case of an immediate threat, your response as a parent will be clear: protect my child. At other times what is being asked of you when your child is anxious may be more ambiguous, both to your child and to you. This can lead to a great deal of confusion and frustration for both of you.

Finally, anxiety is quite contagious. When your child is anxious, you are more vulnerable to your own fear or worry, or perhaps any number of other distressing emotions, such as frustration or anger or sadness. This complicates an already challenging situation.

So I am suggesting that anxiety becomes a problem when your child's brain is reacting to the disturbing fight-or-flight response, or milder episodes of fear, with characteristic sets of thinking and "coping" behaviors that are not helpful in the situation. Fearful and anxious thinking, his and yours, tends to be awash in negative evaluations of the initial response and the event that triggered it: "I'm scared," "Being scared feels really bad," "That dog scared me," "Dogs are scary," "There might be a dog at the park, and I will be scared again if I go."

As I will describe in the pages to come, *anxious behavior* is characterized by avoidance or escape (for example, refusing to go to the park), by freezing up (not leaving your side once you are at the park), or by attempts to get help (begging you to take him home). You leave the house with one agenda ("We're all going to have a nice time at the park") and suddenly find yourself dealing with a new and unwanted agenda: trying to manage your child's upset and your own reactions to that—"For goodness' sake, there isn't a dog in sight and we've been cooped up in the house all day. Buck up! Let's just enjoy ourselves."

How Common Is Anxiety in Children?

Fear and anxiety are commonplace in the lives of children. Virtually every child will experience brief episodes of anxiety at times. The intensity and impact of this anxiety can range from mild to quite devastating. However, to actually "have" an anxiety disorder from the viewpoint of mental health professionals, certain diagnostic criteria must be met. I will describe these diagnostic criteria and the assessment process in a moment.

Many studies have looked at how common anxiety is in children—its prevalence, as we say. Looking at the research as a whole, we can see that somewhere between 6 and 20 percent of children experience anxiety to such a degree that we can say they have a diagnosable anxiety disorder (Connolly & Bernstein, 2007). The reason for the wide range in prevalence estimates has to do with how each study defines and measures anxiety, the ages of the children studied, and other variables. What is certain, though, is that anxiety is the single most commonly diagnosed mental health condition in children. Further, one in four individuals will experience significant anxiety at some time in their lives. Most of these people will report that their anxiety started sometime in childhood.

Does Anxiety Run in Families?

Anxiety does run in families, yet we also know that the majority of children who have anxious parents will not develop an anxiety disorder. However, children of anxious parents are still seven times more likely to develop anxiety than are children of nonanxious parents. Siblings of anxious children are more likely to be anxious themselves.

Specific phobias (for example, fear of heights) seem to have the weakest genetic connection whereas panic disorder seems to have the strongest. This makes sense if a simple phobia (described in detail below) has developed out of a frightening event (the dog incident) occurring in the child's life. On the other hand, panic disorder is largely neurophysiology run amok, and we inherit our nervous system, and its sensitivities, from our parents.

But the relationship between genetics and outcome is rarely straightforward. Let's take heart disease, for example. We know that heart disease runs in families. And yet we also know that many factors go into determining who will eventually develop heart disease.

If someone is born with a high risk for heart disease, there are now many avenues for preventing the development of actual pathology. In addition to the new medications (such as statins) that can lower cholesterol, we know that exercise, diet, and even mental health all play an important role in heart health. People with a long family history of heart disease can make any number of changes to their own life in order to reduce their risk, sometimes considerably.

In a similar way, a child may be born with a genetic predisposition to anxiety, but a hundred other factors will influence whether or not that child will eventually develop an anxiety disorder. I'll discuss some of the more important factors or influences in the chapters to come.

THE STANDARD DIAGNOSTIC MODEL

Most psychologists, psychiatrists, and other mental health professionals use a formal diagnostic system that has been around, with various modifications, since 1952. The "bible" for diagnosis is the *Diagnostic and Statistical Manual of Mental Disorders*, now in its fourth edition (*DSM–IV*, American Psychiatric Association 1994). This is called a formal system not because of its fancy attire, but because it is a system based on the "form" of the behaviors or symptoms in question.

In considering *form*, we ask, "What does the behavior look like?" It is much like botany and the system for identifying plants developed by Carl Linnaeus in the eighteenth century and botanists following after him. In this kind of system, we compare the features of an unfamiliar example (a plant in botany, a set of symptoms in psychology) with a known example. Oak tree leaves all tend to have scallops or lobes around their edges. If a particular leaf has five to nine deep lobes, it is likely a white oak (*Quercus alba*), whereas leaves with twenty-one to twenty-seven shallow lobes suggest the chestnut oak (*Quercus prinus*). If our leaf doesn't match any of the known examples, then we might be looking at a new species altogether.

So if your child experiences what the *DMS-IV* summarizes as "clinically significant anxiety provoked by exposure to certain types of social or performance situations, often leading to avoidance behavior," then he likely has social phobia. Full *DSM–IV* diagnostic criteria for each disorder can run to several paragraphs of symptom descriptions and conditions (such as the fact that the symptom is not caused by a drug reaction).

As such, psychological and psychiatric diagnosis is driven largely by the form or content of the *presenting symptoms* (experiences the child reports) and *signs* (things we observe the child doing). Typically we use the term "symptoms" to cover signs as well.

There are no lab tests for anxiety disorders. No CAT scans or MRIs will tell you that your child has obsessive-compulsive disorder or separation anxiety disorder. Recently there has been some interesting research on brain imaging that describes areas of the brain or types of brain activity that may be different in individuals who experience anxiety. However, very few of these studies to date have been done with children.

Anxiety Diagnosis: Interviews and Checklists

Clinical diagnosis in psychology and psychiatry is still pretty much a low-tech affair. The heart of diagnosis is the clinical interview. It is crucial that the person doing the assessment knows children and child development because emotional and behavioral problems are distressingly common in childhood and vary greatly with age. An experienced clinician can sort out "normal" anxiety from a true anxiety disorder that may require an organized treatment program. Checklists found on the Internet or in parenting magazines can be a useful start, but there is more to diagnosis than checking boxes or even cataloging symptoms, as we shall see.

Going Down the Checklists

There are about a dozen questionnaires (sometimes called rating scales) used in diagnosing anxiety in children. Some of these are completed by the parent, some by the clinician as part of an interview, and some are self-reports completed by the child himself. Questionnaires can take anywhere from a few minutes to thirty or forty minutes to complete. Ages covered varies by questionnaire. Self-report questionnaires are not given to children much below age seven or eight because it's difficult to get reliable information from children younger than this.

Although some look at particular anxiety disorders (for example, obsessive-compulsive disorder), the majority of questionnaires assess a variety of symptoms across the range of anxiety disorders. What matters for our purposes is not whether a scale has a general or specific focus, is administered as part of an interview, or is completed by the parents or as a self-report measure, but that questionnaires can obtain quite a bit of information about the child's symptom picture. But making a diagnosis of an anxiety disorder requires more than a cataloging of symptoms. We must also consider the impact of your child's symptoms on his day-to-day functioning.

Assessing the Impact of Your Child's Symptoms

Assessing any psychological disorder in children or adults must include an understanding of the impact the symptoms have on the person's life. *Impact* may be defined as either distress experienced by the child (the symptoms are unpleasant or distressing) or as significant interference with normal activities for a child that age (for example, refusing to go to school).

Understanding the impact of the symptoms on the child and the larger social network is critical. If the child is experiencing anxiety but is not especially troubled by it or is not experiencing real-life problems as a result of these thoughts and feelings, then it is hard to make the case that the child has a psychological disorder. After all, we define bravery as feeling scared and doing what needs to be done anyway. As we shall see in the next two chapters, sometimes the person most distressed and concerned is not the child, but a parent or perhaps a teacher.

A further consideration is the persistence or duration of the symptoms. Childhood is marked by many unfortunate, unhappy events, and children react with a wide variety of emotions and behaviors. Fortunately, most of these circumstances are very brief in duration and the child can bounce right back and continue to thrive. Psychological disorders are situations that have a persistence to them that goes beyond the usual ups and downs of childhood.

The various *DSM–IV* disorders have requirements for how common the symptoms must be in the person's day-to-day life. Most disorders require that the symptoms be present "more days than not," meaning that the child is rather consistently experiencing the anxious thoughts and feelings or displaying the anxious behaviors.

Additionally, there is the criterion of duration. Actual disorders are more than just brief episodes of upset. To make the diagnosis of anxiety disorder, the symptoms must persist, more days than not, for a minimum length of time. Minimum durations vary by specific diagnosis but generally are either at least one month in duration (separation anxiety disorder, panic disorder) or at least six months (generalized anxiety disorder, specific phobia, social anxiety). Obsessive-compulsive disorder does not have a minimum time that it needs to be present in order to make the diagnosis.

Ruling Out or Ruling In Other Conditions

A visit to your primary care doctor or pediatrician can be a good place to start the diagnostic journey. Because anxiety can often show up as somatic, or bodily, complaints (for example, stomachaches and headaches), it's good to rule out any physical causes such as constipation, vision problems, and so on. Your child's pediatrician can help you organize your concerns and give you his or her sense of whether or not your concerns are appropriate for further investigation with the help a psychologist, psychiatrist, or other mental health provider. Steve Curtis's book *Understanding Your Child's Puzzling Behavior* (2008) is a good guide to this process.

MAJOR CHILD ANXIETY SUBTYPES

What follows is a description of some of the more common childhood anxiety disorders found in the *DSM–IV*. In chapters to come, I will provide descriptions of children that further illustrate some of the ways these disorders show up in the life of a family.

Separation Anxiety

Separation anxiety involves excessive and "inappropriate" (for the child's age) worry and distress when separated from, or anticipating separation from, the parent or primary caregiver. The child's chief concern is that something very bad will happen to the parent or to himself if they are apart. A very young child may not be able to articulate this fear as such. Even older children may not be able to describe anything more than anxious arousal or a vague feeling of dread or anguish.

Separation anxiety often manifests as clinginess and an unwillingness to be apart from the parent or other important caregiver. This could include not wanting to sleep apart from the parent, not wanting to be in a different room or floor of the house, and refusing to go to school. It may show up as tantrums or major upsets when the parent or parents try to leave the home. In older children, there may be an unwillingness to go to a friend's home for a sleepover or to sleep-away camps. Often separation anxiety will present as physical complaints such as stomachaches or headaches when there is threat of separation.

Simple or Specific Phobia

Simple phobia, or *specific phobia*, is diagnosed when specific situations or objects elicit significant anxious arousal in the form of minor or major fight-or-flight responses: freezing up, rapid breathing, rigid muscles, nausea, and crying. Often there is avoidance of the feared object or situations in which the child may encounter the object. A fear of dogs may develop into an unwillingness to go to the park for fear of seeing a dog or to walk down certain streets where dogs live.

Older children (for example, school-age or older) may recognize that the anxiety is unreasonable or out of proportion. Younger children, however, may not see the fear as unreasonable.

Often there is no historical basis for the fear. Recurring and debilitating anxiety after a traumatic experience (for example, a dog bite or a car accident) might fall into the rarer category of post-traumatic stress disorder, depending on how the anxiety is being exhibited.

Fears are quite common during childhood and often include the dark, unfamiliar animals, spiders, heights, and so on. What distinguishes a specific phobia from an ordinary fearful situation is the frequency, intensity, and duration of the fear response and the degree to which the fear interferes with ordinary life tasks, such as moving about the house and neighborhood, going to school, and so on.

Social Phobia or Social Anxiety

Social phobia, or *social anxiety disorder*, is diagnosed when the child reports or demonstrates intense anxiety in the context of common social or public situations, such as going to a baseball game or a shopping mall, or when anticipating social situations, such as birthday parties or sleepovers. The child might believe that he'll be laughed at, ridiculed, or judged negatively. A child with social anxiety may avoid situations that require meeting new people, talking in front of the class, ordering in restaurants, or joining social clubs or teams.

Social anxiety is more than just shyness; it's the anxious thoughts and feelings experienced in the situations as well as a significant and problematic level of avoidance of these situations that impact normal social and academic development.

Panic Disorder and Agoraphobia

Panic disorder and *agoraphobia* (literally "fear of the marketplace" in Greek) are both anxiety about being anxious. Your child might be diagnosed with panic disorder if he's had a history of *panic attacks*, intense physiological fear reactions consisting of a variety of extremely unpleasant bodily sensations and thoughts including pounding heart, sweating, racing pulse, nausea, dizziness, difficulty breathing or feeling that he is choking, and fear that he is going to die. These symptoms are uncommon in young children and more likely first occur in adolescence or young adulthood.

For a child to be diagnosed with panic disorder, he must then develop an intense anxiety around the panic attack recurring. This typically involves being afraid that he might do something embarrassing (such as lose bladder control) should he have a panic attack. This sets up avoidance of situations that might cause intense anxiety or panic attacks. It is this pattern of avoidance that we call agoraphobia.

Panic attacks can come out of the blue or may be triggered by anxiety from an environmental cue (the sudden appearance of a spider) or an internal event (an intense worry or bodily reaction). For example, any child may become winded quite naturally from running around the playground during recess. If this child has experienced a panic attack in the past, his racing heart and his rapid breathing may remind him of how his panic felt, and this could trigger a new attack. The child may then begin to avoid all strenuous activity.

The problem with agoraphobia is that the child's (or parent's) definitions of feared situations become broader over time in an effort to avoid anxiety at all costs. The child who begins to avoid strenuous activity at recess may stop playing on his soccer team, may no longer ride his bike around the neighborhood, or might even resist going up stairs in his house or at school if he thinks such activities might induce another panic attack.

Generalized Anxiety Disorder

Generalized anxiety disorder, or GAD, is the condition of chronic, pervasive worry. The worry is chronic because it is almost constant and very difficult if not impossible to turn off. It is pervasive because, unlike specific phobia or social phobia, the worries are not limited to a particular object or situation but instead cover a broad and ever-changing set of concerns and fears.

Children with this disorder are almost masochistically tuned in to the news and other sources of dread. They can incorporate the latest disaster or threat into their inner broadcast of worry.

Interestingly, children and adults who have GAD worry most often about events that are quite remote in terms of probability. They are often more likely to worry about being kidnapped from their bed at night than about a motor vehicle accident in the family car. Naturally children will worry about car accidents too. But it is a curious feature of this disorder that the worries tend to be about relatively low-probability events and yet are highly resistant to either reassurance from a parent or to any evidence or experience suggesting the worry is unfounded.

Obsessive-Compulsive Disorder

Obsessive-compulsive disorder, or OCD, is characterized by two sets of behaviors: one internal, one external. Obsessions are thoughts that, like the worries in GAD, are strong and scary and very difficult to manage. What makes a scary thought an obsession is the repetitive nature of the thought, its "stickiness." Obsessions are tenacious and relentless. Obsessive thoughts are typically some sort of warning or dire prediction of a bad event or threat in the world: contamination from germs or dog poop, poisoning of some kind, accidents, and bad outcomes, such as a failing grade on a test. Obsessions may involve a child's fear that he will do something bad—for example, shout out an obscenity in church. The child may be troubled by an intrusive sexual or violent image.

Sometimes, but not always, obsessions are accompanied by certain behaviors that are performed in order to ward off the dreaded event or to fix the problem. These are the *compulsions*. Examples include repetitive and excessive behaviors such as frequent hand washing or using hand sanitizers to deal with perceived contamination. Rituals may develop that the child believes will prevent disaster. This might include counting or tapping a certain number of times or repeating phrases or words to himself. Other compulsive behaviors include, for example, repeated checking or requiring the parent to check that they did in fact lock the front door: "Are you sure it's locked? Please check it one more time. Please." There is almost an infinite variety of compulsive behaviors that can be performed.

By definition, a child with OCD is supposed to experience a significant decrease in anxiety when the ritual or compulsive behavior is performed. In my experience, children do not always report this connection between the compulsions and their anxiety. Some may even deny that they are anxious or have compulsions. They will state that they just "like doing it" or don't know why they feel compelled to tap or walk through a doorway twice if they forget to cross the threshold with their left foot first instead of their right. Some children have what are called "just so" obsessive-compulsive behaviors; certain routines must be done "just so" or the child becomes unhappy.

In addition to performing rituals, the child may actively avoid situations that are associated with the threat: someone with contamination obsessions, for example, may avoid using bathrooms in public places or at school. Often there will be efforts to get help or reassurance from a parent, such as "Is this clean?" or "If I eat this, will I get sick?" The child may or may not see the obsessive thoughts as unreasonable or his reactions as unusual or over-the-top.

It must be recognized that rituals and routines are quite common in the life of any child. Virtually all children like predictability and structure. Many children, especially very young ones, can be sharply insistent that things be done a certain way. Story time, bath time, bedtime, food presentation—all are common areas of high expectation and moderate rigidity. For young children, or any child when he is distressed, consistency and familiar routines are necessary to establish a sense of security and good habits. For example, a consistent and predictable bedtime and routine help a child go to sleep more easily.

What distinguishes ordinary preferences for routine from actual OCD is the level of distress the child feels when things don't go his way, as well as the degree of interference the compulsive behaviors cause in the daily life of the child. By definition, OCD must cost at least an hour of the child's life each day in time spent on compulsive behaviors. However, I have found that even very brief compulsive behaviors can be quite draining for the child and for his parents and teachers, and can create sufficient distress and disruption to his life to justify an OCD diagnosis.

CONSTELLATIONS OF SYMPTOMS

Children are complicated, and mental health professionals rarely see anxiety disorders in their "pure" form. How does one decide what is a germ phobia versus a germ obsession versus a generalized worry about germs? It may not be easy to distinguish social phobia from separation anxiety or, for that matter, school phobia from mere defiance.

This confusion emerges from the simple fact that the boundaries of these disorders are not sharp. Committees made up of clinicians and researchers come up with these diagnostic categories. We should not be surprised when something as complex as a developing human being fails to obediently fit into the proper box. Part of the problem is that, unlike regular medicine, in psychology and psychiatry we do not diagnose and treat actual diseases. We deal in what are called "syndromes." A *syndrome*, according to *Merriam-Webster's Collegiate Dictionary*, is "a group of signs or symptoms that occur together and characterize a particular abnormality or condition" (Merriam-Webster, 2003, p. 1268).

Syndromes become recognized diseases when research and clinical practice allow us to understand them in terms of what causes them, their inevitable course if left untreated, and the known and recognized treatments. Although we can agree, mostly, on how to describe the *DSM-IV* disorders (the form they take), psychologists and psychiatrists do not always agree about what these disorders actually are, what causes them, and what to do about them.

Like a number of other psychologists (Hayes et al. 1996; Scotti et al. 1996), I think of psychological disorders as constellations, like the dozens of clusters of stars that have been given names over the centuries. In reality, there is no such thing as the Big Dipper; it's a collection of stars that most people can pick out in the night sky. Somebody once said, "Hey, that kind of looks like a big dipper," and the name stuck.

It is useful to have constellations because we can navigate by them. Slaves escaping the Confederate states knew to follow the Drinking Gourd (the Big Dipper) north to the free states. Obsessive-compulsive disorder, separation anxiety disorder, attention-deficit/hyperactivity disorder (ADHD), kleptomania, and the more than two hundred other disorders in the *DSM–IV* are constellations of behaviors and reported experiences. These variously named clusters of symptoms may have real origins in a child's neurology or history, but as labels they are no more real than the Big Dipper. But like the Big Dipper in the night sky, we can use these diagnostic constellations to find our way.

Comorbidity

Additionally there is the issue of *comorbidity*, which is the presence of more than one diagnosable condition. Anxiety disorders often have co-occurring, or comorbid, psychological disorders. The most common co-occurring conditions are these:

- Attention-deficit/hyperactivity disorder

- Learning disorders

- Depression (often showing up in later childhood or adolescence)

- Oppositional defiant disorder

To this list of co-occurring conditions, I would add developmental disabilities, which includes mental retardation (intellectual and adaptive functioning that is significantly below average) and pervasive developmental disorders, such as autism or its milder cousin, Asperger's disorder. If your child has a developmental disability, then you likely know that he is at a somewhat increased risk for developing problems with communication and regulation of behavior and emotions, including anxiety.

The high degree of comorbidity with anxiety results from the high degree of overlap between anxiety symptoms and those of other nearby diagnostic constellations. For example, anxiety shares a number of symptoms with attention-deficit/hyperactivity disorder (restlessness, distractibility, failure to finish tasks, forgetfulness, talking excessively). The reasons for the symptoms may differ between the two disorders, but at the level of observable behaviors, and even at the level of thoughts and feelings, these two disorders are often hard to distinguish from each other. Oppositional defiant disorder, learning disorders, and Asperger's disorder all share symptoms with anxiety as well. Effectively treating one disorder will often bring improvement in another.

In the next chapter, I will talk about how anxiety develops alongside a child's development of thinking about and understanding the world. If a child has difficulty thinking and communicating at a level we would expect for his age, or if his thinking is distorted in a way that would be unusual at any age, it can set the stage for increased anxiety and for maladaptive reactions to that anxiety. Conditions such as ADHD or Asperger's disorder deeply affect a child's ability to understand the world, learn from experience, and regulate behavior. To the extent that any of these conditions set the child up for frustration or failure or not fitting in, anxiety will follow close behind.

Standard Treatment: Chasing Symptoms, Losing the Big Picture

Apart from poor diagnostic clarity, another clear limitation of the prevailing formal diagnostic model is the almost exclusive attention to symptom and their frequency, duration, and intensity. When a diagnostic systems such as the *DSM–IV* is focused primarily on symptoms, subsequent treatment for the described disorder will be focused heavily on reducing or eliminating those symptoms.

Medications, parent training, behavior modification, and cognitive therapy (if the child is old enough) all work quite well to reduce symptoms of anxiety. However, the beneficial effects may be short-lived or may not transfer to other settings or other people (for example, school and teachers). In many cases, something more is needed for real and lasting change. Something more can come from a different way of thinking about psychological disorders.

In recent years, medical practitioners and consumers have recognized that physical health is more than the mere absence of disease. We now talk about treatment programs (again, heart health is a good example) that emphasize lifestyle changes, the interplay between the mind and the body and between work and family, and the importance of supportive relationships and other sources of resilience.

Because formal systems emphasize the details of the form of the disorder, they cannot shed any light on how these disorders come about in the first place, how they establish a pernicious foothold in our lives, and, most importantly, how to treat these conditions beyond mere symptom reduction. I believe that, for the most part, all the fine-grained descriptions of disorders in the *DSM–IV* have not led and cannot lead us to better understanding and treatments because they pull us away from the big picture and the basic principles underlying many seemingly different disorders. As psychologists Georg Eifert and John Forsyth point out, these formal diagnostic descriptions give us "the false impression that anxiety disorders are more different from one another than they really are" (Eifert and Forsyth 2005, p. 4). Again, how different really are OCD and phobias? What is needed, again quoting Eifert and Forsyth, is an increased understanding of the "common processes involved in how anxiety-related problems develop and are maintained" (2005, p. 4).

There is so much overlap among the anxiety disorders because there is much overlap in how children (or adults for that matter) respond to challenging circumstances. The overlap is less in the symptoms than in the "common processes involved."

COMMON PROCESSES IN ANXIETY

I am going to suggest that all of the anxiety subtypes have two things in common. First, the child experiences some distressing or uncomfortable bodily sensation, emotion, thought, or memory. The presence and interplay among these thoughts and feelings is what we label the fearful or anxious emotion itself. For obsessive-compulsive disorder, it might be intrusive thoughts and dread regarding germs. For generalized anxiety disorder, it might be lying awake in bed with a queasy stomach and a head full of thoughts about intruders. For panic disorder, it can be a racing heart, rapid breathing, and thoughts of impending death. Regardless of the actual specifics, these experiences are uniformly regarded by the child as distressing, unpleasant, or dangerous. And when his anxiety shows up, as a parent, you feel your child's distress along with your own similar emotions, including, perhaps, helplessness and frustration.

Second, in order for these thoughts and feelings to rise to the level of a psychological disorder, the child's day-to-day functioning must be affected. Interestingly it was not until the fourth edition of the *DSM* came out in 1994 that virtually all psychological diagnoses had to include "significant interference with the person's normal routine, occupational (or academic) functioning, or usual social activities or relationships" (American Psychiatric Association 1994, p. 410). In other words, it takes more than just the presence of anxious thoughts and feelings to make a diagnosis; there must also be a negative impact on the person's functioning in daily life. At the heart of this book is the recognition that functioning is most often compromised not by the thoughts and feelings directly but by the child's and the parent's *reactions to* those thoughts and feelings. These reactions, by child or parent, most often take the form of avoidance or inappropriate control strategies.

Avoidance and Control

For both children and adults, the true negative impact of anxiety almost always takes one of two general forms, and often both: first, avoidance of the situations that cause, or might cause, the anxious thoughts and feelings, and second, maladaptive attempts at control of one's thoughts and feelings or of the environment. It is a major premise of this book that impaired functioning in the face of anxiety results from these efforts to avoid or control one's life at the expense of living it and learning from it.

For example, an obsessive-compulsive child's rituals and reactions are an attempt to control (ward off or dispel) uncomfortable thoughts and feelings, such as about germs. Similarly, this child will likely avoid situations that could arouse germ fears: touching doorknobs, for example. The child facing another night of intruder fears and worries may insist that a parent sleep in his room. A teenager might try to self-medicate panic symptoms with alcohol (both control and avoidance).

These strategies are maladaptive because they may work in the short run to help the child control, reduce, or avoid anxious thoughts and feelings, but in the long run they interfere with the day-to-day tasks and expectations of childhood (sleeping on one's own, going to school). Additionally, excessive avoidance and control do not allow a child to learn to truly adapt to challenges and difficulty and to learn appropriate coping and problem-solving skills. Hence, control and avoidance strategies must continue or even expand in order to keep the child's symptoms at bay. In this scenario, the wolf is always at the door.

In coming chapters, we'll take a closer look at control and avoidance in your child's life, when it's okay, and what you can do about it when it's a problem. There are, in fact, many things you or your child can avoid without great cost to the quality of your lives. For example, I don't like provoking my fight-or-flight response, so I avoid bungee jumping, high-stakes gambling, and other activities where anxiety is equated with entertainment. I cannot, however, live a happy and productive life if I do not fly on airplanes. Air travel is just too efficient and too necessary for me to reach my goals and to maintain the life I want. At the same time, I hate air travel. It invites considerable anxiety days before my departure, right through claiming my baggage and dealing with ground transportation. But to avoid flying would have a large and negative impact on my life. So I cope and endure and it's not fun, but it literally gets me where I need to go.

Your child's anxiety may be provoked by a myriad of events and possibilities: swimming lessons, trying out for the school play, accepting an invitation to a party, returning to school after a two-week winter break, the dog down the street, a nightmare. Some of these circumstances can be avoided or controlled with little negative impact. Others, such as school, cannot be avoided or controlled so easily.

As I mentioned in the introduction, goals, such as learning to swim, getting a part in the school play, flying to Disneyland, and so on, can provide a context in which anxiety becomes just "part of the deal"—unpleasant but not necessarily a deal breaker. In chapter 5, we will explore the values and goals that you hold and want manifested in the life of your family and which will provide the contexts for courageous action. A clear connection with your values and goals can help sort out questions of when, as a parent, to lean back, yield, and accommodate and when to lean in and move your child forward with compassionate strength.

Your Child's Need for Understanding and Help

You are reading this book because your child has developed any number of subtle and not-so-subtle means for alerting you to his anxious distress and getting you to come to his aid. Some anxious behaviors—clinging, withdrawing, pleading to not go somewhere or to be taken home, imploring you not to go somewhere, asking questions, asking for reassurance, refusing to do something or to stop doing something—are obvious and transparent; that is, they are clearly related to some fearful or anxiety-provoking situation. On the other hand, some anxious behaviors may or may not be clearly related to anxiety. These include stomachaches and headaches; hyper, silly, or immature behavior; sadness and crying; and defiance or anger.

Your child hopes for help in the form of rescue or reassurance. He hopes for—and needs, evens demands—your assistance in avoiding and controlling his anxiety. That is the agenda—to avoid or control anxiety— and your child has developed and continues to develop many strategies to achieve that end. A second and related issue is the unfortunate fact that your child's methods for conveying his anxious thoughts, feelings, and needs may be confusing, aversive, immature, inappropriate, out of proportion, or otherwise off-putting to you. You may then respond with your own confusion, anxiety, and distress. This launches an unhelpful chain of reactions and counterreactions that serves only to make both you and your child miserable and frustrated.

WHERE YOU COME IN

Fear and anxiety happen. What is important is what happens next. How does your child communicate and deal with the fear and anxiety? Is it a helpful and adaptive response, or is it a brittle reaction that only serves to increase the power anxiety has over his life?

Seeking help, rescue, or reassurance is related to your child's own efforts to control or avoid the anxiety. The goal is to get you, the all-powerful and merciful parent, to step in and provide the control that is eluding your child. Alternatively, the goal of the child's behavior may be to obtain your approval of and assistance with an avoidance strategy—for example, getting an excused absence from school.

However well intended, any complicity we have as parents in the use of avoidance or control as a reaction to our child's anxiety has the potential to create and strengthen these maladaptive strategies and prevent real growth and adaptation. Again, the process is maladaptive because it short-circuits the child's development of age-appropriate coping and adaptive strategies, specifically the capacity to tolerate distress, self-soothe, or solve problems on his own. As with control and avoidance strategies that repeatedly fail, seeking your help in the wrong way or at the wrong times leads only to more anxiety, an increased intolerance of anxiety, and further need for rescue or escape. Hence, a vicious cycle develops.

This last point is central to our discussion of childhood anxiety and what we as parents can do about it. Children certainly need us parents for all kinds of help, support, guidance, protection, and so on. Unfortunately, when the help-seeking process becomes coercive, confusing, or otherwise provokes considerable negative emotion in a parent, it is very difficult for us to be responsive to our child's needs. Instead, we find ourselves reacting to our child's distress with our own attempts at control or avoidance, which are also likely to be maladaptive in the long run.

SUMMARY AND A LOOK AHEAD

I have described some of the core features of fear and anxiety, its roots in our biologically driven security system, and how it manifests itself in panic, dread, obsessions, and so on. I also described the limits of the traditional medical model with its emphasis on symptoms and reducing or eliminating those symptoms as the goal of treatment.

In place of the symptom-based approach, I am offering another view, which is based on this question: "What is it that the child is trying to achieve through these behaviors that show up when he is anxious?" The short answer is relief. But at what cost?

In the chapters that follow, I will emphasize general principles for how you can respond to maladaptive avoidance and control behaviors provoked by your child's anxiety. I will be looking at issues specific to the various anxiety disorders (generalized anxiety disorder, separation anxiety disorder, and so on), but the emphasis will be less on this or that anxiety subtype than on how children at various stages of development experience thoughts and feelings, and the actions they take when in distress. In the next chapter, I will describe how anxiety presents itself at various ages and how emotional development and cognitive development go hand in hand.

CHAPTER 2

Child Development and the Nature of Anxiety

Anxiety is a natural part of growing up because growing up is difficult and scary. As I mentioned in the previous chapter, anxiety is the most common mental health issue in this country and most anxiety begins in childhood (Kessler et al. 2005). Left alone, anxiety can become a debilitating and persistent problem. Understood and treated, anxiety can become mere background noise that needn't interfere with life's demands and joys.

I have described anxiety as it is seen from the standpoint of standard psychiatric and psychological diagnosis: formal, symptom-oriented, the "what" of anxiety. This chapter looks at the way anxiety emerges from the interaction between a child's biology and her earliest experiences. Biology is represented by the child's nervous system and the self-protection and self-regulation mechanisms she is born with. Experiences take the form of her earliest interactions with the world, especially the world of other people.

ANXIETY ACROSS THE YEARS

Most clinical psychology textbooks and many books for parents of anxious children provide a description of how fear and anxiety may show up and change across childhood, along with the situations that provoke these thoughts and feelings. Here is mine:

Infancy Through Preschool

- Stranger anxiety: fear responses when the infant encounters adults who are not the primary caregiver (emerges at around seven to nine months of age and fades around twelve months)

- Separation anxiety: may be seen as shyness if the child is unwilling to separate from the parent, typically in social situations

- Unfamiliar and overarousing objects and events: big dogs, insects, thunderstorms, loud and sudden noises, and other objects or events that elicit fear responses from which worries may develop

Elementary School Years

- Dangers in the world: physical harm (for example, accidents), burglars, fires, earthquakes, car and plane crashes, terrorist attacks, and so on

- The dark and places and events associated with it: bedtime, closets, the basement, cemeteries at midnight

- Being alone

- Illness

- Social rejection

- Academic failure

- Disruption to the family (for example, divorce)

- Death

Middle and High School Years

- Humiliation

- Loss of popularity or athletic or academic standing

- Sex and intimacy

- The future

This is clearly an incomplete list. Additionally, these are generalities based on clinical reports, and not all children will respond with fear or anxiety to these situations at these particular ages or perhaps at any age. Typically fears will peak in frequency and intensity between the ages of seven and nine, while anxiety steadily rises from ages four to twelve (Muris et al. 2000). The trends also show us that the form of the anxiety changes as the child's thinking develops and experiences broaden. Fear of harm gives way to worries about emotional distress and competence.

THE ABCS OF ANXIETY

When psychologists look at troublesome behavior patterns, we ask a lot of questions about what a child is feeling, thinking, and doing: How does your stomach feel? What worries do you have? What do you do when that worry shows up? The behaviors a child or her parent describes make up the particular anxiety syndrome we're hoping to treat. I am including thoughts and feelings under the general term "behavior," as these are things a person does, even if this kind of behavior cannot be observed by others and even if it is not done voluntarily. As a psychologist, I want to know exactly what the problem looks like from outside and within the individual. I also want to get some ideas about the events that caused both the *private behaviors* (thoughts and feelings experienced by the child) as well as the *public behaviors* (actions observable to all, such as freezing up or crying). Finally, I ask questions about what happens next: does the child seek help, run away, or trudge on?

To help you understand and effectively respond to your child's anxiety, it will be important for you to ask similar questions in systematic way. To help in that task, psychologists use a technique we simply call the ABCs. In the pages to come, I will show you how to use this technique to look at the patterns of behavior that impact you and your child. Simply put, the ABCs describe the chain of events we call fear and anxiety. The chain starts with circumstances or triggers that appear to provoke the fear and anxiety: a barking dog, a big test in school. Next are the private and public behaviors making up the anxiety disorder: your child's feelings, thoughts, and actions. Finally, we are interested in what happens next: the reactions of the child's world, especially the social world, to those anxious behaviors. This gives us three sets of situations or events, behaviors, and reactions, which are listed in three columns labeled A, B, and C, or activators, behaviors, and consequences.

Activators	Behaviors	Consequences

In the examples and exercises to come, the first column will contain brief descriptions of the events or conditions immediately preceding the child's anxious behaviors. These are assumed to be the triggers or situations that provoked or contributed to the behavior pattern that followed. In behavior therapy talk, the triggers or preceding conditions are called the *antecedents* to the behavior. I sometimes refer to these what-happened-just-before-the-anxiety-showed-up situations and events as *activators*, as in what activated the fear or anxiety reaction?

Try identifying the activator(s) in the following situation: While walking down the street, a barking dog suddenly appeared on the other side of a fence running along the sidewalk. Presumed activators would be listed in the first column. The barking dog is a likely activator for a child's anxiety. However, as we'll see, if the child has been frightened by this dog before, just walking down that street could activate some anxious thoughts, feelings, or behaviors.

The behavior of interest is simply called the *behavior*. For example, the sudden presence of the dog triggers a fear response. The fear or worries, or any other behaviors, such as crying or a stomachache, would go under B in the middle column.

We complete the analysis with a description of what follows the behavior of interest: the fearful, crying child's father puts an arm around her and gently pulls her away from the dog. This is an example of the *consequences* that follow the behavior, which are listed in the third column. We often think of a consequence as something doled out by the adult, usually a punishment. Here I am simply referring to what follows the behavior, regardless of whether it is judged to be a good thing or a bad thing or who or what caused it to occur.

Together we have the ABCs: the *activator* (or *antecedent*) conditions or triggers, the *behavior* itself, and the *consequences* (there may be several) that follow. Right now let's just focus on the first two: the behaviors of interest and the events that precede them.

EXERCISE: Your Child's Anxious Behaviors and the Events That Trigger Them

First, list three or four anxious behaviors (observable actions, thoughts, or feelings) that your child struggles with. Write these in the behavior column. Be as specific as you can. Instead of listing "nervous," "helpless," or "out of control," describe what she does: "paces back and forth," "repeatedly says, 'I can't do it,'" "lies on the floor, wailing."

Next, in the activator column, list the events or conditions that tend to set off these behaviors on a fairly reliable basis. For example, "going to a birthday party," "doing homework," or "bedtime." Here, too, be as specific as you can be. Is it every birthday party or just ones at homes she's never been to before? Is it all homework, most often the writing assignments, or whatever is at the beginning of that night's set of work? Is it bedtime every night, on a particular night of the week, or when your spouse works late?

Please leave the consequences column empty for now. I will have more to say about consequences later.

Activators	Behaviors	Consequences

As you look at this list, you may see that your child's anxiety can present itself in many varied behaviors—outward events such as actions, verbal language, and body language, as well as inner, or private events such as thoughts and feelings. Some of these behaviors are unambiguous: your child saying, "I'm scared," for example. Other behaviors may only suggest fear or anxiety, such as restlessness, frustration, defiance, or poor sleep.

The activators can also be many and varied. There may be obvious triggers such as a barking dog or heading to school on the day of a big test. Other activators can be less obvious but still set the stage for a fear or anxiety reaction. These activators include hunger, fatigue, unstructured time, an ill or absent parent, and others. If you are asked, "What triggers your child's anxiety?" and your first answer is "It depends," then these less obvious but important activators may be at work.

In the pages to come, I will use this ABC technique to describe anxious behaviors, activators, and consequences in fictional case examples drawn from my clinical work. I will also return to this technique in the form of exercises that will help you better understand the "what" and the "why" of your own child's anxiety. But first, I want to describe how anxiety can uniquely develop in a child.

THE ORIGINS OF ANXIETY

As I described in the previous chapter, fear is the quite natural and automatic reaction to a real or perceived threat in the moment. Anxiety, on the other hand, is the *anticipation* of danger or discomfort. It is distress here and now regarding a possible future. Like fear, anxiety stems from natural and automatic processes that shape our experiences of the world within minutes of our arriving in it. From those earliest experiences onward, the world, especially our social world, shapes and refines our perceptions and reactions.

Temperament

A child comes into the world with a set of innate, biologically driven characteristics that affect how she typically reacts to stimulation and subsequently her ability to self-regulate when her equilibrium is thrown off. For example, even a newborn will turn her head away from Uncle Harry when he gets too enthusiastic with the rattle toy. Turning away is one strategy an overwhelmed baby uses to cut down on stimulation. This is the beginning of avoidance.

On the other hand, if something is interesting and not overwhelming, the baby will turn and look at it and later approach it when mobility (crawling, walking) is attained. Simple stuff, but they're just babies after all. It gets plenty complicated later.

If Uncle Harry is not picking up on his niece's discomfort and continues to be intrusive with the rattle, the baby may go to the next level of self-protection: wailing. Dad arrives, picks up the baby, and begins to coo and rock her. The baby settles down quickly. These transactions between Uncle Harry and the baby and between the baby and her father represent aspects of what we call temperament.

Temperament is the starter set of very basic predispositions and stock reactions with which each of us is born. In his book *The Difficult Child*, Stanley Turecki defined temperament as "the natural, in-born style of behavior of each individual. It is the *how* of behavior, not the why" (1985, p. 13, original emphasis). Temperament is the characteristic way each infant reacts to the world around her, often described in terms of being high or low on various traits such as the intensity of her reactions, the predictability or regularity of bodily functions, activity level, approaching versus avoiding novelty, and prevailing quality of mood (happy or unhappy), to name a few.

The Rhythm and Tone of Temperament

Temperament involves behavioral rhythms and emotional tone. Some infants sleep and poop on a very predictable schedule from their very first days. Others have cycles that are much harder to predict. Some infants and toddlers are drawn to novelty and action, while others are more hesitant and watchful. Some infants are chronically fussy, easily disturbed, and difficult to soothe. Others are positive, mellow, and easy to comfort when they become upset. These dimensions of temperament set the stage for how the infant will interface with the world, especially the world of people, starting with the parents.

There Is No Such Thing as a Baby

Temperament governs the degree and quality of a child's transactions with the world. I use the term "transaction" because this is a two-way street. You behave toward your baby in some way that affects her. She responds, and her response affects you and sets up your next action, and so on. The British psychiatrist D. W. Winnicott (1965) said, "There is no such thing as a baby" (p. 39), meaning that a baby can never be seen in isolation from her caregivers and all the many transactions that pass between them. These early transactions are the stuff of your child's earliest learning experiences, the creation of her personality, as well as her views of herself and the world around her, especially her social world.

It used to be thought that certain temperament styles were in and of themselves problematic. Authors who first described temperament, such as Turecki, thought there was such a thing as a "difficult child," meaning a temperament marked by poor or unpredictable rhythms, negative mood, withdrawal or avoidance, and difficulty being consoled once upset. We now know that when it comes to successful parent-child transactions, two factors matter more than the temperament style itself. One factor is the parents' expectations for the kind of child they will have. The second is how adaptable the parents can be in light of the kind of child they actually get.

All parents anticipate what their child will be like. This picture of their future child will be painted in terms of temperament, even if the parents are unaware of the concept. You spent countless hours thinking about your child and what she would be like: her physical features, her moods, her personality, and so on. These expectations emerged from your experiences over many years, including your family of origin, your exposure to infants and children over the years, your younger children's older siblings, books you have read, and even the popular culture. Looking back on these expectations and from the vantage point of now knowing your child, how accurate were you? Did she meet your expectations, or did she surprise you in unexpected ways?

If parents expect a mellow child and get a boisterous one, this can set up miscommunication, frustration, irritation, and conflict. Similarly a mellow child born into a raucous family could cause confusion, concern, and probably some fairly intrusive—at least from the child's point of view—parenting or "uncle-ing."

The second and very important factor, as we noted above, is how adaptable the parents can be in response to their child, whatever her temperament style. Uncle Harry was not responsive to his niece's cues, and this may have gotten their relationship off to a rocky start. Harry and the baby will likely have many more opportunities to get to know each other and make the necessary adjustments. But if Uncle Harry does not adjust his style of interacting, his niece may develop some quite durable and automatic reactions to him that might color their relationship, and perhaps other similar relationships, in the child's life for many years to come.

Syndromes Emerge from the Primordial Temperament Ooze

Most research suggests that some psychological disorders or syndromes can be identified in preschool children; anxiety is one of these. But very young children's problematic feelings and behaviors cannot be well differentiated, and they are often lumped into one of two categories: behavioral inhibition or behavioral disinhibition, otherwise known as being out of control.

Behavioral inhibition can derive from a temperament style in some children characterized by outright avoidance of novelty or highly arousing situations. This is different from the child who may simply be slow to warm up to new or challenging situations. Inhibited children may show characteristics of low adaptability to change and a low activity level overall, and tend to be mild in their reactions to the world around them. These infants and toddlers may be thought of as quiet and shy, and may appear unwilling to take risks. Children identified as behaviorally inhibited as young as age two have a significantly higher likelihood of developing an anxiety disorder than do ordinary children, although some will simply grow out of these characteristic behavior patterns (Turner, Beidel, and Epstein 1991).

Children with behavioral disinhibition generally will have traits opposite those of shy, quiet child. These are the young children who are exploring the world with high energy, reacting strongly (either positively or negatively) to events, seeking novelty and change, and showing high adaptability. Few children, however, are always either inhibited or disinhibited. The following example of Abby illustrates the extremes of mood and behavior that anxiety can invite into your life.

■ Abby: "Pantrums"

Abby is a small and delicate-looking four-year-old girl. She moves slowly and gracefully as if under water. From infancy, her parents and family members described her as shy or introverted. She rarely speaks outside the home, and then only in a whisper close to her mother's ear. Abby is in preschool and will play quietly by herself, though often near other children and adults. She will accept invitations to play with other children but does not initiate play with others.

From the day she came home from the hospital, Abby had difficulty self-regulating and getting in sync with the rhythms around her. She tended to startle, become upset, and withdraw in response to ordinary stimulation in her world: the telephone ringing, someone other than her mother picking her up or getting close, a diaper change. When Abby became overwhelmed, she was very difficult to console. She would cry and shake for an hour or more, and would only calm down with the passage of time and not, it seemed, because of any soothing or comforting by her parents.

Abby is overwhelmed by unfamiliar environments. This is most evident when she is out in the community with someone other than her parents. On a trip to the mall with her grandmother, Abby wet herself because she was would not tell her grandmother that she needed to use the bathroom. Abby later told her mother that she was afraid to use the bathroom at the mall because "it's too loud in there." The ABCs of this event might be described this way:

Activators	Behaviors	Consequences
At the mall with Grandma. Needed to use restroom.	Wouldn't say she needed to use the restroom.	Accident, taken home from mall, crying.

Abby's temperament style made it difficult for her parents, Catherine and Wayne, to understand and address her needs. Because Abby was the firstborn child, her parents had no clue what was typical of an infant in terms of sensitivity or reactions to the world around her. Abby's behaviors confused and frightened them. Positive, energetic, and lively people, they had imagined a child who would embrace the world with a positive and eager demeanor. Yes, Catherine had been shy as a child and Wayne had experienced a panic attack or two in high school, but they'd grown out of these conditions without much fuss or serious impact on their lives. Catherine and Wayne assumed they must be doing something wrong. Mutual frustration marked Abby's relationships from the beginning.

Like many children with strong behavioral inhibition, Abby has difficulty adapting to change and coping with stressful events. When her tolerance has been exceeded, Abby can go from being very inhibited to extreme disinhibition. She will have sudden and very intense tantrums when she is overwhelmed and frightened. During these episodes, Abby can be quite distraught, physically out of control, and completely unable to give or receive verbal communication. She will cry, scream, throw herself on the floor, flail her arms and legs, and hit, kick, or bite anyone who comes within range. At other times, Abby might weep hysterically and cling to her mother. I call these extreme reactions "pantrums" because they appear to be a cross between a panic attack and a tantrum. In Abby's case, they can last up to an hour. Afterward Abby's parents are exhausted, angry, and discouraged. Again, when described in terms of activators, behaviors, and consequences, these episodes (greatly simplified) may be described this way:

Activators	Behaviors	Consequences
Birthday party: Catherine insisted Abby look at friend's mother, say hello.	Pantrum: screaming, arching back, kicking.	Abby removed from party, taken home; Catherine exhausted, angry, and discouraged.

Her parents' inability to manage Abby's behavior saddened, frustrated, and eventually angered them. Relatives were subtly critical of Catherine's parenting techniques and offered many "tried-and-true" solutions, all of which failed. Discouragement set in. Her parents' reactions to Abby's upsets became more rigid and less patient. Catherine's reactions were either to walk away in disgust when Abby was upset, tearfully plead with her to calm down, or bark at her to pull herself together. Later Catherine would be awash in guilt and anger, and then more guilt for feeling angry.

Going anywhere in public or to any social event, especially with extended family, became a source of profound anxiety and dread for Catherine. If these activities could be avoided, they were. As such, the whole family's world became smaller and more tense. Avoidance and control had taken over.

HOW DEVELOPMENT INFLUENCES ANXIETY

Abby and her parents were stuck in an unhelpful cycle of upset, reaction, further upset, avoidance, and control. Her exquisitely sensitive fight-or-flight system, combined with few natural and flexible self-soothing skills, meant that Abby was going to react strongly and negatively to many common life events. What does the future hold for Abby? Will she continue to struggle with these reactions and pantrums, or will she grow out of them? What will influence her trajectory?

As an infant, your child was first afraid of immediate disturbances that overwhelmed her or threatened her survival in some way: loud and sudden noises, the dark, and being alone are typical. Later she developed a more sophisticated thinking style that allowed her to think beyond the immediate situation to imagine, and become disturbed by, all manner of events that were nonexistent or perhaps real but remote. In other words, over time she learned to react not to just what was actually happening to her (fear), but also to what her mind told her might happen to her (anxiety). All of this came about because of the development of more sophisticated ways of thinking as she grew. And thinking develops as language develops. Each person's history with anxiety is their history of thinking and language development.

Our Earliest Style of Thinking: All-or-None

As your child grows from infant to toddler to school-age child and beyond, she learns a startling amount in what is really a very short time. Language acquisition is a case in point. When a child is between the ages of two and three, she picks up dozens of new words every week and incorporates them into her vocabulary.

Your child is also learning how to think. Her particular style of thinking will be a product of her biology (for example, temperament as well as basic brain wiring determined by genetic inheritance) interacting with her experiences as she grows up. Some children, for example, develop a style of thinking that is very methodical, linear, and oriented to detail. Others show flashes of creativity and intuition as their signature style. Everyone, however, starts out in infancy with pretty much the same thinking style: taking in information and organizing it in the simplest way possible, into *this* and *that*.

As infants, we start our exploration of the world by dividing everything into two kinds of things. For example, infants seem to be born with an instinctual preference for high-contrast objects to look at. It makes sense that babies' brains would be wired to look for contrast. Having been thrust into this new and chaotic visual world, they must pick out the edges of things so that they can begin to figure out that there are such things as individual *things*. Our auditory system is also wired to pick out individual sounds and then to develop a sense for where one word leaves off and another begins. If sounds flowed seamlessly together, language would be impossible.

It's Bad, It's Good, It's Okay

So infants and young children (up to about age four or five) have this very binary, all-or-none mode of organizing their world: this is good versus this is bad, I must approach this versus I must avoid that, I am safe versus I am in mortal danger, I am calm and content versus I am going ballistic.

Being fed and held are good experiences—really good. Diaper rash and Uncle Harry armed with a rattle are bad experiences—really bad.

Over the first several years of life, as an infant and a toddler, a child begins to remember and think about (judge) what has happened to her. These judgments are cast in absolute terms of all good or all bad. You are the best father in the world except when you are the worst father in the world. Those extremes are the only two realities, and your status as a father can shatter in an instant for the smallest of reasons. This is tough on everyone.

The young child has little capacity for seeing beyond the immediate situation, good or bad. This makes it very difficult to console herself that it will be better soon or to tell herself that it's not so bad after all. The ability to eventually see the shades of gray in life, to have an "okay" day instead of the best day or the worst day of your life, to have a more supple and adaptive view of yourself and the world, is a developmental achievement.

What allows young children to outgrow this rigid, brittle, all-or-none thinking style? Flexible thinking and language. The development of more flexible thinking gives your child the capacity for going beyond the immediate situation and for considering alternatives to the all-good or all-bad mode of organizing the world and her experiences in it. The development of language enables your child to communicate her experiences—"I'm feeling scared"—to important others such as you, other adults, siblings, and peers. Language allows your child to talk herself through difficult situations, hopefully in a flexible and adaptive manner: "This is scary now, but it will be okay." Finally, language allows you and others to communicate your own experiences back to her, especially your experience of her in that moment: "You look scared right now. I wonder what you're thinking?"

Language, Expectations, and Flexible Thinking

During the second year of life, a child's behaviors become more complex, including the behaviors we call thoughts and feelings, and language emerges. You can then begin to get some insight into what's going on inside your child's mind. Even before she could talk, it was clear that your child had strong ideas about what she wanted and what was supposed to happen. Children have a strong capacity for imagining the world. They can anticipate events. They have strong expectations. Much before age five they have little or no flexibility regarding their expectations or how they will react when their expectations are not met.

As is typical of her age, Abby has very strong expectations about what will and must happen. Her mother described the following typical scenario: Abby would be playing by herself or engaged in some pleasant activity with her mother. She would ask for a cup of apple juice. Catherine would go into the kitchen and come back with the apple juice in a small plastic cup, one of several in a variety of colors. She would hand Abby the cup of juice and Abby would immediately begin to wail. Major pantrum. When she was able to calm down, Abby would tell her mother that she "wanted" the juice in the blue cup, not the red cup Catherine had given her. I put "wanted" in quotes because at this age children "want" things the way I "want" to continue to breathe. Everything they want is something vital to their existence, even though it may seem absurd and trivial to us as adults since we have our world all sorted out into what's truly important and what's not important—and, to us, the color of the cup isn't important.

Depending on her mood and energy level that day, Abby's mother might argue with her four-year-old that apple juice is apple juice and who cares what color the cup is? She finds that this is not a helpful strategy. Clearly Abby cares. But again, this is beyond mere caring. Bringing the juice in the red cup is violating Abby's expectations; it is messing with her reality, or at least her strong and rigid ideas about what reality is supposed to look like.

Your Anxious Child's Reality vs. Your Reality

When Abby asked for her apple juice, she imagined what would happen next. She's had that ability for a couple of years now. She knows what's going to happen next; her loving and all-powerful mother will respond to her request, go obtain that wonderful golden liquid using the magical powers possessed by adults, and bring her the juice in the blue cup, just as she imagined it. That's how she saw it unfold in her mind. That's how it was going to be.

Bringing the juice in the red cup violated her expectations, and at four years of age, children have limited capacity for tolerating variation in what life hands them versus what they expect. On some days, they have no capacity for variation. At those times, the wrong color cup is sufficient to elicit a fight-or-flight reaction, and in some cases, a pantrum. Sadly, we all know adults who have not made much progress on this.

It's really not until about age five that children can muster a reasonably solid, consistent capacity to be flexible in the face of changes to their plans or expectations: "I got my juice. Not my favorite cup, but what the heck. Let's get on with Candyland." Unfortunately, as discussed below, this new and wonderful capacity for flexibility can evaporate when the child is already stressed in some way—hungry, tired, and so on—or when the violation is just too big.

Fusion in the World out There

It is a developmental achievement for your child to separate one aspect of a situation from another, such as the color of the cup from the fact that it contains the desired apple juice. Prior to about five years of age, features of a situation may be and tend to be fused together and all of a piece. Ask a child how to cook something and you will get some interesting answers. For example, to cook a chicken, you put the chicken in the oven, go to church, come home, wash your hands, and eat the chicken. To a very young child, going to church and washing your hands are an integral part of cooking a chicken.

This fusion of features of the environment is just one example of the "magical" thinking that is characteristic of preschool children. Things just happen in the world. They have not yet developed solid and consistent rules for cause and effect or a sense of what are the critical variables and what is mere detail. For the very young child, every variable can be critical—no detail is too small to stress over. The color of the cup is an integral part of obtaining the apple juice. Reading the story first, then getting tucked in, then arranging the pillows just so *is* (not *are*, they are not three separate things) an integral part of, fused with, being able to go to sleep at night. Mess with any of it, and you risk provoking the fight-or-flight reaction because you are messing with your child's reality.

Fusion Between Our Inner and Outer Worlds

It's not just features of the environment that can be fused together and treated as whole and inseparable units. Very young children unknowingly fuse the inner world of thoughts and feelings with the world outside, the world of objects and events.

This kind of fusion has been called "psychic equivalence" (Fonagy and Target 2000), "cognitive fusion" (Shafran, Thordarson, and Rachman 1996), or "literality" (Hayes, Strosahl, and Wilson 1999). Each of these terms describes the human tendency to treat thoughts and feelings as if they were directly connected to events in the external world. Your child operates as if her thoughts are true, accurate, and literal representations of reality. Heck, they aren't even representations, they *are* reality! At young ages and during stress, your child cannot consider that her thoughts and feelings might be inaccurate, distorted, or no longer applicable. That dog scared her. Dogs are scary. All of them. Forever.

Worse still, if a child's thoughts and feelings are literal reality, then the memory of that dog is equivalent to the barking dog hitting the fence again, right here and now. So she may respond to a memory with as much anxious arousal as she did when the event happened.

So, if thoughts are literally true, then it is very difficult for them to change once they've been hatched. If your child's initial thoughts were that the dog was trying to tear her limb from limb, there is no way she is going to accept the possibility that the dog just wanted to play. Her mind will resist considering alternative explanations or information that contradicts the thoughts she originally associated with the event. She will cling to "all dogs are dangerous" because she believes it is literally true and it has become a rule that she believes must be followed strictly in order to keep her safe. Alternative realities such as "You've played with that dog before and he was just excited to see you" or "Didn't you see his tail was wagging?" are going to be a hard sell.

Fusion in the World Inside

In such an undifferentiated mind, an infant doesn't just *have* those feelings. She *is* those feelings. This is similar to the fusion of aspects of the environment (the juice and the color of the cup). In the case of the world inside the child, her thoughts and feelings and even sense of self can become fused. It's built into language, at least in English: I say "I *am* scared" just as I say "I *am* Chris."

For adults who have some distance on fused thinking and perceiving, it sounds odd to say, "I am diaper rash." But we do say "I am hungry" (or tired or angry). In most cases, this semantic oddity is benign. But, as we shall see over the next several chapters, overidentifying with our thoughts and feelings can become problematic and a major source of remaining stuck in unhelpful behavioral patterns. For example, if "I am scared" is as real and enduring as "I am Chris" or "I am a male," then I have little hope for changing *being* scared. But if I can instead think, "I'm acting scared" or "I'm having some worries right now," other ways of acting or thinking might be possible.

As adults, it's difficult to appreciate these old ways of thinking because we've grown beyond them in such profound ways. But even the most mature among us can still touch upon or even dive into these more rigid and primitive thinking styles when tired, upset, or otherwise stressed. Under these circumstances, we can hear ourselves revert to a more binary and rigid way of thinking about the world and others in it: "This always happens…," "You never…," "I must have…" This kind of thinking is as unhelpful to you and me as adults as it is to our children. And, as you know, once you're there, getting out of it can be tricky.

Regression: Moving Backward Developmentally

Regression is the term we use to describe a child's reverting to a younger developmental stage when stressed by events. We all do this to some extent when we feel maxed out in our work or other demands; we go back to the basics, to simplistic ways of thinking about things and reacting to problems and demands. This can be a good survival mechanism when we fall back on what we know best—the old "I can do this in my sleep" mode. But regression can also sharply limit your child's, and your own, flexibility and creativity just when you both need them most.

Your child always seems to be living at the ragged edge of her competence. Every day in school, in sports, in music lessons, dealing with peers or siblings, life pushes her right up to the limits of her skills and resilience. This is the zone where we learn best, the optimal balance of drawing on what we know and can do and applying it to new challenges that stretch our abilities. But the tipping point into frustration and failure hovers close by. When she crosses that line and the alarm bells go off ("I'm failing!"), your child can pull way back and retreat into a frame of mind characteristic of a much younger child. When this happens, you can see a sudden return to that immature all-or-none thinking style. With the more immature thinking style comes less mature behavior: acting out instead of talking it out, and getting stuck in unhelpful attempts at avoidance or control.

This can be upsetting in its own right. Your six- or eight- or ten-year-old is suddenly, functionally three. If your child would just shrink when she did this, it would be less confusing. A moment ago, she was capable of at least some rational thought and communication. Now she's acting like a three-year-old. Well, for all intents and purposes, she is three or thereabouts at the moment. And she is no happier about it than you are.

GROWING THE BRAIN, GROWING THINKING

So you have a child who is occasionally or frequently immersed in this literal, binary, and fused way of thinking. You want her to have a more supple and inquisitive way of thinking about her thoughts and feelings, and how these thoughts and feelings are connected, or not, to events in the world. How do we get her there?

Much of this change, and the ability to remain at a more mature level of functioning without too much regression, will happen through basic development or maturation. Some of this development is pulled along by the growth of neurological structures, mostly the frontal lobes of the brain (right behind the forehead), which allow for more flexible and abstract ways of thinking. The frontal lobes of the brain are responsible for a variety of mental tasks, including time concepts, flexibility of thought, and the ability to step back and think about your own thinking.

Time concepts, for example, are almost nonexistent for the infant and toddler. Even in school-age children, from about age six to twelve, the understanding of past, present, and future is limited. This means there can be little in the way of coping thoughts such as "It will be better later" or "I'll just think about some pleasant memory to hold me over until Mom arrives to make me feel better." There is some debate about when these kinds of self-soothing mental capacities emerge. But realistically, until about age four or five, and even beyond, coping is fragile, life is all-or-none, and the anxiety alarm system is always ready to go off.

The eventual maturation of brain structures helps. But for a long period of time, your child is going to need to "borrow" your frontal lobes so that she can navigate challenging situations. Flexible and accurate thinking is a developmental achievement only in part because it emerges from biological maturation. Flexible and accurate thinking is also something your child is going to learn from you.

Thinking About Thoughts

That skill of being able to step back in your mind and think about your own thinking is called *metacognition*, and it is vital for managing your actions in the face of strong emotions and troublesome thoughts. For example, Abby does not know that she is stuck in her insistence that the cup be blue and not red. She cannot think, "Here I am fussing over the color of the cup." If she could, she might be able to consider not fussing over the color of the cup. But for Abby at that moment, the color of the cup and fussing over it is all there is; it fills up her world so much that nothing else exists and there are no other options but to do what she is doing. She has no mental map that can guide her out of the in-the-moment upset that is consuming her and toward alternatives. As I will describe below in the case of a ten-year-old girl with obsessive-compulsive disorder, knowing that what you're thinking is unreasonable doesn't guarantee reasonable behavior. But it's a start.

Talking About Feelings

Recently psychologists have begun to talk about the ability to reflect on our emotions in much the same way as the ability to think about our own thinking. John Gottman and his colleagues at the University of Washington have studied *metaemotion*, stepping back and having thoughts and feelings about our feelings (Gottman 1997). As your child's brain develops and as she accumulates experiences, she will learn to think about her experiences, initially in those very black-and-white terms but eventually with more sophistication and subtlety. For example, children will learn that there is a difference between being angry and being frustrated, between being scared and being nervous. Later they will add annoyed or perhaps pensive to their vocabulary and create even more range in their thinking and more possibility for responding.

Thinking about our thoughts and feelings may not be a uniquely human trait, but our ability to reflect on the world and on our own mental and emotional states and those of others creates much of what we think of as making us human. Stepping back and considering your own and another's experiences is fundamental to empathy, and with that, to the creation of society. Reflecting on experiences gives rise to art and poetry, religion and science, music and philosophy. Thinking about our thoughts and feelings also makes anxiety and a host of other psychological conditions possible.

Anxiety Is Bad

If we didn't have the capacity to think about our thoughts and feelings, we would certainly have fear, but probably not anxiety. Like other animals, we would quickly learn what is dangerous and do our best to avoid those situations. Should we encounter something dangerous, our fight-or-flight response would kick in and we would react with survival behaviors. But as far as we know, animals do not sit around and stress about what they have been through or anticipate with dread what may happen in the future. As far as we know, animals do not create elaborate rituals in the service of warding off bad events, nor do they remain stuck in behavior patterns that aren't helpful.

Anxious children wouldn't be engaging in anxious avoidance and control behaviors if they did not have an opinion about being anxious. That opinion is likely to be that anxiety is bad. Why not? It's not pleasant to be fearful and to have the body launched into fight-or-flight mode. It's not fun to be dwelling on worries. Additionally, there are many messages from family, friends, and the culture regarding anxiety and anxious behaviors. These messages are uniformly negative: anxiety is something to be avoided, it is a sign of weakness (especially in males), and if you are going to be anxious, the least you can do is not show it, buck up, and carry on. The prevailing culture gives little room for acceptance of anxious states.

Again, at a physiological, survival-mechanism level, we're not supposed to be okay with anxiety any more than a smoke alarm is supposed to play a lullaby. It's our ancient warning system saying that we are about to be eaten by something larger than us. But in modern times and in our relatively safe societies, the fight-or-flight reaction is often over-the-top, if not a false alarm altogether.

While thinking about our thoughts and feelings can get us into a lot of trouble, these capacities are also our salvation. As I will describe in the next chapter, thinking about thoughts and feelings is the very process by which your child learns to take that helpful step back from her immediate experience in the moment (frustration, fear, anxiety, confusion) and consider the full range of possibilities for action available to her. Clinical researchers have a number of names for this process, such as "mentalizing" or "cognitive defusion." By any name, it is what allows us to escape the grip of literal, all-or-none thinking when it comes to anxiety-provoking situations. Flexible thinking about our thoughts and feelings can open up an anxiety-provoking situation and provide a new perspective or shift the context in ways that make better decisions possible, even if the anxious thoughts and feelings don't change much or at all. Sometimes this can be as simple as noticing how far-out your thoughts are getting and shifting the focus to the situation that is literally at hand: "I need to grab the doorknob and turn it." This was the case for Beth, as we'll see below.

■ Beth: Obsessive-Compulsive Disorder

Beth is a ten-year-old girl with obsessive worries about contamination and disgusting things. At one time, she was washing her hands dozens of times a day because of fears she had touched something contaminated. From the time she learned about germs in preschool, Beth fretted about contact with "the bugs we can't see." Beth would not touch doorknobs, especially in bathrooms, including at home. She would cry and plead for her parents to come and open the bathroom door for her. In the bathroom at school, Beth would have to wait for someone to come in or leave, thereby opening the door for her.

Over time, thoughts about germs subsided, and Beth then worried that she'd somehow accidentally stepped in or touched dog poop. She would not walk on grass or dirt without spending a great deal of time examining the ground around her for signs of dog droppings. She frequently asked her parents if something on the ground or on some object (especially her shoes) was in fact dog poop. These examinations consumed a great deal of Beth's time, and she was unable to play at recess or enjoy family outings.

After a few months, each specific worry receded, only to be replaced by another. Beth had read about carbon monoxide poisoning in homes and was frantic until her parents relented and installed a carbon monoxide detector in their home. She then worried that the device was somehow defective and not functional. She sought constant reassurance from her parents that the equipment was in working order. She would often stay up very late at night for fear of going to sleep and the family perishing. The idea came into her mind that she needed to repeat "dixonom nobrac" ("carbon monoxide" backward) over and over. That seemed to work to keep the family alive. Beth fell asleep only when too tired to stay awake any longer.

Beth's parents, Al and Peggy, did the ABCs list, looking for the activators, behaviors, and consequences in Beth's anxiety-provoking situations. Behaviors of interest included expressions of fear and upset (for example, agitation and crying), along with frequent requests and demands for help negotiating situations that provoked anxiety. The help Beth asked for was often in the form of Al or Peggy examining the immediate area for signs of contamination, providing permission to avoid or direct assistance in avoiding the feared material (for example, germs), plus frequent reassurance that she and the rest of the family were safe. The content of her thoughts came and went: germs, dog poop, carbon monoxide. The two constants were a theme of contamination or poisoning leading to potential harm and Beth's distressed demands for help in avoiding or controlling her anxiety.

Although many situations provoked Beth's worries, the exact activators were often unclear since she didn't have anxiety every time she was in a bathroom or at the park. Al and Peggy did notice that Beth's worries seemed to be worse when there was a lot going on in her life: lots of playdates, after-school activities such as gymnastics (she never expressed worries about the gym mats or other equipment being contaminated), or heightened academic demands at certain times of the school year.

Additionally, at ten years of age, Beth is mature enough to be able to think about her thoughts, feelings, and actions. She can tell you that she knows her anxieties are unreasonable. She will say, "I know it's dirt on my shoe and not dog poop, but my brain doesn't care." But even with this ability to step back a little from her inner world, Beth can easily become trapped in unhelpful behavior patterns simply because the thinking and behavior habits are so entrenched through years of practice. There is always the "but what if it *is*?" thought that trumps all others.

Chains of Events, Actions, and Reactions

You can think of these ABCs as a chain of events where a consequence can be the activator for yet another behavior, which provokes another consequence, and so on. Beth's ABCs might look like this (as described by her mother). I've numbered the steps to show the sequence of events.

Activators	Behaviors	Consequences
1. Big social studies test that day	2. Stuck in bathroom, demanding I open door for her.	3. Told her there was nothing to worry about and that she could do it herself.
4. Still stuck in bathroom.	5. Crying and pleading for twenty minutes.	6. Father opened the door for her but told her angrily that she's too big to be doing this.

I will return to Beth and her ABCs in the chapters that follow. Right now I just want to point out that for Beth, once a worry took hold in her mind, it became amplified and drowned out every other thought. Thoughts of catastrophe overwhelmed her: "The carbon monoxide detector is dead, and this odorless and colorless gas will seep into the house, killing us in our beds as we sleep, or maybe I'll survive and be left an orphan, sent to an orphanage like the one in *Annie*, never to see my friends or my dog again," and so on. For Beth, anxious thinking takes the form of one thought ("What if...?") expanding in her mind to produce a raft of dire and paralyzing predictions about the future. She sees one possible "tree," and it expands into an overwhelming forest of catastrophe. The picture becomes too big, and she cannot bring it down to size.

Classic Anxiety

As children get older and begin school, their thinking and their world expands. New information comes their way and new ways of thinking beyond the immediate situation become possible. These developmental achievements bring new opportunities for learning and further growth. They also bring new ways in which anxiety can show up and take hold of a child.

Beth experiences an extraordinary amount of worries and fears regarding potential mishaps and scary outcomes. In her case, these revolve around the theme of contamination and the what-ifs that follow. I think of hers as "classic anxiety": when too much thinking, too much information, runs wild in a child's mind: What if burglars break into the house at night? What if there's lead on my little brother's toys and he gets poisoned? What if I forget my lines in the play and I'm humiliated? What if my parents get a divorce?

The Disney movie *A Bug's Life* has a scene that nicely illustrates classic anxiety. A twist on the old fable, the storyline is of ants that are being extorted by lazy, scary grasshoppers. The grasshoppers demand that the good and hardworking ants pay them tribute in the form of food, which the ants must harvest for them. Due to circumstances I needn't go into here, the ants are being forced to give what may be all of their food to the grasshoppers. The ants quickly assume that they will not have enough of the harvest left to avoid starvation in the coming winter. Panic ensues. From one fact ("We must give even more food to the grasshoppers!"), catastrophic conclusions are drawn in their little ant minds ("We will surely starve!"). The picture has become too big and the ants become overwhelmed, frightened, and paralyzed, much like your own child might in the face of overwhelming anxious thoughts.

When your child's picture of the world or the future gets too big, then someone, probably you, needs to help her refocus to a perspective that is less overwhelming, one that points the way to a possible solution to the problem, to the extent that there is a problem to be solved. What the ants need to do in that moment is simple and specific: solve the problem by collectively taking a deep breath and focusing on gathering more food. When your child's picture of the world gets too big, she can feel overwhelmed and panic-stricken. On the other hand, your child's focus at times can become too small, fixated on one detail, one aspect of a situation, at the expense of the big picture and the guidance it can provide. That's the problem Sterling has, as we'll see below.

■ Sterling: When the Picture Gets Too Small

Sterling is eight. He has a very high IQ and is in the third grade. Sterling's mother, Angela, reports that he is typically in a happy mood, except when he is "going ballistic" about something, usually a situation that requires taking on a new challenge or venturing into new territory. For example, Sterling is extremely reluctant to try any activity without assurance that he will do it very well, if not perfectly, the first time. He has tried a number of sports (tee ball, soccer, gymnastics) and any number of activities (bike riding, swimming, piano), giving them all up after the first mistake or apprehensive moment. When this happens, he will scream, hit himself, say he's stupid and no good, and refuse to continue.

At other times, Sterling, when faced with a challenging task such as a homework assignment or a chore, will lapse into what his mother calls "robot talk," a grating monotone in which Sterling claims to not be a human and to not know how to do homework or whatever is being asked of him. If pressed, he may begin to run around the room in circles saying that he has to get his anxiety out. These behaviors are starting to show up at school. Sterling's teacher is confused and his classmates are starting to be wary of him.

Sterling is a stickler for routine and structure. He has a strong memory for detail and will notice if anything in the environment is changed. On the other hand, Sterling can be oblivious to the most obvious social cues coming from adults or peers.

Angela reported an episode of what she was certain was obsessive-compulsive behavior. She and Sterling were trying to get out of the house in the morning. It was a Monday after Sterling had a three-day weekend at his father's house. (Sterling's parents divorced when he was three years old.) On that morning, Sterling seemed especially agitated and anxious. At one point, he sat on the couch and would not move. He was fully dressed and otherwise ready to go to school, but he kept tying and retying his shoes (something he'd only recently learned to do). As Angela tried to hurry him, Sterling broke down, sobbing and frantically yelling that he had to get the loops on his shoelaces, two per shoe, to be exactly the same length.

Looking at the ABCs of this last event gives us the following description from Angela's point of view.

Activators	Behaviors	Consequences
1. Monday morning after weekend at his father's	2. Pacing, whining	3. Ignored him/gave him space.
4. Lost track of time; now time to leave for school; didn't give him his usual five-minute warning.	5. Sitting on the couch, chewing on sleeve	6. Told him gently to get his shoes on, it was time to go to school; he could probably hear the tension and worry in my voice.
	7. Tying, untying, and retying his shoes; clearly upset	8. Asked him to tell me what he was anxious about.
	9. Crying and yelling that he needed the laces to be the same length	10. Held him on my lap until he calmed down; late for school, late for work.

Sterling's anxieties show up in the form of intense upset (similar to the pantrums Abby shows) and in avoidance and control behaviors (running around in circles, claiming he can't do a task, engaging in routines). The activators for his anxiety are typically situations that challenge or threaten his competence. The consequences are complex, as we shall see, and involve a great deal of interaction between Sterling and his mother.

Sterling has a much more difficult time than Beth describing what is going on inside him. In spite of being eight, his thinking style does not yet consistently show much capacity for thinking about his thoughts and feelings. He has learned, through his mother, to call his upset "anxiety," but he is not typically worried or distressed except under these challenging circumstances. When under pressure, Sterling's thinking zeroes in on one small detail of the situation, such as the soccer ball or the length of his shoelace loops, and he attempts to control that one thing with all his might. Of course, complete control is impossible and his inability to achieve that needed control plunges him into an intense and all-consuming reaction. Angela must then step in and manage his upset with soothing behaviors (holding and rocking) typically used for a much younger child.

Sterling lacks basic emotional vocabulary to communicate what he's experiencing. Articulating his frustration with his shoelaces was actually a small, positive step. More often he will only say things like "I can't" or "I won't" over and over, or he screams or engages in unhelpful actions such as running around in circles or running away.

While Sterling is clearly and chronically anxious, he is not especially worried. Sterling is not giving his inner world that much thought at all. All he knows is that he is upset and stuck. He then reacts to the upsetting situations in his world, provoking reactions in his mother and other adults so that they might understand him and step in to manage him when he can't manage himself.

Modern Anxiety

Beth and Sterling illustrate two quite different reactions to challenging situations. Because of Beth's maturity, she has the cognitive skills to think well beyond the immediate situation and imagine all sorts of possibilities, including deadly ones. Her attempts to manage the dreadful possibilities, in order to manage her anxiety, are unhelpful and also limit her life in many ways. This is what I think of as classic anxiety.

Sterling, on the other hand, shows a second style of reacting to challenges. Because he is very prone to regression, Sterling's thinking can suddenly become literal, concrete, all-or-none, and fragile. Compared to his more expansive and flexible age-appropriate thinking, his view of himself and the world then becomes *too small*. Like someone wearing blinders, a child can suddenly focus on a detail of a situation at the expense of the big picture, the tree instead of the forest, and this detail assumes huge and overwhelming proportions. This is upsetting in and of itself. The problem can then be compounded by a severe restricting of response options that goes along with a restriction in perspective. For reasons I will describe below, I call this "modern anxiety" in order to distinguish it from the classic variety.

This analogy may help you appreciate what modern anxiety feels like: Imagine walking through a very dark house with only a flashlight that shines a very narrow, focused beam. Only a small bit of the room is illuminated at a time. Objects are disconnected and only partially revealed. This in itself may feel somewhat anxiety provoking. You sweep your small spot of light around the room. You see a few books. They appear to be on a small table. Or maybe it's a large table. There's a doorknob and something large looming next to it. On your left, a faint noise attracts your attention. You move the light that way. A clock and then a picture. The clock is ticking. What are they resting on? Is that a mantle shelf? From your right, there's a loud noise. You wildly swing the light in that direction. You shine the light back and forth, trying to find the source of the sound. Was it the door? It seems to still be closed. But now where did that large object go that was next to the door?

Compare this with walking through the same room with all the lights on. Now you can take in the various objects and their relationships to one another with ease and a sense of perspective and context. On your right, there's an ironing board propped up next to the door that obviously opens into a closet. While your attention is drawn to a ticking clock on the fireplace mantle, you see the ironing board move out of the corner of your eye. As you turn your head, you see it fall to the floor with a loud crash. Having the larger frame of reference or perspective helps make sense of what you are seeing, and it can alert you to what is happening so that events can be less confusing or startling. But for many children, this sense of a larger picture eludes them or may simply abandon them just when they need it most. This makes the world, like the dark room, a scary and anxiety-provoking place.

Think of events that can activate your child's intense, anxious reactions. How often do they involve an event that lands right in your child's pathway: "They're out of chocolate ice cream" or "We have to leave now." It is unexpected, even if you, as the adult, could have predicted it. It looms before her, obscuring the goal or destination she'd been working toward a moment earlier: to get some ice cream or to finish the video game before school. With the goal suddenly gone from sight, she is lost and overwhelmed. The behavior that follows is fight or flight.

Modern anxiety is marked less by persistent worry than by a chronic or recurring fear and panic that is whipped up suddenly, wreaks havoc, and then is gone. The child is overwhelmed and insecure, and her primary reaction is one of desperate attempts to control the situation. This often means getting you, the adult, to control the situation.

We can return to the movie *A Bug's Life* to illustrate modern anxiety. In the opening scene, a leaf falls from a tree to the ground. It floats gently down and lands smack on top of a column of ants bearing food for the grasshoppers. Several ants are flattened under the leaf and the long line of bearers halts. The leaf has become a roadblock. The ants, being ants, are accustomed to following the trail set out by the ants ahead of them without having to think about it. With the leaf in the way, they are bewildered and panic-stricken, not knowing what to do. An old ant appears off to one side and tells the others, "You can go around the leaf." Confused and uncertain at first, the ants hesitate. The old ant continues to tell them, gently but insistently, "You can go around the leaf." After some reluctance, the ants carefully step around the leaf. Once one or two safely make it to the other side, the others follow readily and the column marches on. The slight detour around the leaf is now an accepted part of the path.

I call this modern anxiety because it seems to be associated with certain styles of thinking and interacting with the world. I have observed this in some anxious children who also have other psychological conditions that have been getting a lot of attention in the last twenty years. These include attention-deficit/hyperactivity disorder and learning disabilities, as well as some newer syndromes you may have heard of, such as sensory integration disorder, Asperger's disorder, and nonverbal learning disability. Children with these conditions tend to have concrete, literal, detail-oriented, and linear thinking styles. This style is very useful for certain kinds of perceiving and problem solving (for example, engineering), but it can be a liability when dealing with the more intuitive, social-emotional aspects of one's world and for seeing the big picture, the road map through and out of frustrating and upsetting situations.

Because of their strong detail orientation and a deficiency in seeing the bigger picture, these children may have difficulty ascertaining abstract social rules, certain social cues (for example, facial expressions), and other important types of information about the outer world of others as well as their own inner world of emotions. The resulting confusion and uncertainty is a breeding ground for anxiety. This kind of anxiety can show up as an intense need for sameness and consistency, for predictability, for control over the environment (especially people), intense negative reactions when expectations are violated, and avoidance of situations that are ambiguous or pose a threat to their competence and sense of control.

Depending on the form this kind of anxiety takes, it may be given a label such as obsessive-compulsive disorder, separation anxiety, social phobia, school phobia, or others. The common theme, however, is that the child has difficulty interpreting the world and feeling successful in it. Every day is an overwhelming challenge. Tension and frustration are the result.

Think of Sterling on that Monday morning. There were many factors conspiring to raise his anxiety level and his overall sensitivity: the transition back from his father's house late the night before, heading back to school after the weekend, his mother saying he had to get his shoes on and leave the house now (without his usual five-minute warning), struggling with this new shoe-tying skill, and perhaps others. It was all too much, with only the prospect of more challenges and threats to his security and competence in store for him that day at school. So Sterling's mind latched onto one small thing that he might have some chance of controlling—those shoelaces. But, unfortunately, because he was a stressed eight-year-old, the old, fragile all-or-none thinking was just under the surface, and his sole criterion for successful control was perfection. But perfection in the form of shoelaces tied exactly as he imagined wasn't in the cards that morning. If life wasn't perfectly good, then it was perfectly awful, and as his world shattered, Sterling's reaction reflected his frustration, despair, and helplessness.

SUMMARY AND A LOOK AHEAD

In this chapter, I've described how anxiety can emerge out of quite normal developmental processes involving temperament—your child's inborn tendencies to approach or withdraw, to be passive or reactive, to remain upset or to quickly find her equilibrium. These biologically based predispositions set the stage for your child's reactions (behaviors) in certain situations (activators). Does she shy away from new situations or dash headlong into them? Will her reactions to strange or novel events (Uncle Harry) be mild or intense? Will she recover quickly or slowly when upset? Add to this your child's early style of thinking—fused, rigid, and all-or-none—and the potential exists for developing habitual patterns of thinking about the world around her (it's unpredictable, scary, and frustrating) and reacting to that world in ways that are not helpful (regression, pantrums, excessive avoidance and control).

However, life's challenges are the fertile ground for growth. For example, having one's expectations violated is inevitable and most children will use these experiences to develop the capacity for flexibility in their expectations and to defuse and focus on the important elements of a situation ("I got my juice") and de-emphasize the inconsequential elements (the color of the cup). These kinds of frustrations, if not too overwhelming and handled reasonably well by the adults, promote growth in terms of viewing the world more accurately and flexibly, as well as learning distress tolerance and self-soothing.

Anxiety is also inevitable. Like frustration, anxiety becomes a problem when the child's reactions to anxious thoughts and feelings overemphasize avoidance and control at the expense of viewing the world accurately and learning to tolerate distress and to self-soothe. To this I would also add that avoidance and control reactions interfere with learning more socially acceptable forms of communicating one's feelings and needs and obtaining help from adults.

What both classic and modern anxiety call for is a shift from focusing on the problem (the anxiety a situation provokes) to focusing on the solution (getting to what the situation is asking of us at the moment). As in *A Bug's Life*, the focus shifts from thoughts and feelings to what needs to happen next: "We need to get started on harvesting what we can" and "We need to get around the leaf."

As a parent, you play the role of that elder ant. You provide the perspective and point out what needs to happen next so that your child can get unstuck and start moving forward, even if it's just one small step at a time: "I need to use the bathroom." "I need to get out of the bathroom." "I need to get my shoes tied and be on my way to school." If the focus is on taking this next small step, and then the next, and then the next, fear and anxiety do not necessarily go away. They may, however, retreat to the background enough to move forward with life and to experience success in dealing with life's challenges, and thus to grow in self-confidence.

In the next chapter, I will describe the *process* of anxiety or, more accurately, the process of how your child gets stuck in these unhelpful reactions marked by avoidance and inappropriate control. You and your child participate in this process through the anxiety dance: the subtle and not-so-subtle actions and reactions that you both perform in the face of fearful and anxious situations. I will describe how these interactions become choreographed and how they are maintained in your lives, often in spite of valiant efforts to change the dance. In the short run, your child must rely on you for rescue and reassurance. As she grows and becomes more skilled at managing anxiety-provoking situations, she will be able to help herself get free from struggles with anxiety without undue avoidance and control. In the pages to come, I will show you how you can use the power of your relationship with your child to help her grow into that capability.

CHAPTER 3

Responsive Parenting and the Process of Anxiety

In chapter 1, I described the "what" of anxiety: constellations of symptoms that are distressing to your child and to you. In the last chapter, I made the case for how anxiety develops through the interplay between biological tendencies (temperament) and early experiences in the world. The result is the vast array of behaviors that we use to identify the various anxiety disorders: fears, worries, obsessions, compulsions, and attempts at avoidance and control.

This chapter is about the process of anxiety: how it becomes established in your child's life as a disorder rather than simply the transient feelings and worries all children have at some time. Central to this process is how your child gets you to join him in the struggle in order to help him avoid, escape, or control his distressing thoughts and feelings.

An anxiety disorder is not simply the presence of anxious thoughts and feelings. An anxiety disorder is about becoming stuck—stuck in a pattern of anxious upset; inflexible, unhelpful thinking; and maladaptive avoidance and control strategies. Avoidance and control interfere with important life activities, such as being able to go places, interacting appropriately with peers and siblings, taking on reasonable risks, and many others.

In this chapter, I will describe how anxious reactions to common activators can strengthen the habit of avoiding situations—such as school, social activities, and so on—that are necessary for your child's health and development. I will describe how these reactions are a problem because your child engages in ineffective and costly control strategies that prevent him from mastering more useful ways of dealing with distress and obtaining help from others.

I will also describe how you, the parent, become involved in the "anxiety dance" through the activation of your own distressing thoughts and feelings. I will offer an explanation for why it is so hard to change these unhelpful behavior patterns. Finally, I will describe a new approach to managing anxious situations that will allow you to stop *reacting* to your anxious child and start *responding* to him.

THE ANXIETY GAMBIT

A *gambit* is an opening move in chess in which a player sacrifices a pawn or other piece in order to gain an advantage. More generally, a gambit is any maneuver by which a person hopes to gain an advantage, often by inviting another person to take part in the maneuver in some way. It is an invitation to collaborate, to experience something together, to dance. I want to suggest that your child's anxious behavior is a gambit—not the anxious feelings and thoughts themselves, but your child's behaviors in the face of anxiety, his reactions to his own thoughts and feelings. These behaviors serve to get you, or some other adult, to react along with him.

Think of your child's common fears and anxieties and how they show up. Think of what activates them and the behaviors that he engages in. Think of the consequences of those behaviors. More often than not, those consequences will directly involve you or another person. Most likely, it is you. The problem that drew you to this book is probably best described as a series of events: a situation, a reaction, a counterreaction, a counter-counterreaction, and so on and on until the whole episode crashes or runs out of gas. Your child invites you to participate in his anxiety—as a witness, a confidante, a cheerleader, a taskmaster, a lifeguard.

There is a natural process at work here and it necessarily involves you. It necessarily involves your own thoughts and feelings, as I will describe below. The question is, will the process also involve *your* efforts at avoidance and control, or will you be the one to show your child a better way? If there is a better way to manage anxious situations, it must come from an understanding of the processes underlying your child's anxious behaviors and your current reactions to those behaviors. That's where we're going now.

ABC-Dance

Let's look briefly again at the children I described in the last chapter. In certain activating situations, Abby, our four-year old, becomes withdrawn, mute, and paralyzed. At other times, she is wildly upset. Catherine and Wayne are confused and upset by Abby's behaviors. They can only guess at what is going on inside her mind and what she wants. As such, it is painfully difficult to know how to respond, and they frequently feel frustrated and discouraged by repeated failures to help Abby feel better and engage the world rather than retreat from it. As with Abby herself, their reactions tend to be very all-or-none. On the one hand, Catherine and Wayne lean in forcefully, imposing expectations and limits and insisting that Abby do certain behaviors in spite of her obvious reluctance. On the other hand, in the face of despair or anger, they may throw up their hands, retreat, and avoid dealing with her altogether. Adding a fourth column to our previous tables—again from the parents' point of view—their dance looks something like this:

Activator	Behavior	Consequence	Dance
Birthday party at a home Abby has never been to. All the other children are being very social.	Abby clings to my leg and refuses to say hello to the birthday girl. All the other mothers are watching.	Feel intense embarrassment and anger. Not sure what I was thinking.	Pulled Abby out of the party and drove home with clenched jaw. Put Abby in her room. I cried for 20 minutes in my room. Later she acted as if nothing had happened.

This fourth column, described as "Dance," is a change from the simple ABC model from the last chapter. Here the fourth column is meant to link what the parent thinks and feels (the immediate and personally felt consequence of her child's anxious behavior) and what the parent does next. Note that "All the other mothers are watching" is not a behavior of Abby's. But this thought of Catherine's is a definite activator for the kind of feelings and thoughts she experiences next.

Now let's look at the situation with Beth and Sterling, whom we also met in the previous chapter. We'll start with Beth. The dance between Beth and her parents, Al and Peggy, seems relatively straightforward: Beth becomes overwhelmed by anxious thoughts and feelings and uses a variety of strategies to obtain help and reassurance from her parents. Her parents have thoughts and feelings about Beth's thoughts and feelings, and about Beth's help seeking. Al and Peggy then react in characteristic ways, as we see here:

Activator	Behavior	Consequence	Dance
Coming home from a pleasant walk.	Beth asked if mud on her shoe is dog poop.	Had the thought, "When is she going to grow out of this?" Felt discouraged.	Told her, "No, that's not dog poop. Look closely. See it's just dirt. Honestly, Beth!"

Beth's behavior in the face of anxiety invites her parents to participate. Like Abby's parents, they are good parents. They care about Beth and want her to feel good and to meet life's challenges. They provide what help and reassurance they can. They do their best to help Beth while recognizing they mustn't indulge her completely. But where do they draw the line? How do they balance help and reassurance against enabling? And how can they avoid having the dance move into yet more unhappy feelings such as anger, resentment, and discouragement?

When he is in the throes of fear and anxiety, Sterling, like Abby, has great difficulty expressing his inner world in terms that make sense and are useful to his mother, Angela. As a single mother working full-time and with little support from extended family, it's easy for Angela to become discouraged and deeply saddened by her son's obvious pain. Angela just wants her son to be happy. Her most common tactic in the face of Sterling's upset is to try to reduce the pressure each of them feels in the moment and to yield to demands and expectations in the hope that Sterling will feel better. When Sterling feels better, Angela feels relieved. Sterling does feel better, but he is not maturing and not gaining important self-control skills. Angela's relief is always short-lived. In terms of activators, behaviors, consequences, and now dance, a typical problem situation, from Angela's vantage point, might look like this:

Activator	Behavior	Consequence	Dance
Doing homework late in the evening. Long day for both of us.	Sterling sitting in front of his homework and screaming over and over, "I can't do it."	Feeling tired and discouraged. Trying not to feel impatient.	Took a deep breath and said, "It will be okay. Let's find some homework that you can do."

You could say that Angela's helping Sterling escape the difficult homework activator is just another consequence, even a reward, in response to his anxious behavior. You would be correct. However, I am calling this segment of the chain of events the "dance" because it is the point in the chain when one or both partners take the situation in a particular direction. This could be in the direction of avoiding, escaping, and controlling anxiety. Or, as we'll see, it could be in the direction of communication, support, problem solving, and keeping your goal in sight.

EXERCISE: Your Anxiety Dance

Using the following table, describe a common anxiety event starring your child and yourself. As in the examples above, briefly describe the activating conditions, your child's behavior, the consequence of that behavior in terms of your own thoughts and feelings, and the dance that follows, that is, what you typically do next, plus any thoughts and feelings that might show up following your actions. Although there can be long chains of activators, behaviors, consequences, and dance moves stretching seamlessly across many minutes or even hours, this will necessarily be a brief and perhaps simplistic description of what actually happens in your life.

Activator	Behavior	Consequence	Dance

As I mentioned in the first chapter, I'm interested in the common features of anxiety behaviors. I suggested that avoidance and control are two common themes in your child's behavior pattern when he is fearful or anxious. Upon examination, these behaviors are often an attempt to get *you* to help *him* avoid or control these distressing thoughts and feelings. No doubt he has become quite good at it. This is because, without having to think about it, your child can count on your own upset, your own distressing thoughts and feelings, when he displays anxious behaviors. He counts on your distress as a motivator to help him avoid and control because, at those times, you too will be motivated to avoid or control how *you* feel. This isn't a malicious act, and your child doesn't appreciate the cost of doing business this way; he's just trying to get his needs met in the most efficient way possible.

Negative Reinforcement

You may have heard the term "negative reinforcement." Most people believe it is the same as punishment, but it's really not. Negative reinforcement is a technical term coming out of behavior modification therapies. Anytime the words *reinforcement* or *reinforcer* are used in this type of therapy, you are talking about increasing the likelihood that a behavior will occur in the future. You know that a reward can act as a reinforcer to increase behavior you want—that's positive reinforcement.

So what is negative reinforcement? In *negative reinforcement*, the likelihood of any action increases if that action can reliably help someone avoid or escape something unpleasant or threatening. For example, you get in your car, start it up, and immediately hear that annoying buzzing or chiming reminding you to fasten your seat belt. You quickly fasten the seat belt to escape that sound, or perhaps you buckle up right away, thereby avoiding that noise altogether. Then you race to the day care center to pick up your child before you're hit with the dollar-a-minute late charge. As you're speeding along, you notice a motorcycle cop ahead pointing a radar gun in your direction. You immediately slow down to within the speed limit to avoid getting a ticket. You pick up your child at day care and he starts fussing the moment he sees you. You know he's acting this way because he's hungry (a friend calls this "hypoglyscreamia"). But you anticipated his hunger and brought a snack, which terminates the fussing once your child has eaten.

Fastening your seat belt, driving within the speed limit, and providing the snack are all behaviors that you are likely to do in the future because they allowed you to escape or avoid something aversive: your car's seatbelt buzzer, the traffic ticket, your child's fussing. Escaping or avoiding the annoying buzzer, the ticket, the fussing—all negative or aversive experiences—is the *reinforcer* for your behavior (buckling your seat belt, driving the speed limit, bringing a snack); this is negative reinforcement.

Right now you can probably think of many examples of daily behavior that is shaped up and maintained by negative reinforcement. From wearing a seat belt in the car to flossing your teeth, you are trying to avoid unpleasantness in the immediate or distant future. And you are likely teaching your child these behaviors to help him stay safe and healthy. In the following exercise, I would like you to think about a few situations from your everyday life that invite actions meant to help you escape or avoid unpleasant consequences.

EXERCISE: Everyday Escape and Avoidance

After reading the examples below, add a few of your own.

Situation	Action Taken	Unpleasantness Escaped or Avoided
Rainy streets	Driving slowly	Car accident
Crying infant	Picking up infant	Infant's crying (he quiets down)
Bills due	Paying bills on time	Late fee

By definition these are actions you have learned and continue to perform because they keep you, or your child, out of harm's way or somehow help you or your child escape or avoid unpleasantness. Negative reinforcement is big in your life, and it is very big in the life of your child.

I am going to go out on a limb here and state that negative reinforcement is the single most important mechanism at work in your child's pattern of anxious behaviors, regardless of his particular diagnosis. It looms large among the common processes that underlie the various anxiety disorders. As we've seen in the ABCD tables above, a child's anxiety can be described in terms of a chain of events: activators, behaviors, and consequences (for you and for the child). Your child's behavior evokes thoughts and feelings in you that, as we shall see, are and must be similar to what he's experiencing in that moment. They are probably no more pleasant for you than they are for him. You are *both* motivated to avoid or escape these distressing thoughts and feelings. Your next actions (what I refer to as the dance) are likely helping *both* you and your child escape or avoid this unpleasantness—what we might call ABCD-Escape/Avoidance. The goal of the anxiety dance is to escape or avoid the upset that you and your child are experiencing.

Abby's mother takes her home from the birthday party. Beth's father opens the bathroom door for her. Sterling's mother cuts him some slack on his homework. The relief they each then feel, both parent and child—even if brief, even if mixed with many other thoughts and feelings—will serve as a reinforcer for the same or a similar action in the future. Abby will cling to her mother. Beth will plead and cry. Sterling will scream, "I can't, I can't." Catherine will escape the situation with Abby but feel angry about it. Peggy will reassure Beth that mud is just mud but will feel discouraged. Angela will soothe Sterling and help him find some other work to do but will wonder if he's ever going to be able to manage without her.

Think about how your child's anxiety shows up and what happens next. Could it be described, in the simplest and most generic terms, as follows?

Activator	Behavior	Consequence	Dance	Escape/ Avoidance
A challenging situation	Your child expresses fear or anxiety through his words and behaviors.	You think and feel distressing things: your own anxiety, frustration, anger, discouragement, and so on.	You do what it takes to end the challenging situation or to get your child to stop feeling his anxiety.	Your distressing thoughts and feelings are reduced, if not eliminated.

Now, avoidance and control aren't always bad. For example, avoiding that speeding ticket is probably a good idea, and having a snack in the car to greet a hungry child (and perhaps avoid a meltdown) is just good planning and parenting. Your child can, and probably should, avoid frightening

TV images and news stories. If your eight-year-old child is frightened by the thought of going alone into the dark basement, it is perfectly acceptable to accompany him. In subsequent chapters, I will describe ways of managing these situations from your role as a parent and "dance partner." However, what I want to emphasize now is that when avoidance and control strategies interfere with daily, age-appropriate expectations, then this "solution" to a child's anxiety creates its own problems.

■ Joshua: Separation Anxiety

Joshua is a six-year-old boy who until the last six months seemed quite happy, independent, and carefree. He enjoyed kindergarten last year and seemed happy this year to be a "big first-grader." However, just before the winter break, Joshua's parents, Sid and Nancy, began to notice a change. He'd become moody and sensitive. Little things began to annoy him, especially the actions of his three-and-a-half-year-old brother, Bradley, who previously had been Joshua's best buddy.

Moodiness became fearfulness. This quickly escalated to a stark inability to be apart from his parents without significant distress. There were prolonged and tearful good-byes at school every morning. The first week after winter break, Joshua was late to school every day but Friday, sometimes by as much as an hour, because he was inconsolable at home and refused to leave the house. He threw tantrums and cried when his grandmother came to spend the evening so that his parents could have a night out. His parents went out anyway, but they did not enjoy their evening and came back early.

Joshua began following his parents from room to room at home. When one of them went to the bathroom, he would wait outside the door. He would insist that his mother or father accompany him if he went from one floor of the house to the other. Sometimes they accommodated him, but with clear impatience and anger. Sometimes they held out, insisting he was big enough to go upstairs by himself. Tears and immobility were the result.

Bedtime was the worst. Joshua had been a great sleeper as an infant, though he'd gone through a period of restlessness and waking easily right after his brother, Bradley, was born. No one was getting much sleep then, but after a few months, the sleep issues resolved. Now Joshua was having tremendous difficulty going to sleep at night. He fought the bedtime routine every step of the way—from turning off the electronics to getting into pajamas, brushing teeth, and settling into bed. There were many requests for snacks, drinks, or one more story. After being left in his bed, there were numerous "curtain calls," coming out of his room in tears with complaints of scary bedroom sounds, sights, and worries. Sid and Nancy would put him back in bed each time, with increasing impatience and decreasing sympathy. Hours after the routine began, there were threats of loss of TV and computer privileges the next day, then more anger and tears all around. Threats eventually worked to get him to stay in bed, but sometime around three in the morning, Joshua would quietly slip into his parents' bed. A third of the time Sid and Nancy didn't even notice, a third of the time they took him back to his bed, and a third of the time they just moved over and let him stay.

What is this dance that Joshua and his parents are caught up in? What purpose is it serving? What is each member of this family contributing, losing, and gaining? Looking at the ABCDEs, again from Sid and Nancy's point of view, we see the following pattern: Joshua is quite good at engaging his parents when he is feeling fearful and anxious. He is attempting to get their help, to be rescued from (escape or avoid) the intense thoughts and feelings that arise when he must be apart from them. This need for security and for their help is important enough to Joshua that he will use whatever "skills" he has at his disposal. If these anxious behaviors—the crying, pleading, tantrums, helplessness, and so on—work to escape or avoid the anxiety and fear, even if only a fraction of the time, negative reinforcement will be operating and these behaviors will continue and even become more likely in the future. And practicing a behavior, like any skill, only makes us better at it.

And no, Joshua doesn't appreciate the cost of doing business this way. He is not seeing the strain all this dancing is placing on his parents. Sid and Nancy are barely aware of what is going on, reeling as they are from one distressing episode to the next. Like good dance partners, Joshua and his parents complement each other: his picture has become too big and theirs has become too small. Everyone is feeling helpless, incompetent, frustrated, and anxious. Like Joshua, Sid and Nancy are highly motivated to just make it stop. Everyone has fallen into a pattern of avoidance and control. Through no one's fault, they find themselves in this trap together. They will have to get each other out.

ANXIETY AND PARENT-CHILD TRANSACTIONS

Recall that I used the term "transactions" in chapter 2 to emphasize the mutual influence and change that occurs when parents and their chil-

Activator	Behavior	Consequence	Dance	Escape/Avoidance
A necessary separation from one or both parents	Shaking, crying, pleading with parent not to leave or to accompany him	Nancy: Fatigue, impatience, and frustration, leading to anger. Common thoughts: "I don't have time for this" and "I can't be doing this when he's 16." Sid: Memories of his own nighttime fear and panic as a child. Residual stress from work that day. Desire for peace and quiet at home. Resentment. Common thoughts: "Nancy's not handling this well" and "I'm not going to be unsympathetic like my father was with me."	Nancy: Insisting Joshua be "a big boy" and go to school, go upstairs by himself to get his socks, stay in his bed once he's there, and so on. Threats and bribes follow. Joshua complies or retreats. Sid: Mostly gently assisting Joshua upstairs or back to bed with reassurances that there's nothing to be afraid of. May explode with anger if pushed over the edge. Joshua complies or retreats.	Joshua: Engaging his parents helps reduce his fears and uncertainty, even if the transaction is unpleasant. Nancy: Joshua's eventual compliance affirms her belief that she has to get tough with him. Sid: Joshua's eventual compliance affirms his belief that he must support his son in these moments. Exploding feels bad, but he can blame that on work stress.

dren interact. Parent-child transactions are the earliest and perhaps the most important influence on a child's development. Certainly biology (for example, temperament) is important, and sadly some children are born into the world with considerable neurological deficits or differences that set the stage for later challenges, both behavioral and emotional. But it is the many daily exchanges between you and your child that teach him about the world and himself and how to manage that world and himself. My goal in writing this book is to teach you, the parent, how you can use the power of your relationship with your child in the context of those many daily transactions to increase his competence in the world and eventually reduce his anxiety. And with your increased skill and confidence in handling anxiety-activating situations, you should expect to see a change in your own daily stress and anxiety as well. This is the direction the new dance will take you and your child.

From Parent Regulation to Self-Regulation

Within minutes of his arrival in this world, you directly helped regulate and organize your child's world. You fed him and kept him clean and warm and safe when he could do none of that himself. This provided him with a sense that uncomfortable sensations could be managed. You kept your child from becoming overstimulated, as in, for example, telling Uncle Harry when to back off with the rattle. As your child grew older and began exploring the world, you regulated his exposure to various stimuli, interesting and pleasant as well as noxious or dangerous. When he became overwhelmed, you soothed him. You helped him sort out his various feelings and experiences and gave him words to describe them. And in the process of you caring for him, he's responded to you in ways that have changed you forever.

Now, regardless of how old your child is, he still needs you. There are still scary and overwhelming thoughts and feelings to be recognized, named, and categorized. There is still regulating—of self and of others—to be done. Immediate gratification must be weighed against long-term gain. Sometimes your child can manage these tasks quite well. That is the evidence of his growth and maturity. But at those times when he is overwhelmed and has regressed, regardless of how unreasonable or unimportant or minor the reason, he still needs you to step in and do at least some of this managing for him, at this time, in this situation. That's still part of your parent job description. But *how* you help your child matters, and you will need all your options open and every tool in your toolbox to give him the appropriate help.

How you regulate your child—the strategies you use, the tone and tactics you employ—provides the model for how he will help regulate himself. These strategies, tone, and tactics, along with your child's transactions with many other individuals in his life, become *internalized*—that is, these experiences become a part of who he is, how he thinks, and how he responds to life. Consciously and unconsciously, your child draws on these stored models of communicating, problem identification, and problem solving, and applies them to situations he encounters, now and into the future.

Parent Power

One of our most effective treatment models for childhood behavior problems (defiance, aggression, and so on) is known variously as parent management training, behavioral parent training, and the like. Harnessing the natural value and power of the parent-child relationship, a therapist works directly with the parents to increase their skills for managing a child's behaviors in the face of strong emotions and impulses.

Parents are taught to recognize conditions leading to positive and negative reinforcement. From this knowledge comes the ability to be more *contingent*, which means responding to your child in a way that will increase the chances of a desired behavior occurring again (reward or "reinforcement") or in a way that will decrease an undesired behavior in the future (through punishment or not letting a behavior such as hitting work for the child). The parent learns to adjust the consequences to shift the child's behavior in a positive direction. The effectiveness of these techniques has been demonstrated by decades of clinical experience and research. More recently these parent-centered treatment strategies have been successfully applied to child anxiety (Diamond and Josephson 2005).

The vast majority of books on parenting use some variation of this parent-training model. The focus is on the grown-up making the first move to change the way parent and child interact with each another. Like dance partners learning new steps, the parent leads the child into a new way of doing things, which reduces conflict and increases self-control on the part of the child. Like learning to dance, this requires practice and perseverance.

THE PARENT-CHILD DANCE

Jean Dumas at Purdue University, along with Robert Wahler at the University of Tennessee at Knoxville, has spent many years studying how parents and their children interact. Dr. Dumas describes the "interrelated ways of thinking, feeling, and acting that have become characteristic of people who interact with each other often, such as parents and children" (Dumas 2005, p. 781). Pair figure skaters, pilot and copilot, quarterback and wide receiver all have practiced their routines together so that a series of near seamless actions and reactions lead to a goal of some kind: a gold-medal performance, landing a plane in a thunderstorm, or scoring a touchdown against a tough defense. Repetition makes these procedures or interaction patterns highly efficient and quite automatic. They are meant to work well under pressure.

These "interrelated ways of thinking, feeling, and acting" are your choreography; they describe and dictate the dance routines you and your child perform every day. Your choreographed dance routine likely begins with waking and getting ready for the day and ends with whatever nighttime rituals conclude with your child asleep in his bed—or not asleep, as the case may be. Like Fred Astaire and Ginger Rogers, you and your child dance your way through situation after situation.

Most of these routines—those that are thoughtful and adaptable—help to accomplish necessary and positive tasks. However, some of your routines, as we have seen, are a direct response to fear and anxiety and can result in frustration and dysfunction. Often they are performed with little, if any, conscious awareness. They can be automatic.

Automatic parent-child routines—dances that have been practiced over and over—develop as a way of coping with a stressful or challenging situation and serve some goal, if only our survival. They allow each partner in the transaction an assigned role and each can expect the other to act in predictable ways, now and in similar future situations. You and your child do what you do without giving it much thought. And largely because you're not thinking about what you're doing, these dance routines are highly resistant to change.

Helpful and Unhelpful Dances

Parent-child interactions become quite automatic over time. Like a practiced dance team, parents and children fall into a routine of highly predictable steps. Like most solo behavior routines that you've done a million times, such as playing a song on the piano or driving home from work, these parent-child behavior patterns can be largely out of your awareness while they are happening. You and your child can do them without thinking about them.

Now some automatic behavior patterns are quite useful and adaptive. They are at the heart of multitasking: washing dishes while talking on the phone, performing routine tasks at work, and so on. Additionally, and this is important, we fall back on our most automatic responses when we are stressed, challenged, or feeling insecure in some way. When your child does the regression thing I previously described, he is in many ways reverting to old, automatic behavior patterns—old choreography. Unfortunately, these old dances are often not well-matched to present circumstances.

Joshua's Regression and the Return of Old Choreography

At age six, Joshua had been progressing well in his path to self-regulation. He had become more or less independent in all the basic toileting, eating, and dressing skills. He was developing nicely around peer interactions and using his words to express his emotions and solve problems. He still needed grown-ups for many supportive functions, of course. But he was able to be apart from his parents, interact appropriately with other grown-ups and peers, and rely on his own ability to talk himself through angry, sad, or anxious moments (self-soothing).

But then something happened. Development stalled and even began to reverse itself. Somehow Joshua had been pushed beyond an invisible line of security and confidence. In spite of being proud that he was now in the first grade, he was finding the work challenging and his self-esteem was taking a hit every day. Social situations were complicated. Classmates could be mean, rejecting, or annoying. Life was hard.

In addition to the daily stresses of being "a big first-grader," Joshua was experiencing what I think of as the "gravitational pull" of a younger sibling (three-and-a-half-year-old Bradley), whose life began to look pretty care-free from the vantage point of the older child struggling with demands to be competent and more independent. Many children are quite ambivalent about growing up. Seeing Bradley stay home with Mom most days, play all day when at preschool, recharge with an afternoon nap wrapped in a blankie, and not have to struggle with homework in the evenings brought out in Joshua a deep nostalgia for the good old days when life was easy and his parents kept him safe and comfortable.

Perhaps some part of Joshua's mind saw his growth as proceeding too rapidly; with it came a loss of precious security and an increase in stress. Not knowing how to steer or otherwise control events, Joshua, as I think of it, pulled hard on the emergency brake and sent his development into a skid.

He was now easily disturbed by situations he had previously mastered: going to school, being by himself while a parent was in another part of the house, sleeping on his own. Joshua began to regress to a much less mature level of self-regulation. Language seemed to abandon him when he needed it most, and he returned to nonverbal expressions of emotion in an attempt to get his parents to control his world for him and relieve him of his stress. What his parents saw was a return to crying, wailing, clinging, and throwing tantrums, behaviors they thought Joshua had left behind. It was difficult to know exactly what Joshua was thinking, but one could guess that he was finding it difficult to talk himself through challenging situations, to assure himself that things would be all right, or to even name what he was feeling.

However, grow up he must, and Joshua's falling back on old choreographed behaviors such as crying and relying on his parents to regulate him isn't fitting well with his parents' need for him to be more independent and self-regulating. They feel their own stress and lack of competence and confidence. They in turn fall back on a mixed bag of old and new behaviors: ignoring, cajoling, soothing, and acting out their anger and frustration.

The Cost of Going on Autopilot in the Face of Anxiety

What is important to remember is that we are likely to fall back on old and automatic dance routines when we are tired, stressed, or distracted. It's like going on autopilot. This can be helpful when we're exhausted and just have to get through the day. Adaptive, helpful routines can provide stability, continuity, and predictability in the life of a family. For example, a familiar and comfortable bedtime routine can ease a child into the challenging separation from parents at night. Unhelpful dance routines (for example, avoiding conflict at all costs) get us in trouble and keep us stuck there.

Because our parent-child dance routines are so automatic, we often watch ourselves reacting in these unhelpful ways, regretting our actions but unable to prevent them or even to stop the reaction once it starts. Later we may experience anger, guilt, and self-reproach.

Perhaps this is why so many studies of families with anxious children (for example, Ginsberg and Schlossberg 2002) describe the parents as overcontrolling, overprotective, overly focused on negative emotions generally and anxiety in particular, overly tolerant of avoidance behaviors, and frequently engaged in parent-child conflicts as well as parent-parent conflicts. One parent I worked with referred to her "not proud Mommy moments." We've all had our not proud Mommy or Daddy moments. These "moments"—these conflicts and reactions—are simply more attempts to avoid or control distressing thoughts and feelings, your child's and your own.

Childhood anxiety is more than just the distressing fears and worries. Much of what I've described as problematic childhood anxiety can be described in terms of these parent-child dances (or child-sibling, child-friend, child-teacher, child-grandparent, and so on). Often as not, the dance you and your anxious child fall into is not especially helpful, at least not in the long run. Much of the help you seek for your child's anxiety will be found not in getting rid of anxious thoughts and feelings, but in changing the dance. This means choreographing a positive and useful dance: clear request for help, help offered, help utilized, and your child being able to move on from anxiety and toward the real tasks at hand. As the parent, you will be making the first steps toward a new choreography. Remember the wisdom (slightly paraphrased) of the old ant in *A Bug's Life*: "You and your child can go around the leaf."

Family Anxiety

Because anxiety tends to run in families, it is likely that you yourself had or currently have struggles with anxious thoughts and feelings (Dacey and Fiore 2000). Many parents of anxious children will have their past or present anxiety provoked by seeing their child in distress. Your child's angry and controlling behavior may provoke your own memories of frightening events from your childhood. For example, Abby's mother, Catherine, experienced extreme shyness as a child and regrets that it prevented her from engaging in activities. As an adult and a parent, Catherine now recognizes the importance of social events, school plays, and the like to bring out a shy child and teach her to have courage and to focus on the positive and not the negative. It pains Catherine deeply to see Abby suffer and miss out on what life has to offer. At the same time, Abby's avoidant behavior frustrates and angers Catherine, who, still self-conscious and subject to anxiety herself, fears others will interpret Abby's anxious behaviors as rudeness and think critically of both Abby and her. Her primary reaction is to escape with Abby from the painful situation and then feel angry and resentful afterward.

Similarly, Joshua's father, Sid, vividly remembers his own struggles with separation anxiety. As a result, he tends toward a more "support-ive" stance toward Joshua's fears as opposed to the more "punitive" (as Sid sees it) approach Nancy employs. Additionally, Sid is overwhelmed at work and would prefer not to come home to conflict. His own frustration and resentment show up when he thinks that Nancy can't manage Joshua without provoking an outburst that he, Sid, then has to deal with. Sid's reactions then make wide swings from avoidance of anxiety and conflict through accommodation to attempts at controlling the household through his own tantrums.

Angela too struggles mightily every day as a single, working parent. Sterling's upsets are just one more thing she has to deal with, draining her meager resources of time and energy. Her default dance routine is to look for ways to minimize Sterling's stress, because when he is less anxious and volatile, Angela can get through the day-to-day demands. Unfortunately Sterling is not learning how to manage distress, and his avoidance of age-appropriate though challenging tasks is putting him further behind his peers academically, socially, and physically.

Being the parent of a frequently fearful or anxious child is terribly hard work. The strain will cause your own regression to rigid and binary thinking. As a parent, you then develop one of two general approaches when faced with more than just the occasional anxious situation. On the one hand, you may push your child into anxiety-provoking situations in order to "toughen him up" or in some way to get him exposed to anxiety in an effort to make him confront it and face and overcome his fears. On the other hand, and more typically, you will go in the opposite direction and generally protect your child from anxious situations and in any number of ways assist your child in controlling anxiety that can't be avoided. As I pointed out before, neither avoidance nor control strategies are bad in and of themselves. There are appropriate applications of each. However, applied thoughtlessly and as a reaction to one's own anxiety or frustration, neither the pushing nor the protecting agenda, neither avoidance nor control, works very well in the long run.

So, going back to the point I made in the first chapter, successfully treating an anxiety disorder is not just driving out symptoms. A successful approach requires addressing both the inner world of your child's thoughts and feelings as well as the outer world of automatic parent-child interactions, or dances. This involves thinking beyond the push-pull model of reducing symptoms. The whole interlocking and dynamic parent-child system must be understood and reworked into something that balances coping with risking in the service of a big life. Instead of being *reactive* in the form of old dance routines, you will become *responsive* to your child when he is anxious.

RESPONSIVE PARENTING: THE NEW DANCE

The premise of this book is that child anxiety is largely a problem because of how your child's fears, worries, and needs are being experienced and expressed, and how you, the parent, are being pulled into the struggle to avoid or control your child's thoughts and feelings, as well as your own, resulting in a lack of progress toward appropriate self-regulation and mastery of age-appropriate life skills. He feels stuff, hates it, and reacts according to his old choreography. You feel his stuff plus some of your own stuff, hate it, and react with some of your own old choreography. We're now going to talk about changing all that.

What I will call *responsive parenting* is the new dance. It is helpful parenting that can become efficient with practice, just as any dance will. It can become the new standard and provide that continuity and predictability that's helpful in dance routines. But what defines responsive parenting, and distinguishes it from reactive parenting, is that it is thoughtful and flexible. Unhelpful dances can be barely conscious, brittle, all-or-none patterns of interacting. I like to think of responsive parenting as supple parenting—strong but flexible, just like a good dancer.

Responsive parenting is not merely the consistent and timely applica-tion of consequences (or being "contingent," the term I used earlier). And it is not necessarily being positive all the time. Research shows that mothers of compliant children do not consistently provide positive attention for com-pliance and that positive maternal attention is not an especially effective reinforcer for compliance in children with a history of defiance (Wahler and Meginnis 1997). In short, this means that doling out praise and punish-ment does not fully explain child behavior patterns. Something else must be at work here.

It is true that responsive parenting means delivering feedback to your child in the form of instructions, rules, rewards, and punishments. That is the contingent—or appropriate consequences—part. Beyond that, however, responsive parenting means the feedback you give to your child is appropriate to the situation. The situation includes the child's developmen-tal level at that moment (remember, they regress when stressed and may not be functioning at their chronological age). Additionally, the situation must include goals that go beyond "How can I eliminate this upset, his and mine, as quickly as possible?"

So being responsive means appreciating in the moment that your child is trying to get some need of his met and that this need is probably legiti-mate (he doesn't want to be anxious any more than you do). But there may be several things conspiring to make this go poorly: his timing ("Now!"), the way he is going about trying to get you to help him (having a tantrum, sulking, or something equally unpleasant), or his focus on too narrow a set of outcomes (no anxiety!). You need to think bigger than he can at the moment.

If you can orient yourself to the question "What is my child trying to achieve by all this?" and avoid answers such as "He's trying to shorten my life," you can craft a response that accomplishes several objectives. First, you will let your child know that you get the message behind the behavior even while setting limits on the behavior. These validation techniques are described in detail in chapter 8. Second, children (especially young children) may not even know what they want or what they're actually feeling in the moment. All your child may know is that he is scared and confused and is experiencing a rush of energy and upset and raw need. Your response will give your child a vocabulary that will allow him to better recognize and articulate his needs and his own thoughts and feelings, even, or especially, the difficult ones. Third, your responsive feedback will include suggestions for how he can get his needs met in a better way or for how he can cope with the fact that the need is simply not going to be met at this time.

Responsive parenting means having one foot in the "right here, right now" and one foot in the "big picture." When you are being responsive, you are oriented to your child as he is at that moment while also keeping your sights on what really needs to happen next. You can step back and take it all in, aware of your automatic thoughts and feelings and the habitual reaction patterns hovering nearby. You are aware of what your child is experiencing at this moment, aware of the possibilities for encouraging effective communication, help-seeking skills, and problem-solving skills, if there is in fact a problem to be solved. Coming chapters will describe all these processes and parenting response strategies in detail.

In order for the old dance to change, to really work to enhance your child's growth, the goal of the dance must change from attempts at avoiding and controlling anxiety now to learning to manage life out there in the world *in spite of* anxiety and other difficult thoughts and feelings. It is a change of orientation from "How can I avoid or control what's inside my head and body?" to "How can I best manage the problems and opportunities out here in my life?" Recall what I said about both classic and modern anxiety: what needs to happen when the picture gets too big or too small is to focus on the very thing that needs to happen next.

Responsive Language

One way of increasing your understanding of a situation is to examine the language you use when you describe what bothers you. When we become distressed about something, our thinking changes in predictable ways. Like your child, you can regress to more rigid and primitive thinking; you may, for example, think and speak in all-or-none, black-and-white terms. We hear this in a child's language: "You never...," "She always...," "This will never work." And you can hear it in how you talk to your child and to yourself when engaged in an unhelpful dance. You know from experience that this kind of talk is almost impossible to reason with. When it's you talking to yourself, neither of you is going to get anywhere.

Responsive parenting is all about having a range of possible ways of thinking about a situation and a range of possibilities for what, if anything, to do about it. Having only two possibilities, each lying at an extreme of the possible reactions, is not a good place to be. When we feel we have few options, we tend to feel trapped. When we feel trapped, we feel many distressing emotions and think many unhappy thoughts that can distract us from the task at hand and limit our possibilities. It's a vicious cycle.

Responsive Parenting: Stepping Back From Our Thoughts and Feelings

As a parent and a neurologically intact adult human being, you have your own fight-or-flight system, and it's never more aroused than when your child is in distress. This is, after all, highly adaptive. The human race would have not gotten far if parents weren't protective of their offspring.

Your thoughts and feelings in the face of parenting challenges (anger, anxiety, hopelessness, and so on) are quite automatic themselves. They seem to come out of nowhere and with frightening intensity. You may have disturbing memories from your youth that are triggered by your child's anxiety or rage. You may feel guilty because of some of the thoughts you are having in those stressful moments. You don't choose to have these thoughts and feelings. They are a product of the present circumstances and your complex history. We'll look more deeply into the nature of thoughts and feelings in the next chapter.

Suffice it to say, raising children invites a range and intensity of emotions and painful thoughts we couldn't have imagined possible before becoming parents. These feelings, thoughts, and images threaten to overwhelm us. They certainly can fill our awareness to the point where the child and the situation at hand recede into the background and our distress takes center stage. Citing research in emotion and perception, psychologists Georg Eifert and John Forsyth state that "fear is associated with greater vigilance and a narrowing of attention so that the individual's attention stays focused on the event that elicits the fear" (2005, p. 15). Fear and anxiety overwhelm everything else, blotting out other information that might put the upset into perspective or provide an answer to the problem at hand. The narrowing of attention is like putting anxiety under a microscope; it just makes it look bigger—for both of you.

So when you and your child are caught up in old choreography, doing the anxiety dance together, it is very difficult to shift the focus from the fear and anxiety (and how to get rid of it) to something better, such as returning to the original goal of taking a walk or joining the other kids at the party.

Tough Empathy

It's no accident that your child's behavior provokes your own anxiety (or anger or despair, you name it). In addition to being wired to feel what others close to us feel (remember the tuning fork analogy and sympathetic vibrations), your emotions and thoughts are being provoked because this is a necessary part of the anxiety dance. Your upset serves a purpose. Again, these are processes that are largely out of awareness, but your distress in some ways "benefits" your child. Here's how: In order to be truly helpful to your child, two things must happen. First, he needs to know that you understand how he feels. Second, you must be motivated to help him. The most efficient way your child can generate your understanding and motivation is to make you feel just like he does. And he knows, even at a very young age, how to accomplish this. In fact, at a very young age, prior to adequate language and a working "emotional vocabulary," igniting your anxiety and other emotions may be the only way your child can communicate what he's experiencing.

Provoking similar feelings in you is often the opening gambit in the anxiety dance. You need to understand what it's like for him, to empathize with him. Unfortunately, your child doesn't understand that his behavior is creating a situation that actually makes you *less* able to help him because now you are not exactly at your best, and the dance you then slide into is likely not very helpful in the long run for managing the feelings and the situation. There you are, the both of you, feeling highly distressed. Your child has gotten you to understand him (you're sharing in his anxious upset) and has succeeded in motivating you to help him (you both want that upset to stop, now). But what kind of help is this and at what cost to each person's mental health and the relationship itself?

Now let's say you've bought into the standard diagnostic and treatment models that say the best outcome in any anxious situation is a rapid and massive reduction in symptoms. If you believe that anxiety keeps your child from doing what he needs to do (get on the bicycle, go upstairs on his own), then it follows logically that if you are going to do what you need to do (help him), your anxiety must be eliminated first. After all, in order to be functional, don't we need to have all our thinking and feeling ducks in a neat row?

But as we will see in the next chapter, this goal of controlling thoughts and feelings in order to control our own behavior or the behavior of another is extremely difficult, if not impossible, to achieve. This is why so many reactive parenting patterns are frustrating and ineffective. It's not because we're not doing them right (calmer, more loving, more logical); reactive parenting doesn't work because it can't work. It can't work if the goal is first to manipulate your own and your child's thoughts and feelings as a prerequisite for being able to function adequately.

We are wired to be in tune with our children. They are wired to get us to feel with them. This is the foundation of empathy. It's tough sometimes, but it works to establish understanding and to motivate action. You can make it work better by *responding* to anxiety—your own and your child's—and by choosing actions that will clarify what the situation calls for, solve the problem if it can be solved, and thus further your child's growth.

SUMMARY AND A LOOK AHEAD

Responsive parenting is all about creating possibility. It is going beyond the rigid confines of habitual thinking and reacting. It is clarifying what is happening and what needs to happen. It is remembering what is really important in spite of the tendency for anxiety to narrow your focus. Responsive parenting allows you to be sensitive to your child without diminishing your strength or authority. Neither must you deny what you know is true and valuable. In fact, as I will show you in chapter 5, becoming a responsive parent is the surest way to maintain contact with your larger values and goals and not just react to the discomfort of the moment. Rechoreographing the parent-child dance can turn your child's anxious "help me" behaviors from a liability into an asset; the old dance routine of retreat into avoidance and control can be transformed into dance lessons in how to solve problems and achieve goals, a new routine that will benefit your child all of his life. But this will require a shift in your own mind-set regarding anxiety. In the next chapter, we will take a look at anxiety from a new perspective, one of acceptance and commitment.

CHAPTER 4

Acceptance and Commitment Therapy for Your Child's Anxiety

When anxiety is present, both you and your child are likely to become more reactive and less responsive to each other and to the situation at hand. Avoidance and control can lead to a more restricted life: social and academic challenges are not met, age-appropriate skills for self-regulation and conflict resolution are not developed, and relationships with parents, siblings, and close others become frayed. How can you get unstuck from unhelpful dance routines and automatic reactions?

In this chapter, I will describe a new approach to the treatment of anxiety disorders that promises a way out of the avoidance and control trap. I will ask you to consider changing from your old attempts at managing your child's thoughts and feelings (along with your own) to focusing on the tasks at hand: solving real problems or coping with the challenges life puts in your path, whatever they may be.

Psychotherapy has been around for just over a hundred years. Ways of thinking about emotional and behavioral problems continue to evolve. For many years now, the standard for psychotherapy has been a large class of treatments called cognitive behavioral therapy, or CBT. These psychotherapies have a strong track record for helping adults and children with a variety of psychological concerns.

In general, the goals of CBT have been in line with the prevailing diagnostic model that defines anxiety by its symptoms. As such, the goal of treatment has been to reduce or eliminate those symptoms: no more symptoms, no more anxiety disorder. The assumption is that without anxiety we would readily embrace life and have the skills to do so successfully.

Traditional CBT sets out to alter thinking patterns and behavior patterns so that the individual can act in ways that promote success in life and enjoy the positive feelings that would follow. Typically CBT for anxiety involves three basic steps. Step 1 is to monitor and identify anxious thoughts and feelings. The idea is that we can't change what we're not aware of. This is followed by step 2, using logic and experience to challenge the reasonableness of these thoughts or the necessity of these feelings ("Are we in fact in danger at this moment?" or "Based on your experience, how likely is it that you have in fact stepped in dog poop while walking down the sidewalk?"). Finally, step 3 is an attempt to replace the uncomfortable and unreasonable anxious thoughts and feelings with more positive, encouraging, and pleasant ones ("I am calm," "It doesn't matter if my shoelace loops are not exactly the same length," and so on). In work with children, the emphasis would be more on promoting positive behavior changes (for example, rewarding constructive behaviors in the face of anxiety) and less so on making changes to thinking patterns as such.

The idea for many years was that, as better mental habits are established, reasonable and positive thoughts will then become the norm for that person. With better thoughts come better feelings. With negative feelings out of the way, a person can finally get out of bad behavior patterns and into good ones. This makes sense.

THE LIMITS OF COMMON SENSE

My mother is fond of saying, "Common sense tells us the earth is flat." When it comes to the swirling emotional world you and your child plunge into every day, common sense can be helpful or it can be a trap. The logical or commonsense solution to anxious situations would be to get rid of or minimize the anxious stuff that seems to stand between your child and what she needs to do. Similarly, you may think that, in order to be the parent you need to be at that moment, you must get rid of your own distressing emotions: anxiety, frustration, and the like. This also makes sense.

You would solve this anxiety "problem" the same way you would solve any other problem in your life, by avoiding it altogether or by fixing it. You avoid traffic tickets and accidents by not running red lights. You are mindful of personal hygiene during flu season so as not to spread or pick up germs. You vacuum up the dirt on the rug. You replace the burned-out lightbulb. You pull together a costume for the school play at the last minute. All of these tactics and skills, and hundreds of others, allow your life to run well. After all, you're a parent; you're a good problem solver.

Clearly avoidance and control can be useful and adaptive. Having some control over your child's environment is necessary to maintain health and safety, to prevent her from being overwhelmed by chaos, and to model effective ways of dealing with the world for her. Avoidance and control work well in the world outside the skin: vacuuming a dirty rug, not running with scissors, paying your bills on time, driving carefully in a school zone. All of these measures keep your life and your child's life safe and running smoothly. As she grows, you want her to take on these skills and practices so that she can develop confidence in her ability to manage her life and to be effective in the world out there. But what about the world inside the skin—the world of thoughts and feelings?

THE LIMITS OF CONTROL WHEN IT COMES TO ANXIETY

You've no doubt applied many possible solutions to the problem of anxious thoughts and feelings, your child's or your own. You've taken, or encouraged your child to take, deep breaths to get calm. You've encouraged her to focus on thinking something pleasant, to avoid anxiety-provoking situations, or to snap a rubber band on her wrist every time she has a "bad thought," or told her to just buck up. Perhaps you've gone down the medication route. All of these strategies may have had some limited usefulness. But the anxiety keeps returning, often worse than before.

Control is very elusive in the world inside the skin. Legend has it that the famed Russian author Fyodor Dostoyevsky used to torment his younger brother by telling him to stand in the corner until he *stopped* thinking about a white bear. This is, of course, an impossible situation. After some time, the young boy thinks, "Okay, I can leave now, I'm not thinking about ... oh, heck." You can't know you're *not* thinking about something without *thinking* about it. Fyodor's brother was trapped in the corner.

In psychology, we now call this the white bear problem; attempts at suppressing or otherwise controlling unwanted thoughts and emotions, including anxiety, do not make us feel better and in fact can result in the negative thoughts and emotions becoming stronger and more frequent (for example, Gross and Levenson 1997). The more we are unwilling to have a thought or feeling, the more that very mental activity seems to assert itself in our lives. One common example can be found in getting a case of the giggles in church; the more you try to not think the funny thought, the more it returns. It can also show up as some horrific thought that enters your mind, say from the evening news, that haunts you for a period of time in spite of your best efforts not to think it.

You can try this yourself right now. Don't think about something: your favorite warm pastry or cool drink. Seriously, *don't think about that brownie!* The next time you feel a strong emotion, positive or negative, try not to feel it. See how successful you can be. It's likely that you'll find that thought or feeling stubbornly occupying center stage in your mind.

The more we struggle with the products of the mind, the more we become caught up in them. Although avoidance and control may bring some short-term relief for your child and for you, there is a long-term cost in terms of wear and tear on your relationship with your child, as well as depriving her of opportunities to learn to self-regulate and perhaps master common but distressing situations.

Additionally, if escape, avoidance, or control becomes your child's or your main strategy for dealing with fear and anxiety, over time the number of situations that call for avoidance and control may increase because fear and anxiety are states to be fearful and anxious about. The spiral of dysfunction becomes wider and deeper.

This is a complicated problem for us as individuals, and the problem becomes much more complex within a family. As I described in the last chapter, much of what you are concerned about, much of what drew you to this book, was the fact that your child's anxiety has created patterns of interaction between you and her that are distressing and unhelpful. And, as promised, I will show you how those very parent-child transactions will become the vehicle for changing the focus from anxiety and dysfunction to growth and success.

Riding the Wave of Distress

If there are many situations your child avoids because she is convinced she cannot handle them, then she will be at a disadvantage in terms of developing necessary life skills such as learning to ride a bike or introducing herself to potential friends on the first day of school. One of the more important life skills your child needs to learn is how to tolerate some distress. On the way to most of life's goals, one has to encounter some unpleasant experiences, such as anxiety ("Will I get picked for the baseball team?"), frustration and impatience ("I can't get the hang of bunting"), boredom ("Why did they stick me in left field?"), and so on. It's painful to witness your child's distress. Most times we are not just witnesses but participants in that distress. We get to ride the emotional roller coaster with our children.

For a parent, it can be distressing to watch your child begin the ascent at the beginning of a strong emotional wave. How high will this go? How will she react? In her book *The Blessing of a Skinned Knee* (2001), Wendy Mogel cites the psychologist Miriam Adahan, who suggests that parents often do not allow their child to experience the full "wave pattern" of strong emotions. If you too readily pull your child down from a rising emotion when it first shows up, she will not get to experience the natural rise, crest, and dissipation of that emotion. She will not learn that emotions do just that—they show up, they rise up, they peak, and then they go away—if we let them. All of this means, of course, that you, as the parent and emotional dance partner, get to ride the wave with her, to mix a metaphor.

Avoidance or unnecessary rescuing deprives your child of an opportunity to learn that she can manage her distress and not only survive but prevail. With a successful emotional experience, your child obtains a newfound sense of competence and mastery.

A NEW APPROACH TO ANXIETY

For many years, traditional cognitive behavioral therapy was concerned with the products of the mind. It was predicated on the idea that if the mind is in order, your life will be in order. If your thinking and feeling are okay, then you are okay and your behavior will be okay. But more recently, clinicians and researchers have shown, and your own experience can tell you, that trying to get your thoughts and feelings to be okay for any length of time is an extremely difficult and slippery venture. Your efforts may actually make matters worse, either because the unpleasant thoughts and feelings come back again, often more intensely, or the avoidance and control efforts make life miserable for you and your child.

In the last thirty years or so, a great deal of clinical experience and scientific research has gone into rethinking anxiety and other psychological conditions. The result is a new generation of therapies providing more effective ways of making people's lives richer and healthier.

These new therapies represent the evolution of CBT; they recognize the futility of trying to avoid or control thoughts and feelings in order to have a more effective life. The emphasis instead is on living a more effective life.

Acceptance and Commitment Therapy

Acceptance and commitment therapy (or ACT, pronounced as the word "act" rather than spelled out) is one of these new therapies, and it provides the framework for the approach outlined in this book. ACT was conceived by Dr. Steven Hayes at the University of Nevada at Reno, and I was privileged to study with him there when this treatment model was just being developed.

The two major goals of ACT are (1) fostering acceptance of what *is* in the moment, including negative thoughts and feelings, so that (2) action can be taken toward committed goals, as opposed to trying to control or avoid the negative thoughts and feelings themselves (Eifert and Forsyth 2005). But before I talk about acceptance and committed action, I want to say a little more about thoughts and feelings—what they are and what they are not.

The Survival Value of Anxiety

The brain is the organ of the mind in the same way the heart is the organ of blood circulation. What we know as sight, hearing, touch, taste, and smell are the chemical-electrical activities of the fine and astonishingly complex fibers of our central and peripheral nervous systems. This network is stimulated by events in the world outside our bodies via our various sensory receptors. It's obvious that our senses are important for learning about the world and managing our lives within it. Impairments in hearing or vision can create difficulties for people as they navigate through life. But even sensory systems in perfect working order can be fooled: optical illusions trick the eye, sounds and words can be heard incorrectly, artificial flavors deceive the taste buds.

Additionally, there are the internal or "private" experiences of thoughts, feelings, and memories. As I described earlier (using the terms "metacognition" and "metaemotion"), we can also have thoughts and feelings about thoughts and feelings. A lot of our thinking is "commentary": reflections and judgments about what has happened, is happening, or might happen. And it seems as if a lot of this commentary, this internal monologue, is negative in some way: dire warnings, criticisms of self and others, disappointments dwelled on, and the list goes on. A brief observation of your own mental activity will confirm this. Why are we so negative? Are we all depressed? No, but all that negativity reflects the true purpose of thinking: it is not there to make us content, but to help us stay alive.

For tens of thousands of years, human beings have survived and even flourished in harsh and unforgiving environments without much in the way of fur or fangs. We survived by learning from and remembering our mistakes. Better still, we learned from the mistakes of Thog, our cave neighbor: make mental note, petting saber-toothed tiger bad. Our ancestors came up with and passed on verbal rules and social codes, the vast majority of which concern staying alive, not how to have a good time. It's only been very recently in our history that people have come to pursue, expect, and even demand happiness and contentment in their lives.

With thinking, humans could anticipate the future and prepare for it; they could set aside food for the winter, avoid dangerous animals and places, and keep an eye on the children lest they come to harm. Hoping for the best got you eaten by something faster and with bigger claws, usually before you had a chance to reproduce. Stone Age parents who were not highly anxious about their children did not become Stone Age grandparents. We are all the descendents of these paranoid people.

Fast-forward to the twenty-first century. Technology has advanced and society is enormously more complicated, but our brains are still pretty much 10,000 BC standard issue. Abby is at the birthday party. Can she really trust these wild creatures running around? Fear rises up and Abby freezes as if suddenly finding herself amid a pack of jackals. What is Abby's mother thinking and feeling? For Catherine, there is much more ambivalence; she can see a larger picture and competing goals. On the one hand, there is the need to be successful socially, to face fears and prevail so that these situations will become less fearful. On the other hand, she empathizes with Abby's fear and feels too the pull to escape the situation and run back to the cave where they can be safe. She is not alone in her dark thoughts. It's likely that one or two other parents at the party are ruminating on the possibility of peanut dust in the birthday cake or lead paint on the party favors.

The bottom line here is that the fight-or-flight system and the anxious thoughts that evolved with it got us this far in a brutal world, and some other thought ("Oh, it'll be all right") generated by a sunnier part of our minds is not going to easily override millennia of mental and physiological habit. But it's okay; we don't have to pit one thought against another to see which is really true.

Talking to Ourselves About the World

Language, in the form of thinking, is a double-edged sword. It is language that allows your child to persevere in the face of adversity, her goal shining like a beacon through the storm: "I'm almost there. I can make it!" It is also language that persuades her to abandon all hope minutes later: "This is hopeless."

From an astonishingly early age, language allows your child to learn about the world, herself, and you. This learning is organized and passed on in the form of rules. *Rules* are simply ways of talking to ourselves about actions and their consequences. Rules may be direct: I touch the hot stove, burn my finger, and conclude that stoves are hot and should not be touched. Other rules are derived, that is, developed not by direct experience but through social instruction or one's own deduction. For example, you may tell your child, "The stove is hot. Don't touch it or you'll get hurt." By taking in your words and making them her own, your child does not have to touch the stove in order to establish this rule and subsequently avoids touching not just this stove but other stoves as well.

This ability to derive rules is extremely useful. It makes learning many, many things so much easier and safer. I don't ever have to be poisoned or electrocuted or run over by a bus to know that these are bad events and that they can be avoided in many different ways. I did not have to learn each of these things by direct experience. You want your child to learn as much as possible and as painlessly as possible. Language allows her to do that.

However, remember my description of early language as quirky, rigid, and limited. It is alarmingly easy for any young child, or an older child in distress, to cling to incredibly rigid and unhelpful ideas (rules), such as "If I can't do it perfectly right, then I'm a total loser," "I can't touch that doorknob," or "I can't go upstairs by myself." These thoughts are debilitating because, you will recall, for a child these may not be rules or ideas; they are reality. If I think it, it must be so: "I am…," "I can't…." The picture is too small.

It is your job as a parent to show your child that her thoughts are just that—thoughts. They are not reality itself. Thoughts *represent* reality within our minds so that we can remember, plan, and imagine. The thoughts in own minds may be accurate representations, or they may be way off the mark. Obviously, thinking is an important tool for managing life, but we should regard many of our thoughts with a pinch of healthy skepticism. Thoughts do not predict the future with any accuracy beyond what our experience, or the experience of some knowledgeable person, already tells us. Thoughts have no power other than the power you and your child give them.

It is also a problem when an unhelpful idea (or rule) is derived from one situation and then overgeneralized, as we say, to situations that only appear similar. For example, "That dog scared me" becomes "All dogs are scary and dangerous" or even "All fenced yards have a scary dog in them that I can't see, so I must avoid going by any yard that has a fence I can't see through." Here, as we said earlier, the picture is now too big, and real-life goals, such as walking down that street to a friend's house, start getting squeezed out.

Small picture or big picture, this literal and rigid way of thinking is the norm at certain ages and in strong emotional states; it does not yield easily to reason, cajoling, threats, or even reassurance. From the vantage point of acceptance and commitment therapy, however, we would not insist that your child's thoughts and feelings, her rules and her conclusions, conform to some external definition of reality: "No, Beth. There are no germs on the doorknob." (Actually, there *are* germs on the doorknob. But that's not the point.) As I said, thoughts and feelings are—for your child, in that moment—reality. When you show your child that you can really accept her reality (also known as validation and covered in chapter 8), then behavior change becomes possible. This is because acceptance (to take or receive what is given) is a powerful way of conveying empathy and understanding. When your child is in distress, first and foremost she wants to be understood. Only then will your child be willing to play with reality and see what's possible.

Thoughts and Feelings: Neither Powerful nor Dangerous

As I mentioned in previous chapters, the standard treatment agenda for anxiety and similar emotional conditions is to reduce or eliminate the symptoms—the anxious thoughts and feelings. I think of this as the "hair-ball model"; if your child could just *haaaggckk* up this pesky anxious thought or feeling, everything would be fine. Having coughed up the anxiety, you and your child could then calmly go about your business. This approach naturally stems from the idea that negative thoughts, and especially feelings, are physical things that are produced in the body (the brain) and then grow like weeds in your flower bed, compelling all sorts of behaviors and choking out positive and reasonable thoughts and feelings. This notion has roots in how psychologists and psychiatrists first began thinking about and treating emotional conditions.

It was just over a hundred years ago that pioneering psychologists and psychiatrists, such as Sigmund Freud, first began studying and describing the inner life of human beings. At that time, the main scientific models came from physics. Physics at the turn of the twentieth century talked about forces such as gravity and described objects big (planets) and small (the newly discovered atoms) bouncing around and into each other like billiard balls. It was all very much a push-pull system; add heat to a container of gas molecules and they would push against the container to expand it if it were elastic enough or rupture it if the container were too rigid. Emotions and thoughts were described as if they were any other physical substance and as if they operated under the same push-pull, expand-contract rules of the prevailing scientific theories.

But thoughts, feelings, physical sensations, and memories are not physical substances. They are products of the mind. They are the result of electrical activity in the brain, often in combination with some chemical (hormone or endocrine) responses in other parts of the body. When these conditions are activated, we get the typical experience of fear or love, anxiety or jealousy, and so on. When the conditions change, the particular emotional experience is done. Emotions and thoughts are not stored anywhere as physical things to linger or grow or fester. The memories of experiences, emotions, or thoughts are just more electrical activity of the brain. There is no emotional hairball to hack up.

This is not to say that thoughts and feelings are not important or have no power to influence us in many ways. The love for your child, the laughter or sadness a memory can conjure up, the resolve to stick it out in the face of discouragement—these are all experiences that make us human and make life wonderful and rich. Bear with me a little longer while I make my case that the key to no longer being tyrannized by anxiety is not to get rid of those thoughts and feelings (your child's or your own) but to see those mental events, while they're happening, in a broader context—a context that emphasizes understanding, problem solving, skill building, and growth.

Thoughts and Feelings: The Electrical Activity of the Brain

Consider your TV set. The football games or the so-called reality shows appear when the TV is on and tuned in to those programming frequencies or cable channels. The programs are created by the electrical activity of the TV's components. Once the program is over, the sounds and images are no longer in your TV set. Without an actual recording device, the programs are not stored up in your TV. Years of TV programs will not burst forth unexpectedly some day if you don't vent them off somehow or get them out.

And yet we believe that feelings, especially anger, must be gotten out or the angry person will explode or be made to do something awful. Sterling believes, and his mother too, that he must run in circles to get his anxiety out. Running and other activities may feel good when the body is agitated and charged with adrenaline, but there is nothing *in* to be gotten *out*, only a feeling to be passed *through* on the way to yet another feeling.

Your TV will present whatever station it's tuned to, although some stations may come in stronger than others given your location relative to the transmission source. If you switch channels to watch the reality show, the TV will not on its own switch back to the football game, unless your spouse has the remote. Similarly, a computer will run whatever software you direct it to, even something you haven't used in a long time. Your income tax software pops right up and works perfectly well even after not being used for a year.

The brain, on the other hand, does best what it does most. Unlike TVs or computers, the brain will strengthen the electrical activity that is used most frequently. Through repeated use, particular circuits or combinations of brain cells will become physically larger and better connected, making them more likely to become engaged. Neural circuits that are not used will become weaker over time. Can you recall your locker combination from sophomore year in high school? You used it several times a day for many months, but it's long gone now.

If anxiety and anxious reactions are the norm, if this is what your child's brain and body have practiced most, then that is what will show up first and loudest under the right circumstances. That does not mean that anxiety is in there somewhere and someone must conduct an exorcism to expel it. What it does mean is that the combination of endocrine responses and brain activity we call anxiety has been automatically tuned in by the situation at hand. What is required to change the anxiety and subsequent anxious behavior is switching to a better program.

This is tricky, of course. Recall how strong the pull of the anxiety dance can be, having been built up through practice—years of practice for your child and perhaps decades of practice for you. Additionally, the alternative—that is, more responsive dance routines—may be relatively weak due to infrequent use. If you have always done something with your right hand (for example, writing) and then try to do that same task with your left hand, it will feel awkward. More fundamentally, programming may be lacking altogether; for example, you can't speak French if you never learned French.

So if you want better responses from your child or from yourself, then it's less a matter of getting rid of the old feelings and thoughts and reactions, and more a matter of adding and strengthening new responses that will allow the channel to change. In order to add these new responsive programs, we must first step out of our attempts to avoid and control thoughts and feelings, or what we might call "the avoidance and control dance." The new, responsive dance will be focused on effective living in the moment, regardless of what you and your child are thinking and feeling in that moment. This change must start with acceptance of that moment and everything it brings.

THE MANY MEANINGS OF ACCEPTANCE

"Acceptance" is a complex term that has numerous meanings. In any dictionary, you will find several definitions such as these:

- The act of agreeing or consenting to

- The act of regarding as true or valid

- The act of taking or receiving what is offered

- The act of accommodating or reconciling oneself to

Most of us think of acceptance as having the first two meanings: agreeing or recognizing that something is true or valid in some way. It might mean that we acquiesce or give in somehow. It often implies resignation and defeat. There must be many times when, as a parent struggling with day-to-day challenges, you feel resigned or defeated. But giving in to these feelings and thoughts and acting resigned and defeated are rarely helpful to you and to your child. How do you accept your child's fear and anxiety when she is overreacting to something trivial?

I am interested in acceptance from the standpoint of the last two definitions: *acceptance* as the act of acknowledging what *is* at the moment. It is receiving what life is handing you and making the appropriate accommodations. It doesn't mean that you have to agree with or condone or be happy about what's happening. But if I have any hope of effectively dealing with a situation life hands me, I must pay attention to what is going on and do my best to understand it.

I wouldn't want my house to catch on fire, but if it ever did, I would have to accept that fact in order to take appropriate action. If I indulge in denial or self-pity at the expense of action ("My house can't be on fire; I've got friends coming for dinner this weekend"), my home will go up in flames along with me in it.

This view of acceptance is tricky. Again, I am not talking about the "Gee, isn't this great" kind of acceptance. Acceptance is simply the opposite of denial and of ignorance. Taking an unflinching look at the situation at hand is necessary if you're going to come up with the best response rather than just reacting. It doesn't mean you must like what life has handed you. It is not condoning what someone is doing or is not doing. Nor is acceptance, as ACT describes it, a form of resignation. It is not giving up or taking a passive approach to the problems of life. In fact, the way I will use "acceptance" is anything but passive. It is a powerful key that will unlock the potential for real change in your life and in the life of your child.

From the standpoint of clinical psychology, practicing acceptance can be seen as the opposite of attempts at avoidance and control. From childbirth to graduate school to a kitchen remodel, achieving just about any goal worth having will demand acceptance of the process. In order to reach any of these and most other goals, there is a certain amount of effort, apprehension, blood, sweat, tears, anger, regret, and a host of other thoughts and feelings that must be slogged through before we reach the end of the journey.

Parents need to be in command, of course, and I will describe strategies for staying in command in this and the next chapter. But for those first few moments of any challenging event, while we attempt to figure out what on earth is going on with our child and what we need to do about it, acceptance will supplant avoidance and control as the thing we must do first.

Acceptance in the Context of Choices

So why don't we simply avoid or escape everything that is uncomfortable or challenging in some way? Where would you begin if you went on a total and unrestrained avoidance binge—the housework, your job, relatives, spouse, children when they are being demanding or you're simply not in the mood for company? The list is potentially endless, and obviously life would grind to a halt if you avoided everything unpleasant. Let's be honest: if your goal in life were to avoid all things difficult or noxious, it would certainly rule out parenthood.

As an adult, you know that by not avoiding small tasks or problems, you are avoiding even bigger problems. Here's negative reinforcement again. Through years of life experience, you have come to recognize that avoiding tasks such as the dishes, flossing, paying taxes, or tending to your upset child when you least feel like it can result in even larger problems to deal with down the road. So you make your choices, lean into your life, and take on these tasks, even if imperfectly and perhaps without total enthusiasm.

Your child does not have years of life experience to draw on. Lack of experience, combined with the immature thinking processes I described in the previous chapters, make it difficult for her to rise above the urge to simply escape or avoid all things unpleasant. After all, the black-and-white, all-or-none thinking she is often caught up in raises the stakes and limits the options. On a good day, your child may be old enough to have left much of the immature, rigid thinking style behind. But remember that when anxiety shows up, like any stressful event, it will often cause your child to seriously regress, often right back to thinking like a four-year-old or even younger. This makes it extremely difficult for your child to see beyond the immediate unpleasant thoughts and feelings caused by the need to eat her peas, do her homework, or go to school even though she has a stomachache.

Wantingness vs. Willingness

What needs to happen in these situations is not for your child to *want* to go to school with a stomachache but instead for your child to be *willing* to go to school with a stomachache. Being willing to do something is not the same as wanting to do it.

Wantingness, if there is such a word, is a preference. Willingness is a choice. Your child may prefer peppermint ice cream over rocky road. She may prefer not to feel anxious or have a stomachache. But anxiety and the stomachache showing up are not her choice. They are simply two internal events that have shown up, for whatever reason; they are what she is experiencing at that moment. The presence of anxious thoughts and feelings, or stomachaches, does not take away any options. What takes away options is what happens next—the reactions to those events, the subsequent thoughts that limit the options: "If I am thinking *this*, then I can't do *that*," "Before I do can *that*, I have to stop feeling *this*." *Wantingness* reduces every option down to "I must get rid of the bad thoughts and feelings and restore the good ones," ASAP. And if your child feels powerless to do this, she will enlist you in the service of that goal, by whatever means necessary.

On the other hand, *willingness* opens up the possibilities for what you and your child can choose to do next. It's possible that getting rid of a thought or a feeling may be the thing to do next. But more likely, the thing to do next is to take action in the service of some larger (but not too large) picture. Constantly trying to tidy up the internal world as a prerequisite for managing life is what got you here to begin with. After all, you and your child were on your way somewhere, figuratively if not literally, when anxiety showed up and halted you in your tracks. What would it take to get back on track?

The Courage of Our Convictions

We can choose to do something that we don't want to do. It helps enormously if we have a conviction that what we are doing will serve us well, even if only later. This is basic wisdom and maturity, and like all parents you want your child to understand this so that she can become a productive citizen, or at least move out of the basement someday. As parents, we emphasize this willingness thing over and over when it comes to instilling a work ethic and notions of thrift, service to our community, unselfishness, discipline, and so on.

But when it comes to the realm of distressing thoughts and feelings, willingness is a much harder sell, and as parents we are often reluctant to insist upon it. The reason for our reluctance, I would suggest, is that as reasonably successful adults, we have achieved some of this wisdom and maturity based on our experiences and can speak to the benefits of willingness out in the world of work and school. However, we all struggle when it comes to the world of thoughts and feelings, and we ourselves still tend to take evasive action when something unpleasant is thought or felt.

Bravery in the Face of Fear and Anxiety

We define bravery as having fear or anxiety and doing the things we need to do in spite of those feelings. Bravery is the willingness to do something that we are afraid to do. It's hard to imagine a firefighter actually wanting to rush into a burning building. But he or she is willing to do it because of the commitment made to serving the community in that role. Of course, firefighters have training and experience to make success more likely than if you or I dashed into that building. And I imagine firefighters know quite well when not to rush in.

My point is that the firefighter's willingness to rush into that burning building does not eliminate or perhaps even necessarily lessen the fear or anxiety. Willingness is not another trick to control one's feelings. Dr. Steven Hayes, the founder of acceptance and commitment therapy, is fond of saying willingness is, in fact, nothing at all. If you see the firefighter doing his or her job, you are not seeing anything other than the firefighter doing his or her job. You might say, "How courageous!" but you wouldn't say, "How willing!"

Beth, our girl with obsessive-compulsive behaviors, was unwilling to not wash her hands after touching something. Hand washing helped her temporarily placate the thoughts that she might be contaminated by this month's fearful substance. But, of course, the contamination anxiety always returns. If Beth were to be willing to forgo hand washing except in more ordinary circumstances, such as after using the toilet or before meals, what would she be doing? Well, she'd be doing any number of things; she just wouldn't be washing her hands. That "not washing her hands" would be indistinguishable from ordinary life—playing, reading a book, whatever she might be doing with her hands instead of washing them. She would not have a golden glow about her or now want to not wash her hands or be quite happy about not washing. She would just be doing what she would do if not for the hand-washing habit. Sterling would just be heading out the door to school. He would not be not struggling to get his shoelaces under control. Abby would just be engaging peers in play. She would not be not talking to them. Joshua would be heading upstairs on his own.

Unwillingness is many things. Willingness is nothing; it is just doing what's there to be done. It's not "not doing anxiety"; it's just living one's life as needed, even if anxiety is present.

COMMITMENT

In addition to the emphasis on acceptance, the other track that ACT follows is that of commitment. I tell the children I work with that a commitment is a kind of promise; it is declaring that you have a goal and letting people know that you're going to work toward that goal as best you can. Your efforts don't have to be perfect; you just have to keep at it. In some ways, commitment may be necessary before acceptance can happen. Your stated goal and the promise to do your best to achieve it create the context in which acceptance and willingness become possible. I'm sure Steve Hayes considered the name commitment and acceptance therapy, but CAT isn't as cool an acronym as ACT, given the agenda for action that it promotes.

Commitment gives meaning to what your child is being asked to accept as she faces life's challenges. It also makes possible what you do every day as a parent. Another way of saying this is that you and your child need a good story to tell yourselves every day as you both meet obligations and perform tasks in the face of uncomfortable thoughts and feelings. Thoughts and feelings come and go. A good story will carry your child onward.

This story needn't be complicated, and the commitment needn't be grand. In fact, the best stories are often the simple ones that spell out that small next step: "I'm going to really listen the next time someone talks to me," "I'm going to spend one hour on that project today and get as much done as I can," "I'm going to call one friend and invite her over this weekend."

Often the most useful and flexible goals are ones that really have no "finish line"; they are as much about the journey as the destination. They reflect a commitment to live our lives a certain way, every day. To be a good parent, a good student, a loyal friend, a helpful big sister—these are commitments that create breadth and possibility. I can accept some discomfort, some doubt, some anxiety in the service of living these goals each day.

As I mentioned above, commitment is often linked to small actions. If your child is going to be a good student, then what must she do, right now, to further that goal? That "very next thing" could be as simple as getting out of bed, taking with her the various thoughts about the impending disaster that will be her school day. In subsequent chapters, we will spend a great deal more time looking at how this actually works: promoting action in the face of troublesome thoughts and feelings. Right now I just want to recognize the fact that all endeavors, great and small, are made up of little acts that are coherent and purposeful. We will be giving a lot of thought to what can make your child's behaviors coherent and purposeful.

In the way acceptance balances what is with what might be, commitment too is a balancing act. We can't be overly concerned with our goals at the expense of living in this moment. The French philosopher and writer Albert Camus said, "Real generosity toward the future lies in giving all to the present" (1956, p. x). I think this is especially apt for parents. As a parent, you can't help but think about and even fret about your child's future, especially when things aren't going well. But all you have is today to do what you can. And tomorrow will provide more opportunities to do the simple yet profound tasks of raising your child, day by day. If you or I can do what's there to be done every day with commitment and acceptance, the future will take care of itself.

If you can change the day-to-day process to one that is less literal and more responsive, accepting, and committed, you will be laying the foundation of a supportive and mutually satisfying relationship with your child. It is this relationship that will allow any future difficulties to be opportunities for growth, however painful they may be. If family relationships are strong, then having problems doesn't have to be a problem.

Orienting to the Goal: Foreground and Background

Look at the following classic faces/vase illusion. What do you see in this figure? Some people immediately see the white vase or goblet, while others may first perceive the twin faces in black silhouette. Without much mental effort, you can shift back and forth between the two images, the vase and

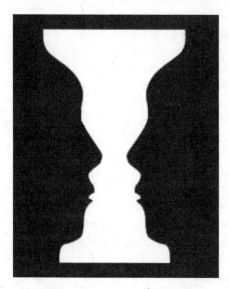

the faces, first seeing one and then the other. So, which is it—the vase or the faces? Obviously it's both. It depends on how you look at it. Specifically it depends on which part of the whole figure you are seeing as foreground and which as background. (These two parts are sometimes called "figure" and "ground," respectively.)

When your mind perceives the black outside portion as background, the white vase pops into the foreground and that is what you see. Relegate the white vase to the background and the faces come into view as figure. Clearly neither section is actually moving

forward or back. It is a perceptual trick your mind can play, and you have control over it, although most people will more naturally see one figure over the other.

Dividing your attention and your focus in everyday life is like this. As you read these words on the page in front of you, there are probably other sensations that you are aware of: noises in the room or outside, an itch on your nose, a thought about the past or the future drifting through your awareness. With some effort, you keep these words in the foreground and the rest of your awareness in the background. The sound of the furnace turning on would likely remain in the background with little trouble. If you were to hear your child cry out right now, this book would become background instantly, as it should.

Sometimes you choose what will be foreground, and therefore what will be important. Everything else becomes background or drops out of awareness completely. However, when your child is anxious and struggling with you and your mind is thrumming with your own painful thoughts, feelings, and memories, it is easy for all that suffering to push into the foreground and demand your attention. You feel challenged to control the pain as a precondition to doing the right thing. Here the strategy of reacting to your thoughts and feelings, as well as those of your child, with control moves is probably not going to work well, at least not without a significant cost to achieving your goals. You can trust your experience on this.

There is another choice. Instead of your typical reactions, you can learn to overcome the control habit and replace it with a responsive approach. I will be spending the remaining chapters of this book describing how to do that. In the short term, I will say that it is as simple as shifting from the vase to the faces. It is shifting one source of information (anxious thoughts and feelings) to the background and allowing other information (what life is asking of you and your child right now) into the foreground. The vase doesn't have to go away in order to see the faces. The faces can't be permanently in the foreground, but they don't have to be. Sometimes all we need is just a glimpse of where to go and what to do, and we can take the next step—and then the next and then the next.

The Bigger Picture

Willingness is possible when we place our thoughts and feelings in a larger context. In the case of the firefighter, it is the context of "doing the job I was trained to do." In the context of being a parent, there are many things you are willing to do that you do not necessarily want to do because it's "the job I was so not trained to do, but I'm doing it." You could probably right now list hundreds of things that you have done as a parent that you did not want to do, starting perhaps with labor and delivery itself. Certainly all those times you got up in the middle of the night to feed or change your child were acts of willingness and not something you necessarily wanted to do at that hour. The list could go on and on. And, of course, there are some things you are unwilling to do. You make choices as a parent, and these choices are connected to something—an event, a goal, a principle—something that gives direction to your decision making and informs your choices.

Again, when it comes to insisting that your child do her chores when you could just as easily (probably easier) do the task yourself, you can hang tough because you want to instill in your child work habits, character, appreciation, and so on. Her not wanting to do it is a side issue and you work to keep it to the side. But when your child does not want to go to school because she is anxious, that is a much more challenging situation for a parent. The anxious thoughts and feelings are not a side issue; they are front and center. They are dinging, flashing barriers to taking the next necessary step in the life of your child.

Your child does not have the wisdom, maturity, or experience to understand the consequences of her control and avoidance strategies. These consequences are that her anxiety will not be reduced over the long run and may in fact increase, and although she obtains some help from you in managing her feelings, she is creating larger problems in her relationship with you and potentially in her relationships with other individuals in her life, now and into the future.

The fact that your child attempts to get you to solve her anxiety problem is a good thing. She is simply going about it the wrong way and with the wrong goal in mind. Other than that, it's a good thing. She is engaging you in the process because you are her parent. You are her first and her most important teacher in life.

Context and Meaning

One way the picture, big or small, can affect us is through context. Context can change the meaning of words. For example, "Meet me at the bank" could mean at a financial institution or beside a river. Great peals of laughter are appropriate at a comedy club, probably not so at a funeral home. Context includes the many and shifting factors that make up our physical and social environments: Monday versus Saturday, sickness or health, the boss looking over your shoulder, sunshine after a week of rain. These contextual factors form a class of activators called *setting events*. Setting events change how we relate to the world around us. For example, I love cheeseburgers. If I'm hungry (a setting event), a cheeseburger is going to look especially good to me. But if I recently saw a documentary on mad cow disease, that same cheeseburger is going to appear unappetizing. The cheeseburger hasn't changed. How it affects me has changed as the result of the documentary as setting event.

EXERCISE:
Changing Contexts, Changing Experience

In this exercise, I want to illustrate how context can change your experience in subtle and not so subtle ways. I will ask you to describe a common situation you and your child struggle with. Then I will suggest changes in the external context or situation as well as your own internal context (moods or physical states). I want you to see if these changes in context might change what you subsequently think, feel, and do.

1. Think of a situation that provokes a typical anxious reaction from your child. Imagine that reaction now in terms of your thoughts and feelings and your response. Write those down.

Thoughts and feelings _____

Response _____

2. Now imagine your child is behaving that way in each of the following situations or contexts. In light of these contexts (setting events), write down how your thoughts, feelings, and responses might remain the same or change in some way.

You're tired.

Thoughts and feelings _____

Response _____

You're well rested.

Thoughts and feelings _____

Response _____

You're physically ill.

Thoughts and feelings _____

Response _____

Your mother is present.

Thoughts and feelings _____

Response _____

Your spouse is present.

Thoughts and feelings _____

Response _____

Your spouse is out of town.

Thoughts and feelings _____

Response _____

You're at home.

Thoughts and feelings _____

Response _____

You're in public.

Thoughts and feelings _____

Response _____

Your other children are unhappy and causing problems as well.

Thoughts and feelings _____

Response _____

Your other children are happy and content for the moment.

Thoughts and feelings _____

Response _____

You know your child is tired or hungry or in pain.

Thoughts and feelings _____

Response _____

Your child was three years younger and doing the same behavior.

Thoughts and feelings _____

Response _____

Did you find much variability in how you regarded your child's behavior? What changed more, your thoughts and feelings or your likely responses? If there were differences in your experience between the contexts, what do you think accounted for those differences?

Context or setting events affect our perceptions, our thoughts and feelings, and our behavior every day. They account for both the variability and the rigidity of your behavior patterns as well as those of your child. Again, our agenda is not to eliminate anxiety as a condition for successful living. The goal is for you and your child to understand the nature and process of anxiety and to change this process to one that is more forward-looking and useful in achieving your goals. Imagine that the difficult thoughts and feelings you experience as a parent are just tentative information. They are just sensations generated by your body and mind for the purpose of letting you know how things stand at that moment, under those circumstances. Imagine being able to use that information (or to ignore it) in the service of getting your bearings and keeping to your course. Patience with the process is required. This will take time and a great deal of working out the details.

SUMMARY AND A LOOK AHEAD

For much of the last century, the treatment of psychological syndromes centered on getting rid of symptoms or somehow controlling them so they would not control us. More recent thinking suggests there is an alternative view that holds great promise for freedom—not freedom *from* distressing thoughts and feelings but freedom *for* living a vital and interesting life, with all the joys and sorrows that may come.

As parents, we provide the structure and encouragement so that our children can be successful. At the same time, we allow increasing autonomy, exploration, and even failure so that our children can achieve mastery. Responsive parenting is a delicate and lively dance of acceptance and commitment, to take what is offered *and* to continue to work toward one's valued goals and a valued way of living. I know someone who says to her child, "I love you just the way you are, but I love you too much to let you stay that way." You can accept your child for who she is in the moment and still promote her growth and even demand she change her behavior. You can acknowledge her needs and feelings while providing rules and boundaries that ensure a secure and well-functioning family environment.

This new dance can succeed only when you can experience a measure of balance within yourself, when you extend these same possibilities for acceptance and commitment to yourself. When I originally wrote that last sentence, it read "only when you have *achieved* a measure of balance." I changed it because it is a fact that we cannot achieve balance; it is not static or something we can hang on to for long. Life will come along soon enough and knock us off balance again. Responsive parenting is not lying in repose. It is a day-to-day, even minute-to-minute dance, a shifting and correcting and adjusting in response to what your child is doing, to what is going on inside you, to the goals before you. A good place to start creating acceptance and making commitments is through examining and clarifying your values and goals, the subject of our next chapter.

CHAPTER 5

Anxiety in the Context of Values and Goals

As I described in the last chapter, acceptance and commitment therapy seeks to enable people to live a values-driven, goal-directed life. Such a life is not necessarily free of uncomfortable thoughts and feelings, but it is one in which you accept the reality of occasional or even frequent discomfort in order to move toward your goals and what matters to you, which brings a certain kind of peace. It is an *effective* life; problem solving, coping, and adapting take the foreground while avoidance and unhelpful control recede into the background.

As the white bear problem (see chapter 4) illustrates, the anxiety dance keeps you and your child stuck in recurring and ever-expanding cycles of anxiety and efforts to avoid or control that anxiety. You may experience some short-term relief in doing this, but it comes at the expense of fully engaging life and being able to solve problems as they arise. Anxiety becomes entrenched in your lives, but even more problematic, it expands its reach and power.

However, when you and your child emphasize managing the situations life presents to you instead of trying to manage thoughts and feelings, your lives can be more vital, purposeful, and successful. As you and your child become more effective in dealing with anxiety-provoking situations by focusing on your goals, you will find that confidence increases. Over time then, you and your child can expect a gradual lessening of unwarranted fears and worries. You needn't be fearful and anxious about fear and anxiety when these thoughts and feelings do show up, in your child's mind or in yours. As one mother said to me, "When I operate from a place of fear, nothing works well." In this chapter, I will talk about coming to know and articulate the values and goals that will allow you and your child to respond differently to anxiety and fear. Your new responses will be directed toward living your values and moving toward your goals rather than trying to eliminate anxious thoughts and feelings as a prerequisite for living a good life. Once you start focusing on values and goals, you and your child will be able to turn your attention to what you are really trying to accomplish in a particular situation instead of trying to manage and manipulate anxious thoughts and feelings.

You can think of most anxiety as a telemarketer who calls during dinner. You and your child are doing something, heading toward some goal, and now you're being interrupted ("How rude!"). The idea is to politely but firmly say no to the interruption and get back to what you were doing as quickly and smoothly as possible. Because you are the grown-up, more often than not it will be you who decides what goals you and your child are working toward. This is especially true when your child is quite young. As he grows older and take on more responsibility, he will have more say in what his goals will be. Today flossing his teeth or getting to school even when anxious may not be on his to-do list, but they're probably on your list for him.

Finally, at points throughout this chapter, I will offer some exercises and ideas for selecting goals and setting priorities, for knowing what to focus on and what to let go. This will help you change the choreography of the dance you and your child are currently doing.

MAKING SENSE OF THE HARD WORK OF PARENTING

Raising children is hard work and requires tremendous sacrifices, day in and day out, year after year. Let's be honest, if we'd wanted a comfortable and easy life, we would not have become parents. Our children may have made us more angry, sad, frustrated, and anxious than we could ever have thought possible. We may have had feelings of regret, resentment, and jealousy. And those are just the feelings and experiences we're willing to admit! It's also true that our children have brought us great joy, and even the challenging times have, in time, shaped us and helped us grow as people and all that. However, we can't do parenting from the stance of "the good feelings and thoughts will outweigh the bad ones in the long run." They may not. I'm just being honest here.

Let's think back to Angela and Sterling. Angela loves her son dearly, but after fighting him and his feelings in order to simply get out the door in the morning, she is tired, discouraged, and feels like a failure. Good feelings and thoughts are wonderful, but they are rare and fleeting in our lives. We need more than "Where am I on the 'feeling good index'?" as the measure of how our lives are going and whether or not we are succeeding as parents. In fact, the goal of feeling good and not feeling bad is what has gotten Angela and Sterling, and many of us, in the predicament we find ourselves in: trying to manage our insides (thoughts, emotions, and so on) while not giving enough attention and energy to what's going on outside in our lives, such as the actions we must take toward accomplishing what we care about. We need to remember that being a good parent, a responsive parent, doesn't mean we always get to feel good. It means focusing on what our child needs in the moment, within the context of our values and goals, and then taking small steps in that direction.

DEFINING VALUES AND GOALS

Perhaps you're wondering what I mean by values and goals. The first several definitions of "value" in the *Oxford Pocket American Dictionary of Current English* have to do with assessing or attributing worth to something, as in the value of a dollar. Further down you get to "values" as "a person's principles or standards of behavior; one's judgment about what is important in life" (Oxford Dictionaries 2008). From the same source, we find that a "goal" is "the object of a person's ambition or effort; an aim or desired result" and "the destination of a journey" (Oxford Dictionaries 2008). In acceptance and commitment therapy, we say that values are directions and goals are destinations (Eifert and Forsyth 2005). Our principles and ideals tell us where to direct our work and play, and our goals mark the progress we make.

So, for example, I value being a good dad. That is a direction, like a compass heading, to which I endeavor to stay true. How I live out "being a good dad" may take many forms, and I may have many different and varied goals for being a good dad, such as to listen well, to show patience, to set limits, to spend my weekend driving a carload of scouts to some soggy meadow and sleeping on the ground for two nights in the rain, to laugh, to bear anxiety and sorrow. The list is endless—all because I *chose* the direction of being a good dad and reaffirm that choice every day. The other stuff—the goals—then comes with the territory.

My son values being a good student. His goals include getting his work done and turned in on time, doing well on tests, and contributing to the general learning environment at school by participating and not disrupting the learning of his fellow students. On his road to being a good student, he's dealt with and will continue to deal with various obstacles: boredom, fatigue, competing interests, lack of interest, negative comments from the guys who don't think being a good student is cool, and many others.

Values and goals—my own, my son's, yours, your child's—give shape to our commitments and allow us to make the hard choices about what to do when uncomfortable thoughts and feelings show up. What is important now is learning to articulate and live by our values and goals in order to have a full and satisfying life.

Your Family's Values and Goals

The eminent Swiss psychiatrist Carl Jung said, "Life's truly important problems cannot be solved, they can only be outgrown." In line with Jung's wisdom, we are going to take a growth approach to life's problems. The strategies in this book are geared toward growing your child out of the tendency to become stuck in anxiety and to coerce you into rescuing him. In order to accept acceptance, to do willingness, to face and push through fear and anxiety, you and your child need to have an idea of why you are doing this. What's the point of being brave? Where is this willingness going to take you? What is really important to you? What is important to your child? To your family? What are the commitments you would like to have front and center in your life today?

Childhood is a time when, as a parent, you must often step in to guide, direct, and command your child to do things that he might not necessarily choose to do if it were entirely up to him. For example, your child may endorse oral hygiene, good grades, and becoming an accomplished musician. However, would he brush his teeth, do his homework, or practice piano without your "encouragement"? Some children are fantastic self-starters and quite disciplined. Most need at least some prompting and nudging to get through a day's worth of tasks. Many thoughts and feelings get in the way of the simplest tasks—boredom, impatience, resentment, to name a few.

Think of a typical day in the life of your family. If your family is the least bit normal, you're spending a lot of time and energy pushing and cajoling your child into doing things he *needs* to do but does not necessarily *want* to do. This starts with getting him out of bed in the morning and ends with trying to get him to sleep at night. In between are a hundred tasks, demands, and goals that you know are important and necessary, and perhaps he knows this too. But since you're the adult (with perspective and experience), you're going to be the one caring about it and putting your shoulder to the wheel. On that Monday morning, all Sterling cared about, all he could think of, was gaining some control over his shoelaces. Angela had to be the one with an eye on the big picture and the clock.

And that's just the day-to-day stuff. What about the real challenges? Would your child readily plunge into situations that invite him to feel and think terrifying things? Why should he? During the best of times, most school-age children lack the perspective and experience to overcome the in-the-moment thoughts and feelings that encourage avoidance of what's uncomfortable and difficult. It's hard enough for us as adults. How hard must it be for your child?

When anxiety shows up, our plans and goals tend to recede into the background and self-preservation rushes into the foreground. This is true for you, and it is also true for your child. Unfortunately one of you is going to have to maintain a grip on what's important and what needs to happen next. As the mature member of the dance team, that would be you.

What Do You Want for Your Child?

Do you want your child to be a peacemaker, a discoverer of great ideas, a giver of gifts to humanity. To win the Heisman Trophy? To make a gazillion dollars? To be appointed to the Supreme Court? To be happy with who he is? What he strives for himself will depend on what he learns to value. What he can become will depend on his ability to achieve goals in spite of the obstacles he encounters.

What your child learns to value will come from many sources. As the parent, you have a great deal of influence over what your child sees as important and worthwhile in his life. As he grows, there will be many influential people and experiences in his life shaping his values and goals: other adults, peers, and the media, to name just the more obvious ones. But as his parent, you will always have a central role in this process.

Values are the compass heading. Goals are the destination. In real life, these terms overlap somewhat; for example, being a responsible person can be both a value and a goal. I will talk more about this below. For now, let me just state that by clarifying your values and goals, for yourself and for your child, you will be better able to keep focused on an effective direction in the midst of anxious upset, your child's and your own. There will be short-term tasks and goals to orient you to what needs to happen next in order to be effective in those anxiety-provoking situations, and long-term goals focused on the big-picture values of where you and your child need to be heading in order to be the people you want to be.

For example, Angela has the goal of getting out of the house on time in the morning. This goal is based on her big-picture values related to being responsible herself and ensuring that Sterling gets the most out of school by being on time. She also wants Sterling to learn to be responsible generally, and specifically to take over more of his own self-care: small-picture stuff such as bathroom tasks, dressing, eating breakfast, and so on. There is some negative reinforcement at work here too; Angela doesn't want to be late and get on her boss's bad side. She doesn't want the school to think she's the flaky parent of a child who is often tardy.

So when Sterling becomes frantic and stuck in some anxious state, it threatens to derail these many goals that must or could be accomplished in that short amount of time. What's a mother to do?

Looking at Values and Goals

The exercise that follows is intended to help you clarify your own goals and values in life as well as the goals you want for your child. It is necessary to think about your values and goals because these drive parenting behavior. For example, if you care about your child's success in school, you will be more likely to have expectations for good learning habits and strategies. You will do what you can to instill a love of learning and will look for opportunities to encourage effort in learning situations. You will also model eagerness and joy in learning yourself. All these varied behaviors on your part stem from a simple value of learning and the goals of creating that value and those behaviors in your child. Similarly a parent might invest time and energy encouraging athletics, community service, social relationships, fiscal responsibility, and any number of valuable goals. And as your child grows older, you want him to think about his own values and to create his own goals so that he can carry this process into adulthood and use these ideas and strategies to further his life.

In doing this exercise, remember that there are no right or wrong answers. In fact, if you somehow believe that you must care about all of these areas with equal and maximum intensity in order to be a good parent and worthwhile human being, you will surely burn yourself out. Some areas may blend together, such as family and parenting. Values and goals may certainly overlap across life domains. That is often where we get our energy, when various aspects of our lives share common values and goals.

EXERCISE: Values and Goals

This exercise is adapted from the Valued Living Questionnaire (Wilson and Groom 2002). There are ten life domains (such as family or physical self-care) that people commonly value and generate goals for. Look at each of these domains and indicate how much you value each domain on a scale of 0 to 10: 0 is really no value at all, and 10 is very highly valued, a direction in life you simply could not imagine being without.

Next, write down one to three goals for each of these life domains. These could be process goals such as "listening well" or outcome goals such as "take that photography class." (For more on process and outcome goals, see below.) Be as specific as possible; "Taking time to really listen" is more informative than "Be nice."

If you have a parenting partner, it might be helpful if he or she also completed this exercise. How similar or different are the goals you each come up with? Do you each have different means for attaining similar goals (for example, one recreates with high-energy activities, while the other likes to curl up with a book?) Are there areas of conflict? For example, are work and recreation out of balance in your family life? How do you address these differences? How do you achieve balance?

Your Values and Goals

Rate the importance of each on a scale of 0 to 10; then list one to three goals for each.

1. Family (other than marriage or parenting) _____

   Goals:

   1. _____

   2. _____

   3. _____

2. Marriage, couples, intimate relations _____

   Goals:

   1. _____

   2. _____

   3. _____

3. Parenting _____

   Goals:

   1. _____

   2. _____

   3. _____

4. Friends, social life _____

   Goals:

   1. _____

   2. _____

   3. _____

5. Work _____

   Goals:

   1. _____

   2. _____

   3. _____

6. Education, training _____

   Goals:

   1. _____

   2. _____

   3. _____

7. Recreation, fun _____

   Goals:

   1. _____

   2. _____

   3. _____

8. Spirituality _____

   Goals:

   1. _____

   2. _____

   3. _____

9. Citizenship, community _____

   Goals:

   1. _____

   2. _____

   3. _____

10. Physical self-care (diet, exercise, sleep) _____

   Goals:

   1. _____

   2. _____

   3. _____

Now, using the form below, I would like you to do this exercise again, but this time with your child in mind. If your child is old enough, say eight years of age or older, you might sit down with him and talk about these life domains. Assess how important these areas are for him or how he sees himself thinking about them in the future (for example, for marriage or work). Come up with some simple, concrete goals that he can achieve in a relatively short amount of time or on a frequent basis: being more patient with his little sister, flossing, volunteering to help an elderly neighbor with yard work. Talk about how these relate to the values you share. For a younger child, or a child of any age, think about what *you* want for your child in terms of valued directions and representative goals.

Your Child's Values and Goals

Rate the importance of each on a scale of 0 to 10; then list one to three goals for each.

1. Family (other than marriage or parenting) _____

   Goals:

     1. _____

     2. _____

     3. _____

2. Marriage, couples, intimate relations _____

   Goals:

     1. _____

     2. _____

     3. _____

3. Parenting _____

   Goals:

     1. _____

     2. _____

     3. _____

4. Friends, social life _____

   Goals:

     1. _____

     2. _____

     3. _____

5. Work _____

   Goals:

     1. _____

     2. _____

     3. _____

6. Education, training _____

    Goals:

        1. _____

        2. _____

        3. _____

7. Recreation, fun _____

    Goals:

        1. _____

        2. _____

        3. _____

8. Spirituality _____

    Goals:

        1. _____

        2. _____

        3. _____

9. Citizenship, community _____

    Goals:

        1. _____

        2. _____

        3. _____

10. Physical self-care (diet, exercise, sleep) _____

    Goals:

        1. _____

        2. _____

        3. _____

Now, what did you notice? Did you or your child give every domain a value of 10? Were you surprised that, on reflection, some domains weren't ranked very high on the value scale? Did your goals strike you as realistic, impossible, frustratingly elusive, or boring? Are there significant conflicts between your values and goals and those of your parenting partner or your child? Are your goals for your child the recycled, unattained goals of your youth? Are you struck by how many gifts of value you have in your life and how much life has to offer your child? Again, there are no right or wrong answers. The questions that this exercise can generate are possibly endless. Find someone with whom you can continue the discussion. Talk to your child about your goals. Show interest in his.

Goals Take the Foreground

Recall the vase/faces illusion in chapter 4. You can see either the vase or the faces depending on how your mind shifted one or the other from background to foreground. The vase does not disappear when you see the faces; the mind has simply relegated it to the background by a shift in perception. Goals and values can be like that in relation to anxiety. With practice, your mind and your child's mind can learn to let your goals claim the foreground, letting anxiety recede into the background. Anxiety doesn't have to disappear when this happens any more than the vase disappears when you see the faces.

Outcome Goals and Process Goals

In doing the exercise above, you likely found that a number of your goals competed with one another—for example, to find time to get to the gym after work *and* to support your child's efforts at soccer by getting him to practice. A large part of being a responsive parent is being able to sift through all the possible and competing goals in a given situation and come up with the one that will serve everyone best. This is not as hard as it sounds if you've given it some thought ahead of time—and that is what we are doing now.

A few pages ago I mentioned that values and goals can overlap, as in the case of "being a responsible person," for example. It can be useful to think about two kinds of goals: outcome goals and process goals. Again, there will be some overlap between these two in reality. *Outcome goals* are the "destinations" that are fairly clear as to when you have arrived: your child is dressed and fed, the bills have been paid and mailed, Joshua has gone upstairs by himself, Beth has opened the bathroom door on her own, Sterling is off to school, or Abby is looking at someone and saying "hello." *Process goals* describe events or behaviors that can be observed but lack a distinct finish line, or they are some activity that recurs and you're never actually done with it. For example, cooperating, listening, being responsible, being a good student, and being a good dad are all process goals.

So there are outcome goals (getting the shoes tied and getting out the door on time) and there are process goals (listening and cooperating). The key element here is recognizing that you are taking the time to invest in this moment for the sake of the big-picture goals, such as your child developing increased self-awareness or more effective communication and self-regulation skills.

Angela's outcome goal was for Sterling to get out of the house on time. What if her process goals included helping Sterling to understand his thoughts and feelings, perhaps to simply have names for how he feels (frustrated, nervous)? Or perhaps Angela could help Sterling understand the connections among situations, thoughts, feelings, bodily sensations, behaviors, and the consequences of those behaviors, including the reactions or responses of others. For example, Angela might say, "When you've been gone for the weekend, these Monday mornings are so hard! Little things can be so frustrating. I'll bet your stomach's nervous. If you need help with those laces, just ask me." These process goals are clearly oriented to the child's growth and self-awareness, and serve to increase his self-regulation skills over time. The key phrase here is "over time." By taking the long view, Angela can become a more responsive parent by encouraging Sterling's growth (self-regulation) and rechoreographing their automatic dance, which now leads them more toward avoidance and control than to understanding and growth.

This doesn't mean that difficult situations will suddenly work out better. What it means is that anxiety-rich situations can be seen as teaching opportunities wherein you convey to your child that you understand him and his distress. You teach and model a new dance that will allow your child to begin to step back from and understand the situation at hand.

VALUES AND GOALS AS CONTEXT

Shifting values and goals from the background to the foreground creates the context within which choices and effective actions become possible. In the last chapter, I asked you to look at your child's behavior from within various situations (being tired, out in public, and so on). Those different contexts likely changed how you would see, interpret, and respond to your child's behavior. That is the power of context: to alter the meaning of information coming to us, to change our intention, and to guide our actions. In the context of values and goals, what would you be willing to do to ensure that your child grew up strong and capable? Perhaps you'd say, "School is very important and I am going to insist that my child go to school even though he is complaining of a stomachache because I know from my experience [another context] that he will be fine within twenty minutes of my leaving him at school."

In the context of values and goals, what might your child be willing to do, even in the face of fear and anxiety, in order to grow and succeed? "To help my soccer team, I'm going to get in there and attack the ball even though it's scary and I'm having the thought that if I mess up, I'll just die of embarrassment." That may seem like a small and even insignificant achievement. But for many children with anxiety, it could be a very important and brave act that, when repeated in a variety of ways in a variety of situations, becomes a part of their experience, their history. That experience of success, with a new self-image of competence and confidence, becomes the context for further willingness when it's needed. Not that this happens overnight, but it starts here.

Outcome vs. Process Goals as Context

In the coming chapters, I will be talking about specific strategies for you to employ when your child is anxious or fearful. You will essentially be modeling for him the process by which he will better understand what he is experiencing in the moment, communicate that experience to you, ask for your help, and either accept your help or solve the problem himself, all with as little drama and negativity as possible.

To do this in those moments when anxiety interrupts your child's life, it will be important to be clear about your outcome goals and your process goals, and which you will emphasize. For example, Joshua is standing at the bottom of the stairs, unwilling to go up to his bedroom to retrieve his shoes without his mother accompanying him. He is whimpering as his way of communicating this to her. His mother, Nancy, could focus on the small-picture outcome goal of "Joshua goes upstairs by himself." This is the default goal to date, and it has invited much of the stress he and his parents know as the anxiety problem or dance. As an alternative, Nancy could focus on a "medium-picture" outcome goal of "getting the shoes from upstairs." This creates more options for a solution. Nancy could go upstairs with Joshua or go without him and retrieve them herself. The goal would be accomplished, but negative reinforcement would ensure that Joshua whimpered the next time he needed to go upstairs on his own. Both of these options are logical choices in the context of the outcome goals of Joshua going upstairs by himself or the shoes successfully being retrieved. Little else seems possible if those are the goals. But what if there were other possibilities?

A shift can be created by placing the problem in a different context, essentially redefining the problem: what is the *process* involved here, and how can that process be improved? A process goal in this situation would be to address the *how* of what Joshua is doing rather than the *what*. As defined in chapter 3, the process is the dance between Joshua and Nancy in that situation. As I will describe in detail in chapter 8, Joshua's mother could take action to directly address the dance and focus on process goals, such as how Joshua communicates his feelings and thoughts, and how he asks for help. For example, Nancy might respond to Joshua's pleas with "I can tell you're having some scary thoughts about going upstairs by yourself. Am I right?" If Joshua affirms Nancy's perception, she might ask, "What's your brain telling you about going upstairs by yourself?" Perhaps he can describe these thoughts, perhaps not. Nancy would quickly get to the issue: "And you want me to go upstairs with you so that you'll feel safe?" Joshua nods. Nancy now has several options, each one striving for a bit more growth on Joshua's part. Which one she chooses will depend on her reading of the situation (including her own level of frustration and patience), how far along they are in their efforts to change the anxiety dance (see below), and how far she might be able to "stretch" Joshua that day. Quickly taking all this in, Nancy might say, "Okay, let's go," and go on upstairs with him with a minimum of fuss, physical contact, or reassurance. Or she might tell Joshua that she will go upstairs with him, but he must ask her to do so in a clear, strong voice. On the other hand, they may have done all this before with some success and Joshua is ready for a challenge: "I'll be right here at the bottom of the stairs. You run up as quickly as you can and get those shoes so we can go to Grandma's. Hurry now. I'll be right here."

Focusing on the process changes the context. Actually, a process orientation *recognizes* the context. This exchange between Nancy and Joshua was only partially about shoes upstairs or even about scary thoughts and feelings. For Joshua, this has always been about needing to feel secure and protected: "Are you still going to take care of me? Even here? Even now?" Process goals answer that question: "Yes, I'm here for you now. And here's what you need to do to make this work."

EXERCISE: From Outcome to Process Goals

Look back at the goals you and your child came up with in the various life domains in the exercise above. In the left-hand column of the table below, I want you (with your child if he is willing and able) to write down a few of your outcome goals. Now, opposite each of these goals, in the right-hand column, write down one or more process goals that could contribute to the success of that outcome goal. An example is provided.

Outcome Goals	Process Goals
Getting Joshua to go upstairs and get his shoes	Joshua communicating his thoughts and feelings in an age-appropriate manner
	Joshua asking for my help using words

Outcome goals tend to dominate our busy lives. Process goals—such as communicating, listening, or cooperating, to name a few—may seem trivial or thought of as a given. If you find yourself saying things like "I shouldn't have to tell him three times" or "He should be able to do this on his own," you are often dealing with some process that isn't working well—

cooperation or self-reliance, for example. But often process goals describe the very actions and reactions that define your child's anxiety problem: he is not communicating, not listening, or not cooperating; he is not being self-reliant. Process goals are not trivial and they cannot be taken for granted. If you were to feel resentment at having to give this topic so much time and attention, that would be understandable. But focusing on process goals and the means to achieve them is one of the first steps in any effort to change a pattern of behavior, especially one that can be characterized as a dance between two people.

Graybar's Second Law of Human Behavior

Steve Graybar, a good friend of mine in graduate school, used to say, "He who cares least has the most power." I call this Graybar's second law of human behavior and sometimes flip it around to say, "The more you care, the more you must be willing to bear." Graybar's first law of human behavior will be discussed in chapter 8. It can be summed up as "All behavior is a message, and a behavior won't begin to change until the person knows his message has been received."

The more you care, the more you must be willing to bear. I'm bringing up Graybar's second law now because, as a parent, you know that there are certain things you need to care about (process and outcome goals) that your child is not necessarily going to care about, or at least not in the same way or to the same degree. For example, it seems that every mother in Seattle, a city surrounded by water, insists her child learn how to swim. Many kids are perfectly fine with that, and a lot of kids aren't. So attaining the goal of drown proofing your child may involve considerable struggle to get him to swimming lessons and to overcome whatever obstacles—defiance, anxiety, indolence, finances, or your own time constraints—may be in the way. If swimming is a priority goal for you, then you'll likely be willing to endure almost any form of protest from your child in order to achieve that goal.

The question is, how many of those do-or-die goals do you want to be struggling over? How much are you willing to bear to see that certain goals are achieved? As a parent, you have to pick your battles and invest your precious resources of time, money, energy, and goodwill as wisely as possible. Whether it's the quality of the homework, the number of merit badges earned, the soccer goals scored, or the fearful situations overcome, there is a tipping point where we as parents begin to care more about the goal than does our child and we do more than our share of work toward achieving that goal. Sometimes this will be necessary. But often, by assuming too much of the caring and the work involved, we rob our children of the opportunity to strive and struggle, persevere and learn—or perhaps to quit or fail, and learn from that.

How much we should do as parents is a hard call with no easy answer. But the process of discussing goals and priorities, acknowledging competing agendas, honoring one another's thoughts and feelings (even the ones we don't share or agree with) can create a family atmosphere that allows for compromise and cooperation.

One last point along these lines: values and goals are not cattle prods. You don't use them to goad your child into doing something he is unwilling to do: "You *said* you wanted to go to the party." Being aware of values and outcome goals can encourage movement in a positive direction when fear and anxiety show up. If movement has stalled, focusing on the process can help you and your child at least get to a more conscious and responsible choice *not* to move in that direction. An example of the latter might be your child saying, "I've decided not to go to the party" instead of "I *can't* go to the party because I'm too anxious." If your child makes a choice you don't agree with, you can at least hold out for him making that choice well—and being aware that he is, in fact, making a choice.

PLANNING YOUR CAMPAIGN TO CHANGE THE ANXIETY DANCE

Changing behavior is difficult. It is especially difficult in the face of powerful emotions, biologically based survival instincts, forces such as negative reinforcement, and years of habit. Change requires a campaign: a planned and concerted effort over time. As I will describe it in the next chapters, your campaign to address your child's anxiety will be conducted in phases that will overlap somewhat.

Following the clarification of your values and goals, phase 1 involves increasing everyone's awareness of and understanding of the current dance. We'll explore this phase below and in chapter 6, where I will talk about mindfulness. Phase 2 involves teaching and practicing social skills and social understanding, along with breathing and muscle-tone techniques for self-regulation (chapter 7). Giving your child the clear message that you get what he thinks and feels, that you hear the message his anxious behavior sends, is variously called mirroring, reflecting, or validating, and is the objective of phase 3 (chapter 8). Phase 4 involves effectively managing anxious situations, both proactively as well as in response to your child's anxious behaviors (chapter 9).

PHASE 1: INCREASING AWARENESS

Phase 1 in any behavior change campaign involves increasing awareness of what each of the dance partners is actually doing. This phase is vital. As I stated with regard to the anxiety dance, much of what you and your child struggle with operates out of awareness in the moment. In hindsight, you may be able to reconstruct what happened, who felt and thought what, and what action was taken. That awareness after the fact can be useful. But to change the dance, you must change your behavior *while* you're dancing. To do that, you and your child must be aware of what you're doing and what you need to do instead—in that moment. In the next chapter, I will introduce strategies and exercises for increasing your own and your child's awareness of what you are doing when anxiety shows up.

Patience is required during this phase of increasing awareness. You want to get to the change part ASAP. Perhaps you have every reason to believe that your child knows exactly what he's thinking and feeling and could do the right thing if he wanted to. Perhaps you see your child as being at the mercy of his biology or as burdened with a sensitivity that would only be exacerbated by further scrutiny. However, I will show you the importance of investing in increasing awareness as I walk you through each phase of your change campaign in the rest of the book. Awareness is the first phase, and in reality it never stops being important. It is an ongoing and necessary context, an internal process goal.

Awareness puts you and your child in touch with what you are doing, how you are communicating with each other, and whether you are reacting or responding to each other. From there, you begin to see the parent-child transactions (the dance) and the process goals more clearly. I will show you how to articulate and encourage good parent-child transactions through effective communication and problem-solving strategies. These strategies will be covered in chapters 7, 8, and 9. Like awareness, the need for good communication never ends, and you will find yourself often directing your child's attention to the give and take of communication as a step toward achieving other goals, both process and outcome.

Getting There by Degrees

In all of the phases of your behavior change campaign, it will be important to recognize and appreciate something we behavioral psychologists call successive approximations. The term *successive approximations* refers to incremental behavior change. You have an ultimate outcome goal, say, "My child will get out of the house in the morning without my having to prod him." In reality, he probably won't jump from where he is now (your extensive prodding with negative reactions on his part) to that vision of peace and maturity you have in mind. You will both get there by degrees, by successive approximations. Again, the first phase will be increasing awareness of his pattern of avoidance, your prodding, his distressed reaction, and so on. After that, you will expect and encourage some behavior that helps you and your child move in the direction of your ultimate goal. For example, "using words" to convey his thoughts and feelings gets you away from old, regressed forms of communication, such as wailing and flailing, and toward more age-appropriate and fruitful verbal communication, your process goal.

You know what you don't want your child to do when he is anxious: cling, cry inconsolably, freeze, throw a tantrum. What *do* you want him to do when he's fearful or worried? The answer can't be "to be less anxious." That anxiety-provoking situation calls for an appropriate response. What could that be?

Alternative expected behaviors, such as "using your words," are sometimes called the *positive opposites* of what your child is doing now. Diplomacy is the positive opposite of war. It will be important to clarify what you want and what you will expect from your anxious child so that you can teach it, look for it, and encourage it. For example, the positive opposite of whining might be asking for something with a pleasant voice. The positive opposite of avoiding something would be doing that thing. Again, as I described in the last chapter, willingness is not anything special. It's just doing what the situation truly calls for in the context of your process and outcome goals.

As the adult, you will also want to be sure that you demonstrate that same or similar behavior under your own challenging circumstances. It's only fair, and your modeling of the expected, positive opposite behavior and your willingness in the face of your own upset are powerful teaching tools.

EXERCISE: Using Values and Goals to Increase Awareness of Your Anxiety Dance

The first step in rechoreographing your anxiety dance is becoming aware of what you and your child are doing, what you value, and what goals you are trying to achieve. In this exercise, you will use the values you identified earlier to help you and your child increase your awareness of your anxiety dance and thus begin your behavior change campaign. The steps below will carry you through a process that lays the groundwork for learning how to *respond* rather than *react* to anxiety-provoking situations. As you work through this exercise—and as you face any anxiety-provoking situation with your child—keep these two questions in mind:

- What is my goal in this particular situation?

- What values will help me decide what to do?

Take a piece of paper and write down your answer(s) for each step below. An example from Beth's behavior change campaign will illustrate each step.

1. **Name two or three current and recurring anxiety-provoking situations. How frequently does each situation arise?** You might choose, for example, one aspect of getting out of the house in the morning or of your child's bedtime routine. It's best to start with behaviors that occur daily or several times a day, if possible.

Beth's Behavior Change Campaign

Beth and her parents agree to target bathroom contamination fears because she experiences these fears several times a day.

2. **Of those situations, select one over which you have some control.** You likely have more control over situations at home. Control is important because you want to be able to predict how the situation will play out, based on your previous experience, and you need to be reasonably sure that you can control the outcome.

Beth's Behavior Change Campaign

Beth and her parents choose the bathroom at home. It's part of their daily experience with few complicating factors (for example, other people won't be involved). Also, the expectation for Beth's behavior can be simple and consistent.

3. **Think about the situation you've chosen. Name two or three milder and less entrenched behavior patterns, ones that only show up about half the time.**

Beth's Behavior Change Campaign

Beth's fear of contamination and unwillingness to touch the bathroom doorknob isn't especially intense or rigid. Sometimes she can open the door on her own, with or without a lot of anxious thoughts and feelings. These moments present opportunities for her to be aware of and to examine the internal process that ebbs and flows and that sometimes gets in her way. Similarly, Beth's parents' reactions to her bathroom behavior at home are milder and more thoughtful than they often are in other situations (for example, when in public, or when it's late at night and everyone's tired).

4. **Given this situation, what are the primary values—yours and your child's—that will guide your response?** Older children may be able to identify their values; for younger children, you may have to guess.

Beth's Behavior Change Campaign

Because Beth is ten years old, she can understand and articulate at least some of her values. Her value in this situation, which at first glance may seem to be unrelated, is to be a good student and to do well on tests. Her parents' value is to have Beth "act her age."

5. **Identify the anxious thoughts, feelings, and behaviors—both yours and your child's—that show up in this situation.** If your child is very young, you may have to guess as to what he is thinking and feeling.

Beth's Behavior Change Campaign

Beth identifies several anxious thoughts and feelings: She worries that touching the doorknob will contaminate her fingers, then she'll get germs in her mouth and become sick and miss school. She worries that she'll spread these germs to her family. In her thoughts, she berates herself for being so childish and tells herself to just open the door. Thinking about touching the doorknob nauseates her and leaves a bad taste in her mouth. Her typical behavior in response to these thoughts and feelings is to sit on the edge of the tub and call for her mother in a loud wail, even though she knows her father is more likely to just let her out. She calls her father if her mother isn't around. Sometimes Beth will get bored waiting and let herself out of the bathroom, sometimes covering her hand with a tissue.

Beth's parents identified exasperation, resentment, and worries about Beth's future as their common reaction.

6. **Identify the message behind your child's behavior. What is he trying to accomplish in that situation?** Most likely, your child is attempting to get you to help him, to use your considerable adult powers to rid him of his distress, to make it okay. But he may have another goal.

Beth's Behavior Change Campaign

Beth's message seems relatively straightforward: I can't get out of this bathroom because I'm unwilling to touch this germy doorknob and get myself (and maybe others) sick. Beth and her parents identify this as the message and state it explicitly, perhaps for the first time. What was unsaid and implied becomes stated and clear. Small changes in language can change how we see the problem and the solution. For example, using the phrase "I'm unwilling to..." instead of "I'm too anxious to..." shifts the focus away from using thoughts and feelings as reasons for her behavior and toward the context of goals and willingness. Similarly, "I'm choosing not to..." instead of "I can't..." puts the focus on Beth's taking responsibility for her actions. Taking responsibility is a general goal that can be linked to her value of being a good student.

7. **Identify the goals—both process and outcome goals. What can you and your child agree needs to happen in this situation, particularly in light of your values?** An outcome goal might be committed action or willingness, whatever that might mean in this situation. A process goal might be improved communication, help seeking, and cooperation.

Beth's Behavior Change Campaign

Beth's value of being a good student is relevant here because we might speculate that her fear of *not* doing well (for example, on an upcoming test) may underlie her reluctance to let herself out of the bathroom. If she misses the test, she can't fail it. On a more general level, Beth may be feeling a lot of pressure to do well in school, to be responsible and independent. Implicit in the dance is Beth's goal to get a parent to take care of her (process) by opening the door so she can avoid germs on the doorknob (outcome goal). Her parents' goals are to have Beth face her fears and help herself (process), and to have Beth open the door on her own (outcome). This is based on their value of Beth growing up to be self-reliant and responsible.

As part of developing the behavior change campaign, Beth and her parents talk about their values and Beth's ultimate goal, which Beth says is to "not be anxious anymore." Peggy bites her tongue and doesn't tell Beth that her goal is unrealistic. Instead she and Al tell Beth they think it's a great goal, but that they will need to work toward it in steps. Beth's parents talk up the common ground she and they share regarding values and goals: "We all want you to be a good student, which means taking responsibility for what you do, dealing with frustration, getting help when you need it, being willing to do things you sometimes don't want to do (like taking tests) because you want to honor your commitments," and so on. This anxiety campaign, they tell Beth, is all about those same ideas: goals, commitment, willingness, patience, and using your resources (such as parents) wisely.

Together Beth and her parents come up with incremental goals. For Beth, a next-to-ultimate goal is to turn the doorknob, in spite of her anxieties, and let herself out of the bathroom. Short of that, another incremental goal is using a tissue to cover her hand to turn the knob and get out of the bathroom without her parents' assistance. Closer to her current behavior but still a change, Beth will ask, in a calm but clear and strong voice (no wailing), for a parent to help her. She also agrees to tell a parent that she is going to use the bathroom and ask if the parent will please be nearby in case she needs help.

Al and Peggy agree to be more patient with Beth, to suggest what she could do in those situations instead of focusing on what she is doing wrong, and to listen to her worries without being dismissive of them.

As you begin the behavior change campaign, remember that you begin where you are: upset, conflicted about what to do, even confused. Being aware of all these thoughts and feelings is the important first phase of any behavior change and of rechoreographing the anxiety dance. With perseverance, your routine will change from the old dance of avoidance and control to a new dance of understanding, effective problem solving, and growth for both you and your child.

Beth and her parents were able to have a calm and articulate discussion about this situation and their various values and goals. For a young child such as Abby or Joshua, you would want to take more of a lead in directing the conversation and introducing the goals and values. You would keep it brief, simple, and concrete—that is, very specific and observable. For example, "keeping a promise" could be used instead of "keeping a commitment" and "doing it by yourself" might stand in for "taking responsibility." Values, too, would be phrased almost in terms of goals: to be polite, to be helpful, to be kind.

One of the reasons I ask that you first select a situation over which you have some control is that when you're trying to teach a new response in the face of anxiety, surprises are not helpful. Obviously you can't completely predict or control situations that make your child anxious. Often what makes situations anxiety provoking is their ambiguity or the lack of certainty about the outcome, something we'll discuss in chapter 9. Right now we're going for the low-hanging fruit: situations that will give us the best shot at some successful behavior change. So even if you find only one or two optimal situations where you can implement your campaign and start seeing new responses, you will be establishing a new foundation of communication, cooperation, and success that can and eventually will be expanded to other, more complex or highly charged situations. You may find that, in the meantime, the more difficult situations have begun to improve almost on their own.

SUMMARY AND A LOOK AHEAD

In this chapter, I've suggested that clarifying your values and goals provides the context within which the hard work of parenting and the hard work of being a kid can make sense and be worth the struggle. Acting on your values and goals moves you and your child away from the anxiety dance and toward the acceptance dance. It is only after you have begun to move together in the acceptance dance, even if a bit clumsily at first, that you can begin to increase your child's capacity for coping with difficult, anxiety-provoking situations in order to move forward in his life.

Your immediate, phase 1 objective is that you and your child increase your awareness of and, to a degree, acceptance of the current patterns of reaction and counterreaction that divert you both from your actual goals. This means turning your attention toward, as opposed to avoiding, the anxiety-rich situation as well as the thoughts and feelings it occasions.

In those moments, turning toward the discomfort is often the last thing any of us wants to do. You and your child certainly don't want this stuff; you don't want to feel it or think it. But in the service of goals such as understanding and growth, you might be willing to look at it. How else are you and your child going to get to know what you're dealing with? You can't change something if you don't understand it or aren't aware of it. To borrow a phrase from the eminent family therapist Salvador Minuchin (1981), it would be like trying "to stop the music in order to hear it more clearly" (p. 78).

Changing anxiety and the way it controls your life is challenging. Going after anxiety is not like fumigating your house; you don't just bag it and in one move kill off everything nasty inside. The process I am guiding you through is more like fly-fishing. You're going to be changing anxious behaviors one by one, changing the process through small steps toward the goal of a life that isn't controlled by anxiety, of a life that is worth living.

In this chapter, we started clarifying the process and outcome goals you want for your family. Now we'll look for some opportunities to increase awareness and understanding of what you're dealing with on the way to those goals. This is the topic of our next chapter: mindfulness.

CHAPTER 6

Mindfulness in the Midst of Anxiety

So far I have been describing your child's anxiety on a big canvas: behavior patterns, the anxiety dance, values and goals, and coming up with your initial campaign for making changes to the old way of doing things. In this chapter, I will focus on the moment-to-moment behaviors that make up the anxiety dance. The goal is to increase awareness, your child's and your own, of exactly what it is you each are feeling, thinking, and doing in those anxious moments. Any behavior change campaign must begin with becoming aware of what you are doing. This is the only way to rechoreograph the dance.

DEFUSION: REDUCING IDENTIFICATION WITH YOUR THOUGHTS AND FEELINGS

All by itself, becoming more aware of what you are doing can make subtle changes in what you experience. Naming a feeling ("tension"), locating it in space ("the back of my neck"), identifying time and place ("driving home from picking up the kids at after-school care") helps you to step back from the experience and perhaps see it more clearly and from a new and different vantage point. The new vantage point is *you* looking at *it*, the thought or feeling, instead of you and the thought or feeling being fused together. This is the beginning of *defusion*, of reducing your identification with your distressing thoughts and feelings. Instead of experiencing yourself as inseparable from your thoughts and feelings, you become the observer of them. When I have anxious feelings and thoughts, these are something I experience at the moment, not something I *am*: I *have* anxiety. I *am* Chris. Thoughts and feelings come and go; I endure. As we shall see, this shift in how you and your child view and experience thoughts and feelings changes their quality and perhaps makes them less distressing, less urgent.

You and your child are stuck doing the old dances that most often involve the desire for avoidance and control. By definition, these dances are automatic behaviors that you and your child engage in, operating below awareness. To get unstuck or to avoid becoming stuck along the way to your goals, you must first be aware—aware of what's actually going on in the present situation, aware of your dance, aware of your goals, aware of what to do next. Likewise, your child eventually is going to have to do the same.

In this chapter, you'll learn how to increase your awareness so that you can respond (rather than react) to your child's anxiety. In their book *Parenting from the Inside Out* (2003), Daniel Siegel and Mary Hartzell state that "awareness creates the possibility of choice" (p. 70). Another way to say this is that awareness creates possibilities. Out of these possibilities and the increased sense of choice will come a true sense of control for both you and your child—not control over your ever-changing emotions and thoughts, but control of what you both do next when anxiety shows up.

To help you do this, I'll give you exercises later in this chapter that will give you and your child a heightened experience of the world around you and within you. Ironically, with this increased awareness of and attention to your distressing thoughts and feelings comes increased perspective and distance between you and those thoughts and feelings. You and your child will experience defusion—separating yourselves from your thoughts and feelings rather than trying to eliminate them or being suffocated by them.

Increased perspective and defusion create more possibilities for responsive parenting, that is, parenting in keeping with your values and goals. As your child increases her ability to have perspective on her passing thoughts and feelings and identifies less with them, she will find a stability and security within herself that will allow her to better cope with distress and to switch from efforts at avoidance and control to living a vital life right now.

WHY BE AWARE?

Many people seem to believe that anxiety is necessary to stay alert to danger and to ensure their child's survival as well as their own. However, generally speaking, anxiety does not make us more alert to danger or more competent as parents. Yes, there are adrenaline junkies out there and people who believe that they can't get anything done unless they're under pressure from a deadline or other external force. But our experience tells us that we are at our best when we are oriented to the important information in a given situation. We are at our best when we make decisions based on the information out there in the world combined with our experience, and not when we are caught in and reacting to the feelings surging through our stomach or the often negative commentary and speculation that makes up most of our thinking.

On the other hand, anxiety in and of itself does not have to make you or your child *less* effective in reaching your goals. It all depends on what you are oriented to: if you seek to avoid or control the anxiety, then you and your child will be caught up in that task at the expense of more urgent or useful goals.

Dancing Below the Radar

The steps you and your child are now taking in your anxiety dance keep you from moving freely across the dance floor of life. But your attempts to lead your child in another way and to become a more responsive parent have been difficult and frustrating—with good reason. As I mentioned before, you and your child enter into the anxiety dance automatically, and your awareness of it remains below the radar. Together you dance on and on without thinking much about it, if you think about it at all. As you undoubtedly know, anything we do automatically or by habit is very difficult to change. I'm sure you can think of many examples of this from your own life—habits you, your child, your partner, or your parents just can't seem to break.

When my father was a child, his parents taught him to trace the word GOD on his pillow with his finger just before he went to sleep each night. He did that for the rest of his life, I'm sure without giving it any thought and probably without even being aware he was doing it much of the time. A habit such as this could be broken (if one dared to in that particular case), but it would be very difficult. We can't change what we are not even aware of.

So the first phase in changing such patterns, as I mentioned in the last chapter, is to increase your awareness of what you are doing. For example, quitting smoking is hard in part because smokers light up without giving it another thought. Smokers who want to quit are helped by the simple assignment of carrying a small notebook and pen and writing down whenever they have a cigarette. When they do this, smokers become more aware of their habit and its particular patterns. They realize how frequently they light up, the situations that increase the desire to smoke, and so on. This knowledge alone can lead to a reduction in smoking.

In a similar way, you want to increase your awareness of your automatic behavior patterns, thoughts, and feelings that show up when your child is fearful or anxious. One simple strategy is to simply slow down. Resist the frantic urge to solve this problem right now, once and for all. Slow down and watch yourself as you do your old choreographed dance. Obviously some situations (for example, those involving dangerous behavior) need to be dealt with swiftly and decisively. But many of the situations you confront every day are ones that you have been confronting every day for a long time. They are not acute situations. You may be able to slow down and experiment a little, even be a little late to where you're going or serve dinner a few minutes behind schedule as you seek to develop a better understanding of and hopefully better responses to these situations.

So, if you are going to change the automatic behavior patterns that represent your child's anxiety, the first thing you have to do is become more aware of what you are doing. Then, as I'll show you, you can increase your child's awareness of what she is doing in those moments and point her in the direction of better responses.

EXERCISE: Increasing Awareness #1— A Common Procedure

1. Take a sheet of lined paper.

2. Think of a common multistep household procedure you engage in more or less on your own virtually every day, for example, doing the laundry, washing the dishes, or something like that.

3. Before writing anything down, quickly estimate how many individual steps you think this procedure involves. Write that number down.

4. Now start writing out the procedure, step-by-step, from beginning to end.

5. When you're finished, take a look at what you wrote and answer these questions:

   a. How good was your estimate of the number of steps?

b. Is the first step you wrote down really the beginning?

c. What prompts you to begin the procedure? What typically initiates the prompt?

d. Is the last step you wrote down really the end? For example, does the "doing the laundry" procedure include folding the clothes and putting them away?

e. Did you leave any steps out? For example, does the laundry procedure include "Nag children to put clothes away neatly in the proper dresser drawers"?

f. What additional procedures blend with, compete with, or run parallel to this procedure (that is, multitasking or toggling from one procedure to another).

g. What keeps this procedure from happening, going well, or getting finished?

h. Reflecting on what you noticed in doing this exercise, is there a simple change you could make that could make this procedure more efficient or enjoyable?

If you're like most people, you seriously underestimated the number of steps involved. You also likely were surprised by the level of detail you would need to really set out the "operating instructions" for even a relatively straightforward and routine daily procedure you've done hundreds if not thousands of times. You may have noticed that procedures such as these have rather indistinct beginnings and ends; one task blends into another with little sense of closure or control over events. Perhaps you became aware of the competing demands that occur when you attempt this one task and that conspire to erode your efficiency and increase your frustration and sense of futility. And this is just getting the laundry done!

We don't want to be aware of what we're doing much of the time. Many daily tasks are boring or unpleasant, and we'd rather be thinking of something else instead, running on autopilot. Also, if I stop and really think about the futility of doing the laundry, cleaning the gutters, and so on, I just might run off to Baja and never come back. Sometimes I think I can't afford to be aware of what I'm doing, thinking, and feeling. However, as a parent, I can't afford *not* to be aware. Awareness may result in some initial unpleasantness, but it is vital to making needed changes.

EXERCISE: Increasing Awareness #2— A Common Dance with Anxiety

1. Take another sheet of paper.

2. This time I want you to think of a fairly common and difficult situation that invites your child to feel anxiety or some other unpleasant emotion or thought. Give it a name: "Trying to get out the door on Monday morning," "Going to the dentist," "Walking past the house with the big, loud dog in the yard."

3. As before, start writing out the "procedure," the typical sequence of events that defines that situation: what your child does, what you do, your child's subsequent actions, your reactions, and so on.

4. Take a look at what you wrote and consider these questions:

   a. Was the first step you wrote down really the beginning of this event? Is it your sense that the anxiety (your child's or your own) shows up in subtle ways minutes, hours, or even days earlier?

   b. What are the emotional or cognitive steps in this procedure? Are there certain feelings or thoughts (your child's or your own) that appear at predictable points in the chain of events? There may be certain feelings such as your own anxiety, anger, or despair. There may be judgments ("This is unreasonable"), conclusions ("This will never get better"), worries about the future ("He can't be doing this when he's fifteen"), memories, and so on.

   c. When and how does it really end? Do you need to talk about it later? Does your child need to talk about it later? Can this event carry over and affect the tone and success of subsequent tasks and events? Does this weigh on you when you enter the situation and in some way raise the stakes for a positive outcome?

   d. Could there be several variations of this event, for example, one pattern when it goes well and one pattern when it goes badly?

   e. What additional procedures blend with, compete with, or run parallel to this procedure (that is, multitasking or toggling from one procedure to another)?

f. What keeps this procedure from happening, going well, or getting finished?

g. Does anything now come to mind that you or your child could do that might make this procedure more efficient or successful?

What did this exercise and follow-up questions reveal? What showed up for you in the way of thoughts, feelings, bodily sensations, and memories? Where are the points in the procedure where a change in your behavior, or hers, could take the dance in a different and better direction?

MINDFULNESS: THE PRACTICE OF ATTENTION

The word "attention" comes from the Latin *attendere*, meaning "to stretch forward." This fact reminds us that when we are aware and paying attention to something we are moving toward it and not away from it. Attention should not be confused with vigilance, which means to be watchful, on the lookout for danger. Many anxious children are highly vigilant, wary, hesitant, and cautious. This being on the lookout is not stretching forward into life but can actually be a pulling back from life and the tasks at hand. Anxious children can be mislabeled as having an attention *deficit* disorder because their vigilance is taking their minds away from what teachers and others want them to be focusing on. It's hard to stretch forward when you're anxiously looking out.

Attention is a complex set of skills and habits that allows us to stretch forward into life and to engage in effective problem-solving and goal-oriented action. This stretching forward and engaging life happens "at the expense" of the old dance steps where we retreat from life and fall into unhelpful avoidance and control behaviors. Because it is a set of skills and habits, attention can be learned and it can be strengthened through practice.

Although it has been around for centuries, mindfulness is a concept and a practice that has recently found its way into the psychological literature. The term is used to describe an awareness or attention that is both simple and powerful. Typically we use this idea of mindfulness to convey paying strict attention or maybe thinking ahead or outside ourselves such as "Mind the stairs!" or "I want you to be mindful of how much money you're spending," and so on.

Mindfulness has been given various definitions over the years. It is often associated with meditation practices from India, Tibet, and East Asia. However, mindfulness is not a spiritual or religious practice, although it is found in all spiritual and religious traditions in one form or another, both Eastern and Western. It is a way of looking at the world, both outside and inside ourselves. *Mindfulness* is simply the bare awareness and acceptance of one's experience in the moment. That experience is made up of all the many subtle and powerful sensations occurring at any given moment: thoughts, feelings, bodily sensations, and memories.

Definitions of Mindfulness

Jon Kabat-Zinn, one of the first Western scientists to systematically study and apply mindfulness to psychological issues, describes mindfulness as "paying attention in a particular way: on purpose, in the present moment, and nonjudgmentally" (1994, p. 4). This definition bears some elaboration.

First, mindfulness is something you do consciously and for a reason, as opposed to something you do out of habit and with little intention or even awareness. The purpose of mindfulness is to increase your awareness of what is going on around you and within you so that you can both experience it more fully (even the uncomfortable stuff) and so that you can see things more clearly. Seeing things more clearly will help you understand what is really happening (or not happening), and from that understanding you can take real and effective action of some kind.

Second, in the practice of mindfulness, the focus of your attention is what's going on in the present moment. It is an awareness that in fact everything we feel and know and do is happening in the present moment. What else is there? When else is there? Thoughts about the past or the future are still just events happening right now. Right now is where you need to be because that's where you can be most effective in your life and most responsive to your child. Right now is where the action is. That doesn't mean we should never think about the past or plan for the future. But a simple assessment of your thinking about the past and the future will reveal that much of this activity is repetitive, speculative, and not especially useful.

The third component of Kabat-Zinn's definition of mindfulness is interesting. Virtually all definitions of mindfulness state that it is in practice "nonjudgmental." This means that we are to observe what is going on within us and around us without getting into dividing these experiences into good and bad, fair and unfair, or any of the thousand other opinions and evaluations we can apply to thoughts, feelings, and physical sensations. The idea is that dividing up thoughts, feelings, memories, and bodily sensations into good (acceptable) and bad (unacceptable) piles creates frustration and a host of other (bad and unacceptable) feelings. Doing this dividing up or evaluating can pull us toward avoidance and control and is frequently a waste of our time and energy.

With regard to this idea of mindfulness being nonjudgmental, I tend to be pretty inclusive and say that if a judgment is what you happen to be thinking at that moment, then *that too* is part of what you are mindful of. You can be honestly and courageously aware of and accept your judgments: "I am aware that I'm being judgmental right now. How like me!" To say that we can only be mindful if we are not being judgmental invites us to try to avoid or control judgments. Good luck with that.

Those who advocate mindfulness as an approach to increasing mental health and effective action recognize that we must acknowledge and get to know our "negative" thoughts and feelings if we're going to understand how they in fact push our behavior around. What *exactly* is the worry that drives Joshua to insist that his mother accompany him from one floor of the house to another? Does he actually think that harm will somehow come to him if he is alone and that his mother will keep him safe? Or is it, upon reflection, more a vague feeling of unease or dread or loneliness? To answer these questions or to even simply, consciously consider these questions helps put the thoughts and feelings out there a little. Then they are not so much part and parcel of who Joshua is. Curiously observing apprehensive thoughts or feelings is a very different perspective from *being* apprehensive. This is defusion, as I discussed above.

Also, by better understanding our negative thoughts and feelings and the situations that invite them, we are in a better position to solve problems or, if the problems can't be solved, to simply adapt or cope. Understanding can only come from awareness and acceptance. The Buddhist writer Gunaratana reminds us that "you can't examine something fully if you are busy rejecting its existence" (2002, p. 139).

So the point I want to make is that mindfulness practice means that whatever you are thinking and feeling in this or any other moment is noticed fully and without an effort to change it. At least not right away. Again, as Siegel and Hartzell said, "Awareness creates the possibility of choice," the possibility of choosing a different response from what has been your habit. As I keep saying, you cannot change what you are not aware of. Mindful awareness is the prerequisite for change. Finally, and this is important, you and your child will discover that, with a more accepting and mindful perspective, fewer anxious (or angry or frustrated) thoughts and feelings will *need* to change.

Mindfulness and the Anxiety Dance

Mindfulness has been shown to be an effective skill that enhances therapies for a variety of adult psychological conditions such as anxiety, depression, stress, substance abuse, and marital conflicts. Its usefulness in the context of family and parenting is only just now being discovered.

The child psychologist Jean Dumas (2005) teaches mindfulness as part of his work with families and states that it is "both a state of mind and a varied set of practices" (p. 782). By this he means that mindfulness develops out of doing things mindfully. It is much like I described willingness in the previous chapter: mindfulness is simply doing something, anything, with full awareness. It is not actually some different or special behavior. In fact, as I will describe below, everyday experiences (eating, opening a door, doing the dishes) can be opportunities to practice and develop mindfulness.

In describing mindfulness as the antidote to mindless reactions, Dumas says that parents (and their children) can use this type of attention as a way of "stepping back from unproductive ways of coping... in order to see more clearly how best to respond" (2005 p. 783). Sometimes, as we'll see, the best response could be not responding at all. For example, one common unhelpful "dance step" is to rush in and solve a problem for your child without giving her a chance to fumble with it and perhaps come up with her own solution.

So, to summarize, mindfulness practice is consciously stepping back and observing your thoughts, feelings, and actions. It is recognizing that these events are neither fused with you nor alien to you. You don't have to identify with them or reject them. As such, mindfulness becomes an opportunity to be present to your inner life and your outward behavior in a more relaxed and flexible manner. You gain a little more perspective that allows you to begin to see the connections among external events, feelings, thoughts, and impulses. Where these inner and outer events connect and flex we can find *choice points*, places where the dancers can pivot and go in a new direction, perhaps awkwardly at first but smoother and more naturally with practice. From this mindful viewpoint, alternative interpretations, judgments, and actions suggest themselves. Thinking becomes more supple. This all starts with a strong and unflinching attention to what is in the moment so that you can understand what you're dealing with and then better select your response from among the possibilities.

What Mindfulness Is Not

Because of its long association with Buddhism and other religious traditions, there have been a number of misconceptions attached to mindfulness. Here are some points about what mindfulness is not:

■ It is not passive. Mindfulness will actually allow you to stay connected to your values and goals and to act on them more effectively.

■ Mindfulness is not necessarily calm and placid. You can be quite agitated and be mindful of your agitation. You can be mindful and moving briskly through your daily routines. Your child can be mindful during her soccer game and bear down on the ball like a bird of prey. In fact, mindfulness will lead to more effective action because of heightened focus, clarity, and intention.

■ It is not detached. Mindfulness will actually allow a deeper connection between you and your child in the moment. This deeper connection will be felt by her and will itself help soothe and guide her in those challenging moments.

■ It is not liking everything you think and feel. Mindfulness is simply being aware of how things are in the moment. That includes not liking this moment or wanting this moment to be different. And it is recognizing that this moment isn't supposed to be different; it is what it is.

■ It is not a new type of thinking or an attitude change. Mindfulness is a skill that can only be obtained through practice and practical application, through experience.

■ It is not a religious or spiritual practice, although some form of mindfulness meditation can be found in virtually all religious and spiritual traditions. Mindfulness does not require a religious belief system.

Mindfulness Is a Skill

Mindfulness is a skill that must be practiced if you and your child are to become proficient at it. Through repetition, you and your child have developed these quite *un*mindful habits I've been calling anxiety dances.

Practicing mindfulness is necessary to *un*practice your dance. In fact, mindfulness *is* unpracticing dancing with anxiety. Even if you do the exact same dance with your anxious child—and you will for a while as you launch your change campaign—it will not be the same because this time, dancing mindfully, you and your child will be more aware of what you're doing while you're doing it. That is a profound and important step in the direction of real change, even though you both will endure a certain period of awkwardness and frustration on the way to proficiency in mindfulness and changing your behavior patterns. You and your child must keep your goals ahead of you as you slog through the early, difficult stages of changing the dance. The reward will be new and better ways of responding to one another when anxiety runs high.

Practice, Practice, Practice

I am going to give you several mindfulness and defusion exercises, which you and your child should practice often. Fortunately, everyday life gives us innumerable opportunities to practice being mindful. You can do it right now as you read these words, watching other sensations come and go: a noise coming from somewhere, a memory floating like a cloud through the sky of your mind, an itch on your nose, a thought that you should scratch the itch, and so on. All of these sensations can be observed mindfully.

For the sake of practicing mindfulness, the actual content of the thoughts, feelings, sensations, or whatever doesn't matter. Any mindfulness practice supports the development of this skill, no matter how far removed the situation may be from the hot-button issues and situations anxiety throws your way. Any mindfulness practice (eating an orange, for example) will prepare you to be more responsive when faced with a distressingly anxious situation (such as getting out of the house in the morning).

This is an important point to remember: like most skills you need when times get tough, mindfulness and defusion should be practiced when you don't especially need the skill. Doing so will make the skill available to you and your child when needed in the heat of the moment. Firefighters would be ill-prepared if they used their skills only when there was an actual fire. Orchestras practice before a concert. Sports teams practice before a game. You and your child will practice these techniques so that they will be ready and available when you both really need them.

Some defusion and mindfulness techniques—such as the breathing exercises and some of the metaphors that I'll introduce shortly—are good self-soothing strategies when you are anxious or upset in some way. But the truth is, the primary goal is not to distract yourself or your child from anxiety but to orient you to the task at hand, out there in your life, whatever that may be.

MINDFULNESS EXERCISES

In reality, any activity is an opportunity to practice mindfulness or to simply be mindful: walking, eating, having a conversation, riding in the car, filling a glass with water, writing the words of a homework assignment. Done mindfully, many ordinary tasks take on a richer dimension and allow for more awareness, more focus, and ultimately more success. It's like the old saying "If you don't have time to do it right, how will you have time to do it over?" If your child goes through her day half aware of what she's thinking and feeling and doing, how will she learn from her experiences and make the necessary adjustments to her behavior patterns?

Some exercises and metaphors that will allow you and your child to change the way you look at anxiety and other unpleasant thoughts and feelings follow. Changing how your child looks at her anxious thoughts and feelings is the first step in changing what she does in response to them. Changing how you look at your own thoughts and feelings when your child is anxious or fearful is the first step in your becoming more responsive to your child.

It Starts with You

The following exercises are not just for your child. I want you, the parent, to learn and practice these exercises also—for two reasons. First, as I've described, your child's anxiety provokes a range of thoughts and feelings in you. Your ability to respond effectively in that situation will depend on your ability to shift the focus away from trying to change thoughts and feelings (your own and your child's) and toward the task at hand, whatever that may be. For example, Sterling's mother, Angela, notices her frustration rising when her son resists starting his homework. She begins to berate herself for not having enough patience. Noticing this and noticing how these thoughts take her away from focusing on Sterling, Angela pauses to breathe and get her attention back on the task at hand, which is getting Sterling to engage his homework.

Second, as you do this, you will be modeling for your child how to use these exercises and strategies so that she can get untangled from her thoughts and feelings and instead focus on what needs to be accomplished: to seek help from you and others in a more effective way, to support herself in her distress through self-soothing skills, and to develop any number of effective problem-solving or coping strategies. In the situation just described, Angela will articulate or give voice to the frustration with homework Sterling is feeling at that moment and what the actual problem might be. She will give it some context in relation to values and goals and perhaps give Sterling a sense of how far he's come with it. Then she will suggest some ways he can cope and move forward. "Homework has really been tough this year, hasn't it? You really want to do a good job, and sometimes it's hard to know where to start, and that's pretty frustrating. I remember how frustrating second-grade homework was when you first saw it, and now that stuff seems easy. Let's take a few deep breaths and take a minute just to see what the homework is for tonight. Then we can decide where to start." She can then lead him to start his work and move forward with the overall homework task one piece at a time.

EXERCISE: Breathing

Breathing as a technique for self-soothing will be covered in chapter 7. Here I want to introduce a very simple breathing exercise that will help you practice mindful attention. Using the directions below, take some time to practice at the beginning of each day when doing some ordinary activity, such as getting dressed, making coffee, or packing lunches. During the day, you can practice whenever you feel the need to regain your focus on the here and now.

After a day or two of practice, when you feel comfortable and familiar with the technique, I want you to teach it to your child. For young children, you can make it into a concentration game. Practice together during some ordinary and relatively unstructured time, such as driving in the car or winding down at bedtime. Five to ten in-and-out breaths is sufficient practice, if done regularly. The idea here is not to turn you or your child into serious meditators. This is simply a quick and easy way to bring awareness out of your mind and into your body (specifically, your nose) when the mind—yours or your child's—is becoming agitated with anxious thoughts and feelings.

1. Start by breathing naturally through your nose. Find a comfortable rhythm and pace. Your eyes can be open or closed.

2. Now feel the sensation of the breath as it travels in and out of your nose. Notice how you can put your attention right there, at your nos-

trils. With each slow inhalation, notice how the air you take in is cool against the skin around the edges of your nostrils. Notice how, on the out-breath, the air is now warmer, heated by the body. Notice how this warmth makes the sensation of the outgoing air even more subtle against the skin.

3. Keep breathing. Notice how you can detect ever more subtle variations in the quality of the breath: air speed and pressure, temperature, smoothness, little whistling noises, and so on. You will notice the other sensations going on both inside and outside your body. If you find your mind wandering off, gently bring your attention back to your nostrils and your breathing.

4. Feel free to continue as long as you like. As I stated above, five or ten in-out cycles, done with attention, is sufficient practice and perhaps all a young child may be able to do at one time.

As this type of awareness is developed, you and your child will associate mindfulness with feelings of calmness and security even in the midst of busyness or strong emotions. Then even just a few mindful breaths can call up those calm and secure feelings and increase your sense of competence and your responsiveness. A few mindful breaths can take your child out of fusion with her thoughts and feelings and to a recognition that she is still who she is, regardless of what her thoughts and feelings tell her.

EXERCISE: Listening

This is an exercise you can do with your child. If you have a timer or alarm on your watch, set it for a minute or two.

1. Sit comfortably near each other at a time when and in a place where you won't be disturbed.

2. Start the timer and both of you close your eyes. The objective is to listen mindfully and note all the sounds you each hear in that one- or two-minute time period. For example, there may be noises in another part of the house or outside. Someone's stomach may growl. Shifting in your chair may cause a noise. Or there may simply be silence.

3. Notice how your thoughts run to other topics. You or your child may think how silly this seems. She may think, "Who will hear more sounds?" (let her know this is not a competition) or "Why doesn't my brother have to do this?" You may think, "I should get that load of

laundry in just as soon as this is over," and so on. When this happens, gently bring your attention back to listening.

4. When the time is up, compare the sounds you each heard as well as the other thoughts and sensations that came up.

Other Exercises Using Your Five Senses

There are many other ways to practice mindful attention using any of the five senses. In addition to supplying you with vital information, mindfulness is helpful because it involves slowing down, "monotasking," and letting your mind investigate a simple sensation without wrapping a lot of words around the experience. Here are a few simple exercises you can do with your child.

EXERCISE: Guessing Games

You and your child can play "guessing games" with everyday objects. For example, you each collect half a dozen small objects: a key, a paper clip, a thimble, a button, a coin, and so on.

1. Choose one person to go first, then have that person close her eyes while the other person places one of the objects in her hand.

2. The identity of the object will likely be guessed right away, but stay with the object for a little while.

3. Turn the object over in the hand, letting the fingers explore its shape and texture.

We rely so much on our visual sense that it can be interesting to shut that out for a minute and focus instead on other ways of "seeing" the world.

EXERCISE: Fragrances

Take turns passing items with different fragrances under each other's nose: a slice of lemon, a bit of toothpaste on a spoon, a peppermint candy, and so on (nothing too unpleasant).

EXERCISE: Eating a Raisin

This a famous mindfulness exercise. Take one raisin. Eat it simply and slowly, taking several minutes to do so and thereby deeply appreciating its many aspects: size, color, texture, smell, taste, that tiny, grainy crunch followed immediately by a squish as you bite down on it, and so on.

EXERCISE: Living with an Itch

This exercise is somewhat challenging, but it comes close to what I am asking you and your child to do when an unpleasant thought or feeling shows up. Somewhere on your body, right now, there is an itch. It could be on your nose, your forehead, anywhere. All I want you to do is *not scratch it*. Focus on whatever it is you're doing. Right now, you're reading this book. Just keep reading, mindful of the itchy sensation but not acting on it. You are not using reading to distract yourself from the itch (don't scratch!). Reading is your goal right now. It is in the foreground. The itch (still there?) is the distraction. Keep reading. The ability to tolerate some discomfort is key to both avoiding larger problems and achieving many goals. Practice not scratching an itch with your child. Support each other in staying focused on some other task, like playing a game or signing a song. Notice how the itch eventually fades away by itself.

DEFUSION EXERCISES

Defusion, as I previously described it, is the experience of reducing identification with your thoughts and feelings. It is very similar to mindfulness but is more focused on stepping back from the content of your mind to become aware of the separation between yourself and a thought or feeling you are having in the moment. The way you experience the sounds around you is how you want your child to notice her thoughts and feelings: they show up, they are noticed, perhaps thought about, maybe acted upon, but certainly not identified with. No one would say, "I am the ticking of the clock" or "I am that car door shutting." Sounds come and go outside the body. Thoughts and feelings come and go on the inside.

Releasing your identification with all the comings and goings in your mind is the primary goal of defusion and mindfulness exercises. You and your child can begin to experience a solid, secure self at the eye of these mental storms. Remember, you are the observer of each thought or feeling. Thoughts and feelings are something you observe. You are not one and the same. That thought leaves and another one takes its place. Feelings and thoughts come and go, but you remain constant.

Having Thoughts and Feelings

One way of establishing some distance between our selves and our thoughts and feelings is to modify how we talk about these mental experiences. Unfortunately, identifying with our thoughts and feelings is built into our language. For example, by habit I say, "I am anxious," in the same way I would say, "I am Chris." Is anxiety who I am, or is it actually an unpleasant but temporary state brought on by present circumstances interacting with my history and my biology?

I could say instead, "I'm having some anxious thoughts" or "I'm having some worries." More specifically, Beth might say, "I'm having the thought that I will be contaminated by germs if I touch this doorknob." It's a little awkward at first, but the point is to gain a little wiggle room between the "I" and these transient thoughts and feelings. We will talk about validation in chapter 8 and how to provide feedback to your child when she experiences various emotions and thoughts. For now, be mindful of how you are thinking about your thoughts and feelings. See if the opportunity comes up to comment on what your child is thinking and feeling using defusion talk: "You're having some anxiety (worries, anger, frustration) right now" in place of "You're anxious."

Naming or Cataloging Thoughts and Feelings

When it comes to the world of thoughts and feelings, your child began life experiencing powerful and undifferentiated pleasures and pains. It was only through interaction with others that she began to attach words to particular thoughts and feelings: I'm cold, I'm angry, I'm scared, I'm remembering. Experience gives your child an appreciation of differences between and within feelings. Increasing sophistication in naming thoughts and feelings makes us aware of the subtle differences among them. Now she can say, "I'm freezing," "I'm frustrated," "I'm nervous," "I'm reminiscing."

There is a difference between being scared and being nervous, between being angry and being frustrated. Your child can begin to appreciate that there is a range of emotional experiences between the all-or-none extremes I described as so characteristic of the very young child's experience. You want her response to feeling nervous or even pensive to be somewhat different from her reaction to feeling terrified.

Growing up in Southern California, I learned only one word for "snow"; it was "snow." Later, when I moved north and became a skier, I learned to recognize several varieties of snow that had meaning in terms of skiing conditions. Prior to learning these distinctions, I literally could not see the difference between say "corn" or "spring" snow and "powder" or "crud." Once these differences were pointed out to me, I suddenly had the ability to see variations in what before had been a vague and uniform mass of white stuff. With these new words mapped onto the world, I could now use the information my eyes had been giving me all along but my mind could not "see." With more word choices to describe various feeling and thinking states, you and your child can consider more accurate and useful descriptions of mental events.

Naming and cataloging are deceptively simple and very old techniques that require nothing more than simply observing and labeling thoughts and feelings as they show up. I think of *naming*, sometimes called "cubbyholing," as the act of distinguishing one thought or feeling from another, seeing the distinctions among the sensations we have. *Cataloging* is discovering similarities among events inside and outside the skin. In contrast to using naming to divide things up and make distinctions (scared versus nervous), cataloging can help your child begin to notice patterns or simply see the repetition of certain categories of thoughts and feelings.

Your child's (and your own) earliest use of language involved naming, that is, attaching names to the objects in the world: Mama, Dada, cat, variations on the word "bottle," and so on. Giving something a name helps your child communicate with others. She can tell you about her "owie" or ask you to read a book or get her some juice. Being able to name and distinguish apple juice from orange juice allowed your child to think more specifically about and obtain what she wanted. This greatly reduced trial-and-error attempts at getting her needs met and greatly reduced frustration for everyone.

To do naming, you or your child will simply notice a feeling or a thought as it arises and then give it a label : "Here's 'anger'" or "This is another 'nervous' feeling" or "Oh great, another stupid 'I'm stupid' thought." The idea is to keep it simple, to not go off on a thought tangent about that thought or feeling, to just be ready for the next thought, feeling, or memory that drifts, stumbles, or tears through your mind. You notice and name. Notice and name.

Practice naming feelings with your child. When you're feeling an emotion, name it for your child. For example, if you're in traffic, you might say, "I'm frustrated that the traffic is moving so slowly. I'd like to get home to make dinner." Or "I'm really happy that you were able to spend the night at Suzie's house. I know how hard it was for you to be away from home."

Find emotions out in the world. You can speculate together about the inner life of story or movie characters: "How do you think he feels right now? What do you think he wants to do?" You can start a collection of feeling words that you find in newspapers, magazines, and other print material. Cut them out and paste them into a small spiral notebook.

Catherine, the mother of four-year-old Abby, began naming Abby's feelings out loud: "Oh, you're feeling scared about using the bathroom here." She began stating her own feelings out loud so that Abby would learn that grown-ups can have all sorts of thoughts and feelings for various reasons, for example, "I'm distracted because I'm thinking about making dinner."

Without necessarily trying to change Abby's thoughts, feelings, or behavior directly, her mother was simply establishing the vocabulary for emotions that Abby will need to communicate more effectively with her parents and other adults. Additionally, it is through her own internal dialogue that Abby will eventually learn to identify her own thoughts and feelings and take effective action to sooth and regulate herself. This takes inner language—the more accurate the better.

Children of young ages need someone to model how this thinking about thoughts and feelings works. This is the heart of learning to think about one's own and another's thoughts and feelings and to use that information effectively. For children at the age of Beth, Sterling, or even Joshua, naming can add new colors to the emotional palette: scared, anxious, nervous, pensive. Some other distinctions can be helpful. For example, Sterling's struggles with his homework may be a reaction not to anxiety as much as to frustration. Frustration may call for a somewhat different set of problem-solving skills and a different action plan than would anxiety alone.

Angela, however, saw Sterling's behavior almost exclusively through the lens of his having an anxiety disorder, and the immediate goal for her (and for Sterling) in these situations is to avoid or escape that presumed anxiety. But when Angela began slowing down and observing her thoughts and feelings during homework time, she glimpsed a number of emotions, including her own frustration and impatience. This not only helped her empathize with Sterling, but it gave her clues as to what she, and he, needed to do next: recognize their emotions and thoughts and even accept them as a natural part of the situation, draw on whatever reserves of patience they had left at the moment, identify the actual problem that was causing the frustration (an overwhelming stack of homework), and start to work on solving that problem (taking on the homework in smaller, more manageable pieces).

EXERCISE: Putting Cataloging in Practice

Lumping feelings and thoughts into categories helps you and your child step back a bit from the anxious content of those feelings and thoughts: the scary dog, the test coming up tomorrow, the knot in her stomach. Now she can also observe that she is experiencing "fear," "worry" or "apprehension," and "my body acting up."

As with naming, you will help your child give words to experiences, but in cataloging, you connect a particular event, action (or inaction), thought, or feeling to a larger category of emotion or thought.

Angela sees Sterling clenching his fists and growling at his homework. She might say, "I can tell you're *frustrated* right now." Nancy might say to Joshua, "I noticed you were hesitating a long time at the bottom of the stairs. I wonder if *those scary thoughts* were distracting you from heading up to your room?" Al might say to Beth, "I can tell your mind is putting out some *new worry thoughts*."

By observing anxiety in all these manifestations and in a variety of situations, Beth, for example, begins to learn that her feelings and thoughts are connected to events, sometimes rather arbitrarily. She learns that anxiety keeps coming around but with different "causes": two weeks ago it was all about dog poop, last week it was germs on the bathroom faucet, this week it's carbon monoxide. She may begin to notice the merry-go-round nature of these thoughts and feelings: here comes that thought again, right on schedule—and now this one.

Beth can then perhaps begin to appreciate a sense of her own enduring existence against the background of these constantly shifting thoughts and feelings. You could say she remains the sky in the midst of all the changing cloud patterns. Or to return to the faces/vase analogy, Beth places herself in the foreground, while her mental events are in the background. Thoughts and feelings have not been eliminated. They are still there. After all, some thoughts and feelings can be useful. But they no longer occupy the central place in her life—instead she occupies that central place.

Responding Mindfully

Pointing out the changing landscape of fears could help Beth see these thoughts and feelings for what they are: her overzealous mind trying to take care of her by pointing out all these potential dangers in her world. As we will discuss in the coming chapters, this kind of cataloging—as well as other forms of feedback and validation—must to be done with tact and compassion as well as patience. It would not be especially helpful for Beth's father to say, "Oh, you were worried about dog poop last week and now it's this new thing. Next week it will just be something else."

Instead, a more matter-of-fact and compassionate observation might look like this: "Carbon monoxide [by being specific, it shows that Dad was actually listening]. Wow, that would be a scary thought to have. Your mind really works hard at trying to keep you and all the rest of us safe." Dad would then want to strongly resist saying anything more in order to give Beth a chance to comment. If she doesn't, that's fine. The picture has been elaborated. Other opportunities will come up when Dad might casually offer an observation in response to Beth's concern how an event (bedtime) is connected with feelings and thoughts (carbon monoxide poisoning) and actions or intentions (checking to see that the carbon monoxide detector is working or performing some other ritual). Again, the initial idea is to simply make your child aware of her patterns and to let her know that you, the parent, are mindful of the situation, that her concerns are heard with respect and compassion, and that you both can step back and think about these thoughts and feelings rather than just being driven along ahead of them like a cowboy being herded by the cattle.

Anxiety Goggles

This is my variation on Steve Hayes's metaphor of looking through versus looking at a thought" (Hildebrandt, Fletcher, and Hayes 2007). One afternoon I was driving downtown, looking for a particular store. After getting thoroughly lost, I pulled over, pulled out a map, put on my reading glasses, and located where I needed to go. I put the map away and pulled away from the curb. I immediately knew something was wrong; the buildings were bending and weaving; everything was distorted. It took a few moments to realize that I had forgotten to take off my reading glasses. I pulled them off and my eyes, and the visual field, quickly went back to normal.

Prisms and lenses, such as those found in eyeglasses, change the information coming into the eye. This can improve visual acuity, or it can distort it (for example, when you put on someone else's prescription eyeglasses).

Psychologists have studied visual perception for over a hundred years. One favorite research design is to have college students wear goggles that shift their visual field to the left or right, or reverse it so that left becomes right, or flip the visual field so that the world is perceived as upside down. The students then perform tasks such as reaching out and touching a target. Obviously this would be very challenging with one's visual field distorted in these ways. But with practice and time for the brain to get used to the new view, the students can get better at these tasks. This improvement is called *adaptation*.

After the initial, awkward adaptation period, the college students could perform required tasks with great efficiency. Some studies had students adapt to their goggles over several days. With time, they found they could navigate the world, take notes in class, or ride a bicycle, even with prisms that turned their world upside down and backward! Their brains and muscles had adapted to the distorted condition. However, when the college students took their goggles off at the end of the experiment, they were again disoriented and had to readapt to a normal visual world. This is called *aftereffect*.

Likewise, when your child becomes anxious, she is looking at the world through anxiety-colored glasses or goggles. There is a certain amount of distortion that is taken for reality. As I drove, I knew the buildings were not weaving and bending. My immediate assumption was that I was having a stroke or other serious brain event. Your child, on the other hand, believes that what she perceives is real; it is the way things are. There is danger at the top of the stairs. There are lethal germs on that doorknob. There is survival value in this: better safe than sorry. However, as I've discussed, the typical reactions that stem from assuming the world is really this strange and threatening are often unhelpful and costly.

However, if your child can recognize that there is a certain amount of distortion taking place here, that a part of her brain is making the world *seem* scary at this moment, then she may be able to look *at* these thoughts and feelings (for example, "I'm having that 'I will get sick if I touch that doorknob' thought") instead of looking *through* the lens of anxious thoughts and feelings and seeing the world as colored and distorted: "I *will* get sick if I touch that doorknob."

I tell children that on some days those anxiety goggles (or anger goggles or whatever) are really stuck tight to your face and getting them off is a big challenge. For some reason, those pesky thoughts and feelings are just very strong and plentiful today. And, even if you can't get the goggles off right now, you can still know and tell yourself that it's not the world that is that scary and disturbing and confusing, but it's the goggles making the world look that way. Just being able to tell yourself "It's just the goggles" can create enough distance between you and a thought or feeling to give you some wiggle room to make a better choice—to be responsive and not reactive.

EXERCISE: Goggles

For this exercise, you will need a pair of glasses or goggles. They can be swimming goggles or sunglasses or prescription glasses that alter your child's vision. You will also need some small stickers, colored cellophane, or other objects you can stick to the lenses of the glasses. Tiny plastic insects are ideal.

1. Take turns putting on the glasses or goggles—your child first, then you. Have your child describe the change to her vision. Get descriptive and detailed. Have her move her head around and look at different objects and things at different distances. How does movement or distance or color affect what she sees? Then you can describe what you experience with them on.

2. Put some things on the goggles, either one lens or both. Try different colors, stickers that obscure the view, little plastic insects that suddenly look huge and menacing when right up against the eye. What's your child's reaction to these objects? What's yours? Notice how hard it is to look out at the world and focus on it when there's a huge fly right in front of you, or so it seems.

3. Compare these changes in vision to the ways in which anxiety (or anger or sadness) colors or changes a person's perspective on the world. Talk about how your vision (the way you perceive the world around and within you) can be changed or distorted by these emotions or by certain thoughts (for example, "It's not fair"). Point out that a smudge on one's glasses can be annoying, but it is not a problem out in the world. The world at that moment is fine. The problem is in what you are focusing on.

Joshua and his mother played with this idea. They found Joshua's swimming goggles, which had blue lenses. She did not make him wear the goggles when he was anxious about going upstairs or bedtime, which might be construed as punishing or demeaning. Instead they both spent some time just trying out the goggles when Joshua wasn't anxious. They observed that when they put the goggles on, the room initially looked blue, but noticed that the blue seemed to fade the longer they had them on (adaptation). They noticed that the room took on a kind of yellow tint right when the goggles came off (aftereffect). They talked about how some mornings he seemed to be looking at his day through invisible "nervous goggles" that made the world look scary when maybe things weren't quite as dangerous as they seemed. Note the distinction here: I would not tell Joshua that things aren't as scary as they seem. "Scary" is inside Joshua, and his thoughts and feelings are what they are and really don't need to change. Instead, Joshua's mother is working at orienting him to what's outside his skin, in the world, where she wants him to be putting his attention and energy. That world has its challenges—for Joshua, going upstairs by himself feels scary—but his experience will show him that it is not as dangerous as it sometimes seems.

SUMMARY AND A LOOK AHEAD

Responsive parenting draws its wisdom from being in tune with your child, being attentive to and accepting of what is going on in the moment. In our frantic efforts to accomplish all we must, some thoughts and feelings— your child's or your own—are regarded as problems and impediments. This increases both your and your child's frustration, and you move away from effective communication and problem solving (to the extent that there is a problem) to attempts at controlling thoughts and feelings. This would be tolerable if it made you more in tune with your child, but it likely hasn't. Quite the opposite. You and your child regard each other through lenses that distort what you both experience, but adaptation has made that distortion appear normal. Habit has made the anxiety dance automatic.

Mindfulness and defusion bring you into contact with what's actually going on without having to struggle with it. These techniques (and there are many more that space does not allow me to cover) increase your knowledge of what you are in fact dealing with and are not dealing with. Mindfulness practice can provide a measure of calm, a shift in focus that brings your values and goals into the foreground. To again quote Siegel and Hartzell from the beginning of this chapter, "Awareness creates the possibility of choice." Having more choices for responding to a given situation will allow you to break the grip of reactions and to leave behind the old, ineffective anxiety dance.

In the next chapter, I will describe a number of basic strategies for being proactive toward your child's anxiety so that problem reactions might be avoided altogether. These strategies will include some additional breathing exercises, as well as muscle-tone exercises that are intended not to help you escape or control anxiety, but to help you and your child regain a sense of controlling your own behavior when anxiety shows up. I will also describe the importance of good social skills for anxious children. Your child has many dance partners in her life. If these relationships are going well, if she can be effective and positive with others even when anxious and stressed, it will promote confidence and enlarge her support system. Teaching and encouraging these strategies will take us into the second phase of your behavior change plan: establishing appropriate self control and obtaining help from others in way that are in line with one's values and goals.

CHAPTER 7

Basic Skills for Anxious Children and Parents

There are two objectives for this chapter. First, I will discuss the importance of teaching and encouraging social skills in anxious children. Second, I will give you some simple breathing and muscle-tone techniques for taking the edge off anxiety or other troublesome thoughts or feelings (your own and your child's) when they show up.

These skills for managing social interactions and techniques for managing the body will provide you and your child with effective means for managing the situations you encounter—even in the face of powerful emotions and thoughts, such as fear and anxiety. They will also assist you when you're dealing with anger and frustration.

The social skills are meant to be both proactive and responsive. Getting along better with others will reduce the amount of conflict and stress in your child's life as well as the fear and anxiety that come from these conditions. Good social skills will help your child respond to anxious and stressful situations in more effective and positive ways (for example, appropriately communicating feelings and needs and asking for help). Additionally, social skills help children engage successfully with peers, which increases self-esteem and self-confidence.

The techniques for regulating breath and muscle tone are meant to help you and your child cope with fear and anxiety when these feelings and thoughts show up; they will help you buy time and allow you both to stop for a few moments and to avoid falling into the old and unhelpful dance. Instead you will be better able to step back and look at the larger situation, at the *process* rather than the *content*, and to get in touch with your values and goals as I described in the previous chapter. At that point, you will have many more options available to you—more possibilities and more choices for what you will do next.

Consistent with the acceptance and commitment therapy model, the goal here is not to prevent your child from ever becoming anxious again or to get rid of anxiety once it has been evoked. That would just be more unhelpful avoidance and control. The goal instead is to maximize both your own and your child's responsiveness to the problematic situation. The focus will be on working on the problem, if there is one, and managing the situation as best as you can, regardless of what you and your child are thinking and feeling at the time.

Yes, adversity can build character. But what we want to do is reduce your child's habitual fearfulness and anxiety by helping him to live an effective, committed, goal-oriented life and to accept along the way whatever challenges (or adversities) those goals ask him to meet. You are giving him the tools—effective communication and problem-solving skills—to do this. Confidence and security are the antidotes to anxiety.

Learning and practicing these social skills and self-regulation techniques is phase 2 of your behavior change campaign. Phase 1, as you will recall, is increasing awareness and understanding of the situations that invite anxious thoughts and feelings and, with them, the anxiety dance. In reality, these phases never end because new challenges show up throughout the journey of growing up. You and your child will always strive to understand yourselves in light of these challenges. New skills need to be learned in order for you to continue to be effective in your lives. The skills and techniques I present in this chapter will help that process.

PHASE 2: LEARNING SOCIAL SKILLS AND TECHNIQUES

Even if your child does not have social anxiety as such, he must face many situations that involve dealing with others in a way that can generate a lot of anxiety. These situations may include making new friends or managing existing friendships, dealing with peer conflicts such as encounters with bullies or everyday disagreements with playmates, and interacting with adults, familiar or unfamiliar. Being able to succeed in social situations reduces anxiety in the moment as well as in anticipation of social challenges, and leads to increased confidence (Rapee et al. 2000).

I define *social skills* broadly: in addition to the "getting along with peers" and "appropriate greeting" types of social skills we commonly think about,

I think of many everyday parent-child interactions and sibling encounters as requiring specific social skills. For example, for whatever reason, Abby is not demonstrating the social skill of looking at someone and saying hello when she has been greeted by them. Additionally, she has yet to master the social skill of asking for help when she needs it.

Sometimes children (or adults) have a particular social skill in their toolbox (eye contact while listening, for example), but they don't use it consistently or perhaps even at all. We can train a child to make eye contact or to stick out his hand and say hello, but to really make that work and not be ill-timed or robotic, he must have a basic understanding of when and why he needs to use these skills. This social understanding can be lacking in some children by virtue of their cognitive style; it is also lacking in all children at certain ages. A social skill is knowing *how*: I know how to greet someone or how to work through a conflict. Social understanding is knowing *that*: I know that I should greet someone; I know that I can work through a conflict. This awareness is vital if social skills are going to be used when needed.

Michelle Winner, a speech and language pathologist, has spent many years studying the problem of social understanding (or "social cognitions," as she calls them) and how this relates to learning and applying social skills competently (Winner 2002). Winner works with children and young adults who have been diagnosed with a range of conditions such as Asperger's disorder, nonverbal learning disability, attention-deficit/hyperactivity disorder, and learning disorders. Individuals with these conditions may be lacking in the cognitive skills required for effective social interactions—specifically those tasks I described in chapter 2 as being able to think about one's thoughts and feelings and being able to take another's point of view.

All children struggle with perspective taking before the onset of frontal lobe functioning, which occurs around the time they start kindergarten. We can train very young children to say and do many things, including social skills, but to use these skills independently, flexibly, and in novel situations requires mental functions that are fairly sophisticated and, "at certain ages," quite tenuous. I put "at certain ages" in quotes because I want to emphasize that I mean not just children who are young chronologically but also children who, under stress or in the face of anxiety, have regressed to a much younger state.

I'm spending so much time on this because, even though your child may not fit into the category of Asperger's disorder, ADHD, or the other syndromes (the conditions of children that Winner works with), if he at all regresses when anxious or afraid, it is likely that his social skills and understanding regress as well, if not disappear altogether. And when the ability to think about his thoughts and feelings fails him, social skills will be a casualty. On one hand, social failure leads to frustration and the inability to secure help from others; eventually it breeds more anxiety. On the other hand, social success furthers a sense of confidence and security; it also allows your child to access and utilize support from others.

Identifying and Supporting Social Skills and Understanding

As I've said, social understanding goes hand in hand with the basic perspective-taking skills (one's own perspective and that of another's) that your child may do perfectly well under the right circumstances: low stress, familiar people, well-established routines. On the other hand, when your child is failing at some social task (again defined broadly) and anxiety appears to be the main culprit, you may want to check in with his social understanding at that moment and from there encourage a social skill. The two basic techniques for checking in with and encouraging your child's social skills and understanding are modeling social perspective taking by doing it yourself and suggesting your child's next move based on what you observe. Let's look at each of these techniques now.

Model Social Perspective Taking by Doing It Yourself

For better or for worse, much of what our children learn comes from the models in their lives—starting with us, the parents. Your modeling of effective social understanding and skills is clearly important for your child. One of my favorite techniques for doing this is the use of "I wonder..." statements: "I wonder what you're thinking right now," "I wonder if Timmy knows what a Termadon is," "I wonder if your teacher is going to be able to read this." Or, more directly, "You look like you're feeling nervous," "Timmy looks a little confused," "Your teacher expects to be able to read this." These statements alert your child to important information in the current situation: the feelings he is having, what his friend may be thinking, and what his teacher expects in relation to the assignment he is working on.

You can also model perspective taking in your own everyday encounters with others: "I wonder what your father would like to do on his birthday," "Mrs. Smith looked happy to see you," "My boss was in a grumpy mood today."

Suggest Your Child's Next Move Based on What You Observe

Once your child is made aware of his own or another person's perspective and needs, you can suggest a next step. For example, "If you are feeling nervous, maybe we could do some Darth Vader breathing" (see below) or "I'm thinking it would help Timmy enjoy your story if you *briefly* explained what a Termadon is."

Again, from your own experience, you can let your child in on your helpful social strategies: "When my boss is in a grumpy mood like that, I make sure I'm friendly to him, but I give him some space also."

Both of these ways of encouraging your child's social understanding will also be covered in the next chapter when I discuss validation techniques.

AN INTRODUCTION TO BASIC SOCIAL SKILLS

Social skills are most often engaging skills; that is, they make a connection in some way. Because anxious children have been busy practicing their avoidance and control "skills" (retreating, manipulating, and pushing away), they often lack good, accessible engagement skills that can serve them in common social situations. Some children have good skills but lack the flexibility to manage situations that don't go exactly according to plan. Some children have adequate skills but don't recognize the cues telling them to use that particular skill *now*. Finally, social situations can become an arena for conflict between children and their parents. And conflict breeds anxiety. (We'll discuss managing conflict in chapter 9.)

Expected and Unexpected Behaviors

I have borrowed the terms "expected" and "unexpected" behaviors from Michelle Winner (2002), whose work I cited above. These terms describe, respectively, what you want and don't want your child to do. An *expected behavior* is just that—something we expect the child to do. Catherine expects Abby to look at the person who greets her. An *unexpected behavior* is anything the child does that is a problem because it is odd or inappropriate to the situation. People greeting Abby don't expect her to turn away and bury her head in her mother's leg.

Expected and unexpected are terms that I use to replace the "good/bad," "right/wrong," and "appropriate/inappropriate" adjectives for child behavior. Expected and unexpected convey all you need to convey with regard to what you want and need from your child in the moment. And yet I find these terms free of some of the unnecessary moral heaviness or awkward abstractness of statements such as "What you did was wrong" or "What you did was inappropriate." Instead you can say, "What you did was unexpected," "She wasn't expecting you to do that," or "I expect you to look at her next time she says hello." The message is delivered clearly and concretely with a minimum of shaming.

Identifying Expected Behaviors as Social Skills

Teaching your child a few basic social skills can go a long way toward decreasing his anxiety and increasing his willingness to engage with others. If these skills are practiced until they become habits and become the new, more helpful dance in response to anxiety, then expected behaviors can come into the foreground and be activated even when emotions are running high. The resulting social success will encourage your child to engage more, to problem solve more effectively, and to feel more confident and secure in his skills. I like to start by teaching very brief social skills that the child can access and perform with a minimum of fuss.

The following social skills were developed by my former colleagues Don Jackson, Marcia Bennett, and others (Jackson, Jackson, and Monroe 1993). You can consider teaching one of them as is, or you can use these as models for coming up with any number of social skills you might find your child needs. Most expected skills you will teach your child as part of your behavior change campaign should have these features:

- A skill should have a name so that you can identify it and ask for it when expected: "This would a good time to use your Greet Someone skills."

- A skill should be brief. For example, Greet Someone, described below, has four steps; Don't Take the Bait has five; and I Join In with Others is the longest, with six steps. We want these skills to be easy to learn, to practice, and to use. We can always chain skills together to create longer social interactions.

- To the extent possible, a skill's steps should be framed in positive behavior terms. That is to say, you tell your child what you want him to do instead of what not to do. So, in teaching the Greet Someone skill, you wouldn't say, "Don't whine and jump up and down" but instead "Use a pleasant face and voice and keep a calm body," or variations of those expected behaviors.

Here's an outline of some sample social skills.

Greet Someone

1. Use a pleasant face and voice.

2. Keep a calm body.

3. Look at the person.

4. Greet the person by saying something like "Hi, how are you?"

Introduce Yourself

1. Use a pleasant face and voice.

2. Look at the person.

3. Tell the person your name.

4. Ask for the person's name.

Don't Take the Bait (used when someone tries to annoy you)

1. Take a deep breath to get calm.

2. Keep a quiet mouth.

3. Keep a pleasant face.

4. Look away or walk away if you can.

5. Find something else to do.

I Join In with Others

1. Use a pleasant face and voice.

2. Keep a calm body.

3. Watch to see what others are doing.

4. Patiently wait for a good time to join in.

5. Ask if you can join in.

6. Use "please" and "thank you."

I Start a Conversation and Keep It Going

1. Use a pleasant face and voice.

2. Look at the person.

3. Ask questions about the other person.

4. Tell the person something about yourself.

TEACHING AND ENCOURAGING SOCIAL SKILLS

Many times a parent has described to me a recurring sibling conflict, often fighting over limited resources such as the last cookie or Mom's attention. When I ask this parent what she wants her children to do instead of fighting, I often hear, "I want them to work it out." Agreed—but I then ask several follow-up questions: Do these children know *how* to work it out? Do they know *when* to work it out? Does working it out actually *work*?

Teach the Skill Even If You Think Your Child Already Knows It

We often assume that children know what to do in a given situation. If they demonstrate a skill—hitting a baseball, long division, working out a problem with their brother—we expect that they can do that again at will. In mounting your campaign to reduce anxious reactions in your family, you should not assume anything. If you want your children to work it out when there's a dispute, you may have to define what that means exactly (in specific behaviors you can condone), teach and practice it to the point of competence, and then stay on top of its use indefinitely, or at least until they leave home.

This means more work for you initially as you plan how to teach your children to work it out, and then teach and support them as they practice the skill. This may seem like overkill at first or simply something you don't have the time and energy for, but consider the fact that you spend a great deal of time and energy on the anxiety dance now. In the coming weeks and months (and even years), your job as the parent is to teach skills like these, which are an investment in your child's social and emotional success, now and into the future.

Steps for Teaching Social Skills

Find a time when you can talk with your child without competing demands or frothing emotions. This is a neutral time—what we call "a teachable moment." Teaching a skill and practicing it does not have to take a lot of time. In fact, you want to spend just a few minutes on it, but then come back at another teachable moment soon after (later that day or the next day) and review and practice the skill again for a few minutes. This kind of brief but frequent teaching and rehearsing is called massed practice, and it is more effective than a long, drawn-out teaching and drilling session.

Use these steps for teaching a social skill:

1. Find your child in a teachable moment.

2. Identify the problem as much from the child's point of view and needs as possible.

    "I know how much you enjoy talking with people and telling them about what you've been doing. I like that too. Having a conversation with someone is fun. But conversations can be tricky; sometimes they go great and other times they seem hard to get started or they don't go so well—maybe someone gets confused or impatient. Well, starting a conversation and keeping it going is a skill, like riding a bike or tying your shoes. You have to learn how to do it and practice it to be good at it. Let's take a few minutes to talk about starting a conversation and keeping it going."

3. Introduce the skill.

    "When you want to start a conversation and keep it going, here's what people expect: You're going to use a pleasant face and voice, like the face you've got now. Good. You're going to look at the person—just like you're looking at me now. Do the same when it's your turn to listen. You can ask questions about the other person and give them a chance to talk. You can tell them something about yourself. It goes back and forth, like playing catch."

4. Practice the skill.

    "Let's practice starting a conversation and keeping it going."

    Point out the expected behaviors. Gently remind your child of any steps he is leaving out. Make it natural and fun.

Cue the Skill

In real life, look for opportunities to cue the use of the skill you've been practicing. For example, Sterling and his mother are at a church social event. There are some boys there about Sterling's age. Angela leans over and quietly suggests to Sterling that he approach one of the boys, introduce himself, and then start a conversation and keep it going. She quickly reminds him of the steps involved, tells him to go have fun, and nudges him in that direction, all the while breathing mindfully to stay focused on Sterling and not on her own anxiety as she watches him cross the room.

Encourage the Skill

During the initial stages of learning and using a social skill, you can expect that it will be awkward and not without problems or even setbacks. This is the time to make sure that you encourage your child to use these skills and to not give up on them. One reason that the old anxiety dance became established in his life and yours is because it worked; it met everyone's needs for short-term avoidance, control, and survival. You recognize the cost of the dance, and that is why you endeavor to change it. But the appeal of avoidance and control will always be there for you and your child. Short-term relief and quick relief are addictive. Escaping from a situation that provokes fear will result in an immediate reduction in that fear, a great wave of relief. This is the powerful negative reinforcement paradigm I discussed in chapter 3.

If starting a conversation and keeping it going, asking for help when you're frustrated, or any other skill is to become established in your child's life and reliably replace the old dance moves, then somehow these skills will have to work for him. This means that the important adults in his life will have to be vigilant to his use of these skills ("I noticed you started a conversation with Eric") and be right there with support and encouragement ("I'm very proud of you for not taking the bait just now").

Model Good Social Skills Yourself

Clearly you are your child's primary source for information on how he should handle situations. Perhaps later in life he will resolve to do the exact opposite of what you value and do. That's what adolescence is for. But for now, you need to be modeling expected social skills yourself—with him, with other members of your family, with friends, acquaintances, and strangers.

USING BREATHING AND RELAXATION TO HELP COPE WITH ANXIETY

From the perspective of acceptance and commitment therapy, coping with anxious thoughts and feelings means allowing your value-based goals to enter the foreground while your thoughts and feelings recede (but likely do not disappear entirely). You do not have to get rid of your anxiety in order to take effective action. Metaphors such as the anxiety goggles are meant to create some separation between those distressing thoughts and feelings and you or your child, who can then step up and get something done.

This separation between your thoughts and feelings and your mindful, observing self offers some room to reflect on what's going on rather than simply to react. I think of it as something like shifting gears in a car. Unless you've driven automatic transmissions all your life, at some point in your history you learned to drive a stick shift. You put in the clutch to disengage the gears and then move the shift lever from one position to another. You then release the clutch to allow the gears to re-engage and the car to move again, with more power or more control, depending on whether you've shifted up or down. This was very awkward when you first tried it—lots of jerking and stalling—but you eventually learned to do it smoothly and automatically.

The following breathing and muscle relaxation exercises are like shifting gears while you drive. Specifically, they are the putting-in-the-clutch part of the shifting-gears procedure. These techniques can create a space or a pause that will allow you and your child some psychological space and flexibility to quickly examine your options and select your response. However, going back to the analogy of driving a car, the goal is not to put in the clutch and leave your foot there. The goal of driving is not even to shift gears; *it is to get somewhere.* Using the clutch and shifting gears serve the cause of getting you to your destination. They are not the destination itself—not if you ever want to leave your driveway.

Similarly, breathing and muscle relaxation are not new ways to avoid or control anxiety, nor are they meant to be a distraction from those thoughts and feelings (that is, you breathe until anxiety goes away and then you can go back to living). Rather these techniques are simply a means to give your mind, and your child's mind, a chance to reorient to what matters—to your valued direction, your goals, and the effective response the situation calls for right now.

It is true that breathing and relaxation techniques have been known to take the edge off anxious arousal and to help redirect the mind to what matters: your valued direction and goals. That's a good thing. But I just want to emphasize that the real goal for these techniques is helping you and your child reorient to managing the situation and being responsive rather than simply reacting by avoiding or controlling thoughts and feelings.

Now let me return to the fight-or-flight reaction I described in the first chapter. The mind, or brain, and the body are in constant communication; the brain monitors body temperature, posture, muscle tension, levels of oxygen, carbon dioxide, and sugar in the blood, and many other functions. Adjustments are constantly being made. The brain uses information from the body to know what is happening and what it needs to do. Unfortunately, as I have described, false alarms can happen. Recall that the mind of a child with a history of panic may interpret the racing heart and increased breathing of playing hard at recess as a sign of danger: "Is there something I should be afraid of?" The mind will always err on the side of assuming you're in danger. That's its job—to keep you, and it, alive. The alarm is sounded and off goes fight or flight.

There is little your child can do to talk his mind out of being alarmed once these physiological events are set in motion. Using one set of thoughts to try to change another set of thoughts rarely works in the heat of the moment. However, the brain will listen to the body.

If your child can send messages to his brain that all is well down here in the body, the brain may relax and stand down from high-alert status and the nervous system can return to normal. To do this, your child can use two important and very controllable bodily functions: breathing and muscle tone.

You will recall that both breathing and muscle tone are affected by the fight-or-flight response. I will explain to a child that his brain, convinced there is danger, has ordered his breathing and muscles to prepare for fight or flight in response to the perceived threat. Since we can all agree rationally there is no real threat, his task is to somehow get his brain's danger detector to quiet down if not shut off. To do this, he will have to use the bodily functions he has under his control (breathing and muscle tone) to send messages up to his brain that he is in fact not in danger and the brain can stand down. Then he can say to his brain, "Thank you very much for your concern."

Breathing Exercises

Breathing is obviously important to sustain life, but it is also an important part of the fight-or-flight response. Our breathing becomes more rapid and shallow with the onset of fear. A vicious cycle can be created whereby the mind thinks we're in danger and sets off the alarm, and the body's natural reactions to this alarm (including rapid, shallow breathing) is seen by the mind as evidence that there is danger, and the state of alarm is maintained. We want to shut down the alarm reaction by providing the brain with evidence that we are, in fact, all right. We do this by gaining control over the two things we can control: our breathing and our muscles.

Like the mindfulness breathing exercises introduced in the last chapter, the exercises below should be practiced by you and your child together for a few minutes each day. Try them out when fear and anxiety arise. Give them all a try and determine from your own experience which ones in particular you each find most helpful.

Emphasize Breathing Out to Inhibit the Fight-or-Flight Response

The in-breath takes in oxygen. The out-breath expels carbon dioxide. A buildup of carbon dioxide in the blood stream can trigger and maintain anxious arousal, the fight-or-flight response (Woods et al. 1988). When he is anxious or fearful, it can be helpful to have your child emphasize the out-breath—to blow out as much air as possible, and then blow out some more. This should not be done to the point of passing out. It's more simply giving the out-breath its due, since we tend to think of breathing as sucking in air to the neglect of the equally important out-breath. And lowering the carbon dioxide level in the blood does help create a chemical condition that is incompatible with anxious arousal. There are several fun ways to work on developing a long, steady out-breath.

EXERCISE: Whistling, Pinwheels, and Blow Cups

Whistling a tune is practicing breath control. You can also play with pinwheels and blow cups, the pipe-shaped objects with a little basket and ball that you blow into and keep the ball suspended above the basket.

EXERCISE: Cotton-Ball Soccer

Another fun way to develop a long, steady out-breath is cotton-ball soccer, which is played with a cotton ball and soda straws. This can be played with two teams of one to three players each—many more than that and they'll be bonking heads. Each player has a straw. The object is to blow the cotton ball over the table edge on the other team's side.

1. Clear off a smooth, flat surface. (Coffee tables and kitchen tables work well.)

2. Place the cotton ball in the middle of the table.

3. Place the teams on opposite sides of the table.

4. On your signal, players blow through their straws, trying to send the ball toward and over the opposite edge of the table.

Basic Belly or Diaphragmatic Breathing

Belly breathing is very a basic technique that creates awareness of the breath and helps maintain a slow and steady rhythm. Most children, and many adults, believe that we breathe by moving the chest and shoulders up and down. What really causes us to breathe is a dome-shaped muscle, the diaphragm, located behind the ribs at the very bottom of the rib cage. This muscle looks like a big portobello mushroom cap sitting there, attached to the bottom of the lungs. When we breathe in, the diaphragm flattens out, pulling the lungs down and creating a negative pressure in the chest cavity that causes air to rush in. When the diaphragm returns to its dome shape, the lungs are compressed and air is expelled.

EXERCISE: Belly Breathing

To get the most out of each breath, push your belly out a bit when you breathe in to allow room for the diaphragm to flatten out, expanding laterally as it does. This is a very simple technique to teach and to do. You and your child can do this together. As you do the technique, remember that your breath should be calm, natural, steady, and comfortable—not overly energetic or rushed.

1. Sit in a chair comfortably but with a your back straight and feet on the floor.

2. Find your belly button, poke it with your finger, and then place your other hand on your belly just above where your finger is.

3. Breathe in. As you do so, imagine that you are blowing up a balloon that is expanding against your hand. Continue to inflate this balloon with your breath until the inhalation is complete.

4. Breathe out, deflating the balloon until your belly collapses a little underneath your hand.

5. Repeat.

Eight or ten breaths is sufficient practice for one sitting. Practice a couple of times a day; first thing in the morning and at bedtime work well.

Another good way to practice belly breathing is lying on your back. This can be a good way for your child to practice once he's in bed at night. (Be sure you practice this yourself before teaching it to your child.)

1. Have your child lie on his back.

2. Place his hand or a small, light object on his belly just above his belly button. (A rubber duck is ideal.)

3. Ask him to belly breathe. As your child breathes in, the duck rises up as if on a wave that's passing beneath it. As he exhales, the duck sinks back down.

Belly breathing is a great tool for quickly gaining control over the body and steadying the mind when it is alarmed. Belly breathing can be done anywhere, at any time, and it is inconspicuous.

EXERCISE: The Darth Vader Breath

The Darth Vader Breath is my name for what is known in yoga as *ujjayi* (pronounced oo-ji-ee) breathing. This breathing involves a slight narrowing at the high back of the throat just behind and below the nose. This will create a soft rushing of air sound while breathing in and out. It would be a growl if you got the bottom of the throat involved and a snoring sound if it's too high in the nose. Some describe this sound as ocean waves rolling in and out again. The exercise is simple:

1. While slightly narrowing the high back of your throat, breathe in.

2. Continue narrowing the back of your throat and breathe out.

3. Repeat for four or five cycles of inhaling and exhaling.

Narrowing the throat in this way restricts the flow of air just a little, slows down the breath, and allows for a long, even inhalation and exhalation. Like sipping liquid through a straw, *ujjayi* breathing makes it hard to gulp air. Additionally, the sound it makes, like Darth Vader breathing, makes you more conscious of your breath and what it's doing: slow, fast, steady, halting. Practice will help you and your child develop a long, steady, and smooth breathing pattern that will be incompatible with the fight-or-flight response.

EXERCISE: The Ferris-Wheel Breath

This is sometimes called the "square breath" in yoga, although in reality it's more like a rectangle. I want you to imagine a Ferris wheel, the kind you might find at a county fair. Imagine it turning in a slow circle, down one side, up the other. Imagine that you are riding it and it stops—and there you are in the car at the very top, paused in your arc. Now the Ferris wheel starts again and you descend. Now, for the Ferris-Wheel Breath, do the following:

1. Breathe in naturally, counting about once per second. You may get to a count of three, four, or five when the inhalation is complete. How long the breath is isn't important.

2. Breathe out, counting again—one, two, three, four. Do this a few times, breathing in and out naturally, counting as you go.

3. Now breathe in to the top of your inhalation and then pause while you count "one, two"—again about one count per second.

4. Exhale fully. At the bottom of the exhalation, pause and count again—"one, two."

5. Repeat steps 3 and 4 for four or five cycles of inhaling and exhaling.

Like the Ferris wheel pausing in its cycling, your breath will rise, pause, descend, pause, rise again, pause, and so on. This brief pause should not be a straining or gripping action or even really holding your breath. It is a pause, like a diver weightless and motionless in mid-arc after leaping from the board and just before gravity takes him to the water below. The goal is to establish rhythm, control, and mindful awareness of your breath.

Introduce this image to your child and practice the Ferris-Wheel Breath a few minutes each day as you would practice the other techniques. Look for opportunities to gently suggest using the Ferris-Wheel Breath when you notice your child is anxious or upset in some way.

EXERCISE: The Alien Breath

This is a very interesting experience. You are going to breathe in the manner of an alien from a planet where creatures breathe not through their mouths and noses but through the palms of their hands and the soles of their feet.

1. Sit comfortably or lie down and breathe naturally. Hands and feet can be positioned in any way that is comfortable. You can be wearing footwear.

2. Breathe mindfully (see chapter 6): Breathe through your nose and notice the tingly coolness of the air as it passes through your nostrils during the inhalation. Notice the subtle and warm feeling of the air as you exhale through your nose. Notice those sensations now as you breathe in and out.

3. After a few breaths, use your mind to picture the palms of your hands.

4. Breathe in. Use your imagination to feel a sensation of movement across your palms from outside to inside. Feel the air, cool and tingly, pass through your palms and into your hands, and travel up your arms and into your lungs.

5. Breathe out. Use your imagination to feel a sensation of movement from inside to outside. Feel the air leave your lungs and travel down your arms and out through the palms of your hands, warm and subtle.

Weird, isn't it? Now, in the same way, try breathing through the soles of your feet.

1. Breathe in. Feel the cool air enter the bottoms of your feet and travel up your legs and into your chest.

2. Breathe out. With your exhalation, push the air all the way down and out the soles of your feet, the breath warm now from having traveled through your body.

For variation, you can breathe in through your hands and breathe out through your feet, or the reverse. Have fun with it.

This imaginative breathing is subtle and may be difficult for some younger children to grasp. It can be quite intriguing to older children. Alien breathing takes the mind out of the head and creates some distance from the habitual chatter in the brain. This can be especially helpful when you or your child is having difficulty turning the mind off in order to fall asleep.

Classic Tense-and-Release Muscle-Relaxation Techniques

One of the fight-or-flight reactions is muscle tension. A feedback loop becomes established when the brain senses danger, creates muscle tension in reaction to that real or perceived threat, then uses the tense feedback from the muscles as evidence that the body is in fact in danger. In the case of a false alarm, something needs to break your child's brain and body out of this vicious cycle. Getting your child's muscles to relax is more likely than getting your child's brain to calm down directly.

When muscles become tense and tight, it is often difficult to simply relax them. They tend to be locked. The key to reducing muscle tension is to actually tense them a bit more, which will allow the muscles to unlock and relax. You can explain this to your child by comparing the procedure to working some types of window blinds that have a cord that must be pulled down first, making the blinds go up an inch or two, in order to unlock the mechanism that then allows the blinds to go down. These muscle exercises are generally known as tense-and-release muscle relaxation.

As with the breathing exercises, practice these yourself, introduce them to your child, and practice them with him for a few minutes twice a day—typically, morning and night work well. Each exercise isolates and works on a group of muscles. The idea is to use just the group of muscles directly involved in that exercise, letting the rest of the body be relaxed or in its natural state. For example, when doing the Squeezing Lemons exercise as described below, it is unnecessary to contort the face or the rest of the body. He should work on tensing only the "lemon-squeezing muscles" in the hands and forearms, and to some extent in the upper arms. The shoulders and the rest of the body should be at rest.

EXERCISE: Really Small Face, Really Big Face

The idea here is to tighten up and then relax the facial muscles.

1. Scrunch up your face, trying to make it appear as small as possible while you count slowly to five (each number about one second apart).

2. Then make your face as big as you possibly can by opening your mouth and eyes wide, wider, widest, again to a count of five.

3. Relax your face to normal dimensions and take a belly breath.

4. Repeat two more times.

   If done right, this should make your whole head tingle.

EXERCISE: The Turtle

We often carry a lot of tension in our shoulders. We walk around hunched and tight from shoulder blades to upper neck. The resulting posture is emblematic of the stressed and discouraged person. In this exercise, you will take that posture to its extreme and then release it.

1. Just as a turtle might stick its head into its shell, draw your shoulders up to your ears.

2. Hold your shoulders up at your ears for a count of five.

3. Release your shoulders to fall to a more natural position.

4. Take a belly breath.

5. Repeat two more times.

6. With your shoulders down and relaxed, find your collarbone, those two horizontal bones just below and on either side of your throat.

7. In your mind, imagine pulling them apart so that they each move toward the shoulders. You can't really make them move apart, but trying to do so creates an expansion and lift in the upper chest. The chin lifts a little, and the resulting posture is anything but timid and discouraged.

EXERCISE: Squeezing Lemons

When people become stressed, they often ball their hands into fists. Compared to an open hand, there are very few things you can do with a fist, and they mostly involve hitting something. You want your fearful and anxious child to have open hands, to have lots of possibilities for what to do next. So you're going to squeeze some "lemons."

1. Imagine you hold a lemon in each hand.

2. Tighten your hands into fists. Count to five as you drain as much juice from those lemons as you possibly can with one squeeze.

3. Drop the squished lemons and let your hands relax.

4. Take a belly breath.

5. Repeat two more times.

Where and When to Do Relaxation Exercises

People will notice when you and your child do the Really Small Face, Really Big Face. It's not subtle. If either of you is uncomfortable about the attention this exercise attracts from others, you might consider doing it when no one is going to be looking. Similarly other children may be curious about the Turtle exercise if your child is using it in the classroom, although in other situations it can look like nothing more than a good stretch. Squeezing Lemons, on the other hand, can be done discreetly while sitting at one's desk, standing in line, at the dinner table, or any number of situations without drawing unnecessary attention to oneself.

Feeling Safe and Supported: Exercises for Gently Increasing Muscle Tone

Interestingly, there are people for whom relaxing their muscles is actually anxiety provoking. Some individuals may panic while going under anesthesia. It's not clear why this is, although it may represent discomfort with a loss of control. I've known many children who, rather than calming down, only get more wiggly and even agitated when they try the tense-and-release muscle relaxation techniques described in the previous section. For them, I use a different approach.

It can feel comforting to gently increase the muscle tone so that the muscles are hugged to the body or gently and subtly engaged. Thus engaged, the brain seems less likely to interpret the nervous movements as signs that the body is in danger. The fight-or-flight response can stand down.

EXERCISE: Moving Without Moving

You can do this type of muscle-tone exercise sitting or lying down. I will describe it as if you or your child were sitting down.

1. Place the palms of your hands on a flat surface in front of you. That can be a desk or table, or it can simply be the tops of your thighs. Place your feet squarely on the floor in front of you.

2. Lift your fingers without lifting your palms. Feel the tightening of the muscles and tendons in the backs of your hands and in your forearms. Lift your fingers up and down several times. Lift your toes and feel the same sensations in your feet and ankles.

3. Pretend that the palms of your hands are superglued to the surface they are resting on. Now try to move your hands apart from each other. This is sometimes referred to as isometric movement, or what I call "moving without moving." Since your hands are stuck there, you will feel the muscles of your hands and arms, shoulders and chest tighten slightly, but your hands do not move.

4. Now isometrically move your hands toward each other. Notice which muscles become engaged or awaken and which new muscles become involved.

5. Play with different "movements": hands away from your body or toward it, one hand pulling in one direction and the other still or pulling in a different direction.

6. Now do the same with your feet. Notice the muscles that engage and release when your feet are isometrically moved in different directions.

Moving Without Moving can be done in a variety of situations that call for increased awareness of muscle tone as a means for calming the body and the mind. That could be in the classroom (with practice, these movements can be done without much thought and do not have to pose a distraction risk), on long car rides, waiting in line (palms against the sides of your legs or arms folded across your chest with your palms pressing against your biceps), or in bed at night when sleep isn't coming and your body is agitated.

EXERCISE: Spider Push-Ups

This is a version of increasing muscle tone that incorporates a little movement. I think of this technique as giving the muscles a job to do so that the brain can think about more important things.

1. Place the fingertips of one hand against those of the other. If you then turn your hands over so that one palm faces up and the other palm faces down, it looks like a spider (who is missing three legs) doing push-ups on a mirror.

2. Return your palms to their original and upright position.

3. Gently but firmly, slowly, and rhythmically push your palms toward each other. Speed should be moderate to slow—approximately one second to press in and one second to release.

4. To practice, repeat a dozen times or so. Add natural belly breaths. (Your breathing and the Spider Push-Ups don't have to be in sync.)

Spider Push-Ups act as a quick technique to get your child refocused when he becomes restless or agitated. Turning his attention to this simple action can give your child a sense that he is in control of his body. Sitting at his desk in school or in a church pew, he can do these push-ups indefinitely. The idea is that doing Spider Push-Ups will become an automatic motor behavior that will provide the tactile contact many children and adults seem to need when anxious. Spider Push-Ups, done properly, are incompatible with more problematic touching, such as poking a classmate or sister, picking the nose, or picking someone else's nose. Most children will need some coaching and some practicing to get this technique smooth and functioning just below awareness.

Practice—and Then Practice Some More

Practice often. The best time is when emotions and demands are not hot. If you wait until your child is very upset and then bark at him to "breathe like an alien," there is little chance that the technique will be useful and some chance that the very suggestion of these techniques will itself trigger anxiety.

When first teaching and cuing skills, you will want to pick the time, place, and situation to maximize everyone's chances of success. Find a situation when historically anxiety has been mild or even absent but the social skill or breathing or relaxation technique could be useful. Practice the skills and techniques then. Discuss which ones seem to be most helpful; I expect only some will be a good fit for how your child thinks and what he needs. But you won't know which techniques are the helpful ones unless you give them all a try.

SUMMARY AND A LOOK AHEAD

In keeping with the overall goals of acceptance and commitment therapy, the skills, techniques, and exercises described in this chapter are not intended to eliminate or even prevent fear and anxiety in your child's life. However, you can reduce the overall level of stress, frustration, and anxiety in your lives without compromising your values and your goals, and without engaging in unnecessary avoidance and control. The goal of phase 2 in your behavior change campaign is to give you and your child some ways (social skills and self-regulation techniques) of moving quickly through fearful and anxious thoughts and feelings when they do show up and staying focused on the real goals at hand. Creating social success, reducing uncertainty, increasing predictability and consistency, and reducing conflicts can all go a long way to stave off anxious episodes and rechoreograph the parent-child dance.

When fear and anxiety do show up, you will have basic techniques for taking the edge off the anxiety (or frustration, or whatever) long enough for you and your child to orient toward what you're trying to achieve at that moment. The breathing and muscle-tone exercises I presented are meant to create a sense of self-control and to provide that psychological space and flexibility that will allow you and your child to pause, reflect, and make the choice to engage life rather than fight your anxious thoughts and feelings. To a large degree, this requires stepping back and looking at the larger situation—to think about the process more than the particular content you and your child are struggling with at the moment.

In the next chapter, I will describe in detail phase 3 of the behavior change campaign: the process of *validation*, in which you let your child know you have received the message his behavior is trying to convey, and you teach him something about his own inner workings, feelings, needs, and habits, as well as what can be done next.

CHAPTER 8

Acceptance and Validation in the Face of Anxiety

I described in chapter 6 techniques for increasing your own and your child's awareness of the world "out there," as well as for taking interest in your inner world of thoughts and feelings. These mindfulness techniques, along with the defusion exercises from the same chapter, can be used with the breathing and muscle-tone exercises from the last chapter to help create some psychological spaciousness and flexibility when situations bring a lot of anxious thoughts and feelings upon you and your child. The social skills and understanding I discussed in the last chapter also serve to make your child more aware of her important social world and to provide skills for engaging effectively with others, including you, so that the social world becomes a place where your child can feel understood and supported by others when challenges arise.

As I stated at the end of chapter 4, responsive parenting in the face of anxiety is a delicate balance between acceptance and change: "I love you just the way you are, but I love you too much to let you stay that way." We will now look at how the natural power of your relationship with your child will help give your child the message that you accept her and her anxious thoughts and feelings, even as you encourage her to change her anxious behavior.

You will recall that in chapters 5 and 6 I stated that the beginnings of any change process involve becoming more aware of what you are doing. Next, in order for anxious behaviors to change, your child needs to know that you have received the message and understood the need that lies behind the behavior. Giving these messages of understanding involves accurately and respectfully playing your child back to her. This is phase 3 of your campaign to change the anxiety dance, which is the theme of this chapter.

PHASE 3: VALIDATING YOUR CHILD

What does your child want? To help answer this question, Robert Wahler at the University of Tennessee has studied parent-child transactions for many years. In one study (Wahler and Meginnis 1997), school-age children and their mothers were observed playing together. Wahler and his colleagues videotaped these play sessions and counted the times parents praised their child's behavior ("I like the way you did that"), criticized their child's behavior ("You shouldn't be so rough with that"), or simply "mirrored" or verbally described (played back) their child's behavior ("You put that together"). After each session, Wahler interviewed both the child and the parent and asked, among other things, how satisfied they each were with the playtime.

There is a measure in statistics called a *correlation*. It measures how much two things vary together. For example, air temperature is correlated with ice cream consumption; the hotter it is, the more ice cream is consumed in a community. You can see how the two would be related. But a strong correlation doesn't necessarily mean that one thing causes another. The number of bars in a town is often correlated with the number of churches; the more bars a town has, the more churches it tends to have. Both are actually due to population size; the more people in a town, the more bars and the more churches you will find. Bars don't cause churches nor do churches cause bars, so far as we know.

Wahler's group did correlations on their observation and interview data, and they found something interesting. The child's satisfaction of the play session was not correlated at all with the amount of praise a mother gave during the play, but it was correlated with mirroring. The more a mother simply reflected back what her child was doing, the more likely it was that the child was happy with that play experience. Praise did not make for satisfying play for the child. It didn't detract from it. But apparently it wasn't what mattered to these children.

Do happy children pull more mirroring behavior from their parents? It's possible. But I think it's more likely that the direction of this correlation is that mirroring (that is, simply being noticed) made for happy children.

What was the mothers' satisfaction correlated with? The amount of praise they gave. This is not surprising. After all, it has been observed that when we praise our children, we are really praising ourselves.

Being Seen, Being Heard, Being Felt

Wahler's study reminds us that a child's needs can be pretty basic. To just be noticed—it doesn't get more basic than that. Your child needs to know that she matters to you, that she impacts you. And she will impact you in any way it takes to know she's succeeded.

The idea of *mirroring*, reflecting back or playing back, your child in the moment is an important concept and it deserves some thought. People in general, and parents and children in particular, appear to be wired to imitate each other. Observations of three-month-old infants and mothers (few of these studies are done with fathers, unfortunately) interacting face-to-face reveal clear imitation of one another's facial expressions in a dance of action and reaction (Cohn and Tronick 1988). This is where and how the various dances with your child originated. You will recall that, from the very beginning of life, temperament will color and shape the dance.

More recently neuroscientists have been investigating *mirror neurons*: clusters of nerve cells found so far in monkey and human brains that become activated when we observe someone perform an action, especially goal-directed actions (Rizzolatti and Craighero 2004). The clusters of neurons activated in the observer's brain tend to be the very ones responsible for the action taken by the person (or monkey) observed; I observe you reach out and grasp a stick, and my own neural circuits in charge of reaching out and grabbing sticks will "light up." I may not reach out and grab a stick myself, but my brain is poised to do just that. Should observing another's emotions be any different? It is no wonder that neuroscientists are calling mirror neurons the biological roots of empathy.

This gives scientific status to something you've known since the moment you became a parent; when your child behaves in some way, in any way, it affects you. How and to what degree will depend on the behavior itself and your receptivity—your awareness, your mood, your predisposition to like or dislike that behavior, and so on. Importantly, when you behave in some way, in any way, it affects your child.

This is a big responsibility, but it doesn't have to be a problem. This situation of mutual influence would not have come about if it did not have some survival value. In order to be effective and committed parents, we must be affected by our children. In order to learn about the world and how to live in it, our children must be affected by us. The problem comes when riding the emotional waves with your child overtaxes your resilience or outstrips your skills. Then you have to get back to basics: what's the message behind the behavior and how can I let her know I get it?

Graybar's First Law of Human Behavior

Please recall from chapter 5 my reference to Graybar's laws of human behavior. His second law was "He who cares least has the most power," or "The more you care, the more you must be willing to bear." We discussed this idea in relation to your values and goals as a parent. We'll revisit "caring and bearing" in the next chapter. Here I want to repeat and examine Graybar's first law: "All behavior is a message, and a behavior won't begin to change until the person knows the message has been received."

We often attribute challenging or problematic child behavior to attempts to get our attention, as if getting our attention was something pathological. Of course your child tries to get your attention. She tries to get you to understand her and help her. Children need to feel that they make an impact on the world, that their actions matter, and that they can alert important, powerful adults to their distress so that these adults will help them. Unfortunately, they are immature beings and poor communicators of their experiences, and at these critical times they are usually pretty upset to boot. So it's actually understandable that, when your child is at her worst and needs your attention and help the most, her means for accomplishing that goal are often confusing, off-putting, or both.

So your child's anxious behavior has two goals: getting you to understand her and obtaining your help. Sounds simple enough. Yes, you can see she's acting quite anxious. That is clear. Yes, you know just how to help her: reassure her that things will be just fine and give her a stiff nudge in the direction she needs to be heading. Unfortunately, quite often this does not solve the problem. In fact, sometimes it only exacerbates your child's anxious behavior. The crying and hand-wringing, the avoidance and control only increase. What's going on? You told her in the most calm and loving terms that you understood she was anxious. You assured her that there was nothing to be afraid of. You told her exactly what she needed to do to solve the problem. What is the problem?

The wrinkle here is that your child won't accept your help until she has gotten the message—really gotten it—that she has been understood. Some clinicians talk about a child's need to "feel felt." In other words, at a very basic level, your child needs to get that you get her. Words alone may not do it. In fact, as we'll see, you want to encourage using words when your child is upset, but the heart of this kind of communication may go beyond reason, beyond talk, beyond reassurance.

The validation strategies described below will not change your child's anxious behavior as if flipping a switch. What your acts of understanding and acceptance can do is make change possible. If you can let your child know that you get the message that seems to be behind her behavior, then she doesn't have to continue to ramp up the behavior to get your attention and understanding. She may do so anyway, however, especially if she is tired or hungry or in some way regressed and vulnerable to loss of control. By sheer habit alone, ramping up may be part of the picture for a while, even when you are giving all the right responses. That is how automatic your dance has become. But the goal over time is to teach her that there are many ways to get those messages across to you, and that clear and respectful messages will reliably get your attention.

Validation and Possibility: The Art of Playing Back Your Child

There are a number of terms that describe playing back your child to her: reflecting, mirroring, validating. All describe your giving a child the message, through what you say and do, through your tone and body language, that you see, hear, and feel her. You *get* the message. You play that message back to her in a way that not only shows her you get it, but in a way that helps her understand her own message better: "Oh, you're feeling anxious because you're the first person to get here." Your playback can also contain hints at what can be done about the "problem": "I'm wondering if you'd like me to wait with you until some of the other kids get here?"

You may not agree with what she is thinking or feeling at that moment. You may not be happy about it. You may think that her internal experiences and reactive behaviors are uncalled for, over-the-top, immature, or unreasonable. Yet, at that moment, all those inner experiences and outward messages are hers and as real and valid to her as anything. So, if your child is going to learn to change her reactions in that moment and in similar situations in the future, then she has to first understand what it is she experiencing before she can consider that there might be something else she could think, feel, and do. Your child's understanding of herself comes from you understanding her.

You can't help but play your child back in those moments. The question is, how are you going to do it? Will your playback be accurate in terms of helping your child know you get her at that moment? Will your playback show that you can accept the current state of her thoughts and feelings even as you're about to go for a change in her behavior? Will your playback create some room to step back and look *at* the situation, including her thoughts and feelings, instead of looking *through* it? Will your playback suggest flexibility or possibility such that she can recognize some alternatives to the way she sees the world at that moment, how she feels about it, and what she thinks can or cannot be done?

Mirror Neurons and Playing Back Your Child

There seems to be something very natural and important at work in the validation process, and it likely involves the mirror neurons described above. However, successful validation may not be a perfect reflecting back of what your child is doing at the moment. It is a playback with a bit of a twist. Researchers studied the ability of mothers to soothe their eight-month-old infants immediately after the child received a routine vaccination (Fonagy et al. 1995). The mothers who calmed their infants most quickly and effectively did something interesting. Holding the infant so that she and the child were face-to-face, the expert soothing mothers were observed to scrunch their faces in a grimace of pain for just a moment immediately after the child received the injection. Then these mothers went into the typical rocking, cooing, and gentle talking we think of when we see someone calming a distressed child. Other mothers did not spontaneously mirror the child's expression of pain and surprise, but immediately began their soothing strategies. This second group of mothers had infants who were not as quickly soothed.

What were these very young infants getting out of seeing their mothers "feeling their pain"? The pained facial expressions of these mothers were spontaneous; when asked, they could say they were aware of what they were doing then, but it was not a calculated move on their part. It just came naturally. This is mirror neurons at work.

But these successful soothing mothers did something else, something very interesting and also quite unconscious. The expressions they played back to their infants were not purely pained. In addition to grimacing and furrowing their brows and the like, these mothers' faces showed little miniexpressions within the overall pained look: a slight smile, eyes wide in wonderment, an eyebrow raised in surprise. These "competing" miniexpressions may serve to suggest that there is more than one way to think and feel about this experience. The playback message is both "I get it" and, as painful and frightening as life is at this moment, there are other possibilities.

Key Elements in Playing Back Your Child

Playing back your child needs to convey three things: accuracy, possibility, and genuineness, not necessarily in that order. Your playback must be *accurate* in terms of reflecting what she is likely feeling and thinking. She has to know that you get her, that her message has been received. Otherwise she will be compelled to continue giving the message or perhaps amplify it since it's clear *you're not getting it*! Accuracy doesn't mean matching her whine for whine; you don't have to be as regressed as she is in the moment. You needn't throw a tantrum yourself to convey the message "I get it that you're angry, frightened, or disappointed right now." That would likely be overwhelming, shaming, and frightening ("Mom's really losing it!" "Dad can't handle this!"). However, your playback will provide words and other nonverbal messages that convey the inner experience in a way that hits the right notes. Your words, body language, and tone (discussed below) will give shape to these overwhelming forces that threaten her.

While your validating messages convey an accurate reading of what your child experiences, they will also convey *possibility*, new ways of looking at and articulating these emotions and thoughts, new ways of defining the problem, and new ways of managing the situation. This could simply be conveyed in the choice of words you use, providing a more nuanced label for the feeling: Is this anger or frustration? Is this fear or anxiety or nervousness?

As in the example above, your playback might suggest what it is about the situation that invites your child to be anxious ("you're the first one here") and a possible, acceptable solution ("I'll wait with you").

All these little messages put a slight spin on your feedback; like the breathing and muscle-tone exercises from the last chapter, your feedback creates some psychological space in which your child can step back, look at what is really going on, and consider what might be done next. Finally, your validation is an act of real empathy; it must be done with compassion, respect, and genuine concern for your child.

Why Validation Is Challenging for Anxious Parents

Your child's behavior, feelings, or ways of thinking may be unpleasant, unfair, or inconvenient all by themselves. To you, they may also suggest your child is lazy, ungrateful, mean-spirited, or any number of traits that you had hoped wouldn't appear in her. You may believe she is reacting all out of proportion to the event. She is being unreasonable. Nonetheless, it is important that you validate her experience and—after you take your deep belly breath with an emphasis on the exhalation—play her back effectively as your first response. If you don't let her know you get the message, the behavior is likely to continue or even escalate.

A child's behavior, thoughts, or feelings can evoke in us a flood of terrible thoughts and feelings of our own stemming from past or present circumstances. Your child's behavior may remind you of someone of whom you have unpleasant memories (an abusive or unpredictable parent or sibling, for example). These memories and the thoughts and feelings they provoke are hard to bear, and you may have thoughts that if you accept and validate your child at that moment you will be encouraging that behavior and inviting more unpleasantness for you. Understood. However, validating the message behind the behavior is the very thing that will decrease her need to continue conveying her message in that unacceptable way. It is the first step in a process.

Remember the Tuning Forks

A question often comes up: how do I know what to say? More often than not, the message will be quite clear; your child's behavior and words will tell you what's going on inside her. But how can you know what your child thinks and feels when her message is vague or complicated? The answer often comes in the form of a question: what are *you* feeling at that moment?

Recall my example of two tuning forks from the introduction. There is a sympathetic vibration that one induces in the other when placed close to each other. In those challenging situations you face, the thoughts and feelings provoked in you by your child's behavior may be an accurate reflection of what she feels in the moment. This is not a conscious process. Your child is not thinking, "I'm going to push Dad's buttons so that he can feel how I feel." But to be understood at a very deep and real level is a vital need of any child, and she will do whatever it takes to accomplish that. If she lacks the proper words and means to get you to understand her ("I'm scared, please help"), she will use other means (the pantrum or tantrum).

The fact of the matter is, you're probably doing much of this playing back and validation already. My intention is not only to give you some guidelines as to how validation can be done, but also to place the act of validation in a context, that of acceptance and growth. I also want to give you permission to slow down and not feel pressured to always get every uncomfortable feeling tidied up and every negative thought transformed into a positive one. You have to understand something before you can change it. Your child has to feel accepted before she will accept change.

Validation in Practice

Validation (sometimes called reflecting or mirroring) is the response that plays back your child and also demonstrates that you get your child's message and accept the situation (even while you're working at changing it). The basic procedure involves making a simple statement that reflects back what the child conveys to you through her words or actions. Verbal examples include "Ah, I can see that you're nervous right now," "Looks like you're having a sad day," or "You've got a lot of energy today." Nonverbal examples include a deep sigh, a spontaneous cheer (you can validate positive experiences too), or the reflexive, somewhat exaggerated sad face you acquire when your child is hurt or distressed in some way.

Validation is in no way meant to diminish the child's experience or suggest in any way that what she thinks and feels is trivial. It is meant to convey understanding and autonomy: You understand your child and you recognize that she is separate and a little different from you. She's feeling anxiety at the moment, you get that, and you're not feeling anxiety at the moment—or perhaps you are feeling anxious, but you're thinking about it differently.

Through your modeling of how to talk about anxiety and respond to it, if you respond at all, your child comes to understand herself: how she experiences and responds to anxiety. With this increased perspective taking, your child gains autonomy from her thoughts and feelings; she becomes more defused from her thoughts and feelings and is more herself while having those thoughts and feelings.

Acceptance, from the ACT perspective, is the key ingredient that allows you and your child to step back from your thoughts and feelings and gives you both the space in which to consider the possibilities of how to respond. Validation helps a child achieve this. In psychological terms, this stepping back is called *mentalizing*: the ability to think about your thoughts and feelings as if from a distance. As I described earlier, mentalizing is a very important developmental achievement. Again, it allows your child to be her own self; she experiences these unpleasant thoughts and feelings without losing her *self* to them.

Children learn to mentalize—that is, it is a socially taught skill. They learn it from us—both as we play our children back to them and as we mentalize our own experiences, thoughts, and feelings in obvious and appropriate ways. We do this in a spirit of curiosity, even wonderment. It's not an interrogation. We are not extracting a confession from our children regarding their inner life. We may not even get much of an answer to our musings. That's fine. What we're after is just to let them know that their thoughts and feelings are of interest to us and that we can step back and think about what we think and feel.

VARIETIES OF VALIDATION

Let's look at some of the strategies and considerations when validating your child's experiences. Remember, the following examples are just that—examples. They are not scripts to follow. Every situation is different and requires a considerable amount of experimentation to find what works.

The perspective of acceptance and commitment therapy holds that it is possible to validate a person's pain without endorsing or getting caught up in the apparent reason for that pain. As a parent, you are a problem solver and a protector. When unpleasant thoughts or feelings arise in your child, you want to understand the cause and dispatch the bad emotions as quickly as possible. One way of doing that is to dismiss your child's experience as inaccurate or unimportant. For example, "Oh, Joshua, you've been up those stairs a million times. You *know* there's nothing that's going to hurt you."

Another typical parent reaction is to focus on the problem the thought or feeling represents (the content) and then try to solve that problem as quickly as possible. "Sterling, sweetheart, it doesn't matter if your shoelace loops aren't exactly the same length." The shoelaces may not be the point. This situation may be about control, or the lack of it, in Sterling's life.

In contrast, an accepting or validating approach uses defusion to help your child get untangled from unhelpful thoughts and feelings. Remember successive approximations, which we talked about earlier; you are going to get there by small steps. Right now you are interested in getting your child to step back and see the process, even if the process doesn't change much in the short run.

So, rather than negating her child's anxiety and helpless appraisal of the situation, Nancy will try to get Joshua to step back from that scared thought. She'll say something like "Ah, I can see you're having some of those scary thoughts about going upstairs by yourself." Then—and this is the hard part—she will pause long enough to let that validation sink in and prevent herself from jumping in with her solution to this problem before Joshua gets a chance to come up with one of his own.

This pause may last a full minute (breathe) before one of two things happens. First, Joshua may provide more information about what is going on in his mind. Maybe something important happened that day around this theme of feeling scared, helpless, or incompetent, and he needs to process it and maybe talk about it. The tricky part here is to not let the enticing prospect of connecting with her son on this deep level become his way of avoiding getting to the outcome goal of going upstairs to get his shoes.

How to handle this type of situation is something you will just have to learn from experience.

The second response your validation may elicit is an acknowledgment from Joshua that Nancy is correct, along with a request for her company up the stairs. This is another tricky part of the process: what do you do next?

I want you to recognize that you don't always have to rush in and solve the "problem" of your child's discomfort. You both now have the mindfulness skills from chapter 6 that you can bring to bear on this upset and turmoil. Slow down and take a deep breath or two. You can name, or have the child name, the feelings coursing through her: that's fear, here comes hopelessness, now sadness is here. Categorize the thoughts: worry, resentment at having to deal with this now, worry about the future, and so on. Consider your next move: validate, say nothing, go into problem-solving mode, and so on. Breathe some more.

Thinking Out Loud

It is very instructive for your child to hear you think through a problem. It accomplishes a couple of things. First, thinking out loud lets your child know about the thoughts and feelings you are experiencing and gives them some normalcy, whether they are thoughts or feelings of anger, frustration, worries, or regrets. Your child now experiences her mother feeling and thinking all this nasty stuff, and yet Mom's reasonably calm and working through it. This is interesting!

Second, thinking out loud lets your child know that solutions or coping strategies don't always just show up; we often have to go through a process of working things out in our heads, considering the options and the likely consequences of various possible decisions. Working through issues is not magic or the result of special powers that adults possess and kids lack. Working through issues is *work*, and there are ways of doing that work that are more effective than others. Furthermore, this process can take some time. So we all need to be patient with each other and ourselves.

Leave Out the "I Understand"

As a matter of form, I have found over the years that it's best to leave out the opening phrase "I understand" when validating your child's experience. It's hard to say "I understand..." without sounding patronizing. It's better to simply reflect or mirror your child's statement or obvious emotional state. For example, a simple "You're scared" seems to work better than "I understand you're scared." For very upset and very young children, you want to keep your words to a minimum anyway. I like the "Ah" or "Oh" beginnings: "Ah, you're feeling..." or "Oh, you seem to be thinking..."

By keeping the validation simple, it reduces the risk of sounding patronizing or impatient. This is *very* important with older children. Leaving out the "I understand" makes it less likely you'll provoke the classic "No, you don't understand" response. You can always say something like "Let me see if I understand..." and then repeat back what your child has told you. This shows that you're trying, allows your child to hear her own words or a paraphrase, and gives her the opportunity to make corrections, all of which are forms of perspective taking and social understanding.

"I Wonder..." Statements

There are times when your child isn't saying anything, but you just know that something is on her mind. It might be a distressing emotion, or she may just be deep in thought and you're interested in what she's thinking about. In these situations, I recommend using the "I wonder" statements I described in the last chapter. This is a softer way of validating what you believe is going on with your child at the moment.

The "I wonder" technique can introduce a more accurate or nuanced feeling word into the child's vocabulary: "I wonder if you're feeling nervous" in place of the "scared" she habitually uses. If she replies, "No, I'm scared," don't argue about it. Just say okay and move on. Similarly "I wonder" statements can link a feeling or thought with a situation. For example, your child shuts down while doing homework and you remark, "I wonder if you're confused about what to do next." If you're told you're wrong, so be it. You're probably not wrong, but it may be too difficult for your child to accept the connection, or your being right, at that moment. You've still introduced the possibility that things could be seen from a different and more helpful vantage point; if you know that you're confused and you know what's confusing you, "confusion" is now a small piece of the bigger picture. Anxiety too can be a small piece of one's experience within a larger picture.

We Wonder, They Wonder

You want your child to feel that she matters to you, that she is important, and that she occupies your mind. Letting her know that you wonder about her gives your child a solid sense that she has an important place in your life. A related and important aspect of this "wondering" is that you want your child to consider that others are thinking about her, that others have opinions and ideas about her (even if incorrect), and that others share similar thoughts and feelings in similar situations. This recognition that others have thoughts and feelings similar to hers is the basis of empathy. Wondering about one another builds relationships.

Framing

If you've ever had a picture or photograph framed, it is remarkable how a different frame or mat will change the image it surrounds; different colors are enhanced or muted, other visual aspects of the image are emphasized, and so on. In addition to the parts being transformed, the whole can be very different by virtue of this or that style of frame: thickness, color, simple versus elaborate, and so on.

Framing is my term for how you create an awareness of context for your child by putting a frame around a situation, feeling, thought, or behavior. It can change an experience, as we saw in the context exercise in chapter 4.

Framing is as simple as making the connection between external events and inner thoughts and feelings: "There are a lot of kids here you don't know, so I'm guessing that (wondering if) you're feeling nervous." Framing can connect a child's wish with the expected behavior: "I will go with you if you ask me, but you have to ask in a strong, clear voice." As we will see in the next chapter, framing can be used as a means of getting away with being inconsistent as a parent.

Refusal Rights

It is very important to remember that there are *no* incorrect child responses to your validation. Obviously rule violations—aggression, disrespect, running away, and the like—in response to validation must be responded to appropriately, but you must otherwise be prepared to accept just about any reaction to your comments, especially when this process is new to you and your child.

Ideally, following your validating statement, your child would say something like "Why yes, that's exactly how I'm feeling. How astute of you, Father! I feel so ... so validated!" Not likely. Your child may not respond at all. This is common and actually suggests she is digesting what you've just said. Often the response you get will be a shrug, a grunt, or some other bare acknowledgment. Saving face is extremely important to children. Don't press your point and demand that your child confirm your inference. Anything short of a flat-out denial is tacit confirmation that you got the message. And even when your child flat out denies what you've said, you're still probably right.

Your child may come up with a better word than the one you've suggested to describe what she is feeling. I remember a scene from the Jodie Foster movie *Little Man Tate* when Foster, as the mother, comments that her young genius son appears "nervous" prior to a big math contest. He replies, "No, I'm *pensive.*" You may not get that kind of nuanced reply, but by showing that you wonder about (and care about) how your child is feeling and what she is thinking, she will start to wonder about herself and increase her capacity for self-reflection and for describing and communicating what she discovers.

Your caring insight into your child's inner life may get a provocative "Well, duh!" If she is especially deep into her funk, your child may angrily protest that you're wrong about what she's feeling, that you don't understand her, and so on. You must not take the bait and point out that she is clearly upset and this only proves that you were right. Instead, bail out with a simple "Oh, okay" and move on. If you're truly sensing that an opportunity to talk is still alive, you could say something like "Well, you looked anxious, so I was just checking," and then allow her to respond or not.

For many children (and adults), especially when they are upset and feeling vulnerable, validation can feel like an intrusion. This is why it is important to keep your acceptance moves as simple and respectful as possible. These kinds of defensive reactions on your child's part will diminish as your child gets used to your validation, sees you modeling a nondefensive response to her upset, and comes to recognize that your comments are coming from a place of genuine interest and concern.

Ambiguous Messages

There are times when it simply isn't clear what your child is thinking and feeling. She may not even know. So often we are all awash in a mix of feelings: anger and embarrassment, dread and excitement, boredom and impatience, and many more. If your child is obviously upset but unable to be clear and specific about what she thinks and feels, you can always tell her, "You look upset to me, but I can't tell if you're mad or scared or both." With a very young child, you may be doing this a lot as you teach her a variety of feeling words. In the future, she may be able to offer a more definite description of her thoughts and feelings. But again, how she responds is up to her. The hope is that she will accept the invitation to clarify, for herself and for you, what her emotional state is at the moment.

Whole-Body Validation: Go There and Bring Them Back

We often respond to another's moods by assuming the opposite mood in an attempt to bring the individual toward the middle. For example, your child is very agitated and anxious, so you assume a demeanor that is unnaturally calm and self-controlled. When your child is down in the dumps, you may become very perky. This strategy of going in the opposite direction of her mood—"Come on. Let's see that smile!"—can be perceived as invalidating and often serves only to irritate her.

"Go there and bring them back" means that you show some similar emotion yourself when your child experiences strong feelings. I call this *whole-body validation*: the playback involves not just your words but also your body language and your tone of voice to let your child know that you've really been impacted by her, that you really get it. Recall the study I mentioned earlier in this chapter in which mothers who successfully soothed their infants after a vaccination were those who made a pained face just prior to moving into their soothing response. The idea is to go where your child is emotionally and then bring her back.

Not that you start throwing the furniture yourself, but if your child is upset, you can get energized and put some feeling behind your words: "Wow, you're really feeling anxious right now!" If your child feels sad and discouraged, you slow down and with a sigh say, "Gee, sounds like a really, really tough day," followed by another sigh and a respectful silence. That's the "going there" part. You can take the time to do this, assuming the house is not on fire or no one is really throwing the furniture.

The "bring them back" part is your obvious but not necessarily quick modeling of how you and your child can shift the focus so that the upsetting emotional state becomes background and the situation itself, and your possible response to it, become the foreground. You don't rush this part unless, of course, the situation presents some danger of harm. Bringing them back is often initiated with a nice, deep breath, whether you're mirroring an agitated or a depressed state.

For example, Angela may not run around the room speaking in a robot voice as Sterling does, but she may get up and move around a bit when Sterling is agitated. Again, Mom is going to be in control—that's important to Sterling because she is his lifeline. Angela will reflect back whatever Sterling says in a manner that says she knows how he feels or why: "You are just feeling *so* nervous right now." Note that she is not saying he "is" anxious; she wants to create a little defusion here. Note that she says "right now" to suggest to Sterling that this state wasn't here before and won't be here in a while. At some point, Angela would begin to slow down her movements while taking some obvious deep breaths. She would suggest to Sterling that they sit down. If he does not take her up on this offer, she might sit down anyway, take more deep breaths, and wait to see if he will talk while he paces. She might get him to name his feelings or she might give a category, such as "those worries," in which to put his thoughts. All of this is in the service of getting Sterling to step back from his thoughts and feelings and, with his mother's help, to look at them, not through them.

If Nancy finds Joshua sad and scared sitting on the bottom step of the stairs when he is supposed to be going upstairs on his own, she might sit down next to him and just breathe, without saying anything for a minute. She might offer some reflective comments about how he seems to be feeling, what he might be thinking, and why. Nancy takes her time to do this; it is an investment in Joshua's growth and in their success as dance partners. At some point, she will want to engage him in the process of communicating his inner experience to her and moving toward a plan of action to deal with the situation.

Acceptance Is Not Reassurance

In these initial stages of your behavior-change campaign, you will actually do less reassuring and you will find that this helps. You certainly know that reassurance often does not help.

Nancy wants Joshua to go to other parts of the house on his own. In the short term, she is going to undermine the current situation with acceptance. She and Sid have made this situation and Joshua's behavior in it a priority for change. They are committed to creating a new, more responsive dance. Joshua going to other parts of the house on his own is an outcome goal. It is a worthy goal and a doable goal, or at least it will be eventually.

However, the first goals Sid and Nancy will take on are process goals related to increasing Joshua's awareness of what he is doing in those anxious moments and letting him know that they get him, really get him, and what he's experiencing. (See chapter 5 to review outcome and process goals.)

Nancy has rehearsed her response in her mind, and she and Sid have practiced it a few times to work out the details and to anticipate problems in implementing their plan. Now she is confronted by the situation: Joshua is at the bottom of the stairs, tearfully telling his mother that he is too afraid to go upstairs to begin getting ready for bed. As she has practiced, Nancy takes a deep breath, comes up to Joshua, and drops down on one knee so that she can put a hand on his shoulder and look him in the eyes. She states very matter-of-factly, "You're having some scary thoughts and scary feelings because you need to go upstairs on your own and you want me to come with you because it will make you feel safe." She then waits for several seconds to see what Joshua will do next. In the early stages of the program, Joshua will probably simply acknowledge this statement of his mother's and repeat his demand that she escort him upstairs. But the edge will likely be off the intensity of that demand simply because he now knows she gets it. Nancy then says okay and escorts him upstairs.

Will Joshua ever learn to go upstairs by himself? Yes, but that autonomy can only be built on a foundation of security. For whatever reason, Joshua is not up for that now. The recent struggles with being a big first-grader have taken their toll. By taking the time now to articulate and validate his mental and emotional states, Joshua's parents can fill in the gaps that have appeared in his foundation of security. As his parents' understanding and support becomes internalized as self-understanding, self-support, and self-reliance, Joshua will eventually be willing to take some risks and do more for himself.

SUMMARY AND A LOOK AHEAD

Acceptance is the act of acknowledging what *is* at the moment, what life is handing you, and making appropriate accommodations. Acceptance is not giving in or merely tolerating a bad situation. It is looking life's challenges in the eye and choosing to be equal to the task.

Validation is the act of conveying to your child that you get how she is thinking and feeling at the moment, that—not that you like it or condone it or want it—you have received the message behind her behavior. You get her at that moment and you play her back in a way that creates both understanding and possibility. Possibility comes from the use of defusion strategies ("You're *having* one of those feelings"). Validation may be verbal ("You're having those scary thoughts again") or nonverbal (a sigh, a frown, or a hug). Acts of validation make up phase 3 of your campaign to change the anxiety dance.

When you wonder about and give expression to your child's inner life, she will be better able to step back and think about it too. As she thinks about her thoughts and feelings in useful, accurate, and flexible ways, she will be able to avoid becoming reactive and rigid in the face of uncomfortable thoughts and feelings. Your modeling of useful coping and problem-solving strategies will teach her how to cope.

In the next chapter, I will describe phase 4 of your campaign: changing reactions to responses, reducing anxious behaviors, and increasing coping behaviors. I will address situations where children may engage in behaviors that are unsafe or simply unacceptable. As a parent, you must be able to create clear and reasonably consistent boundaries so that your child feels safe and acts appropriately. These situations when your child is in distress at the same time as she is acting out are often difficult to navigate. In the next chapter, I will talk about how you can balance acceptance with change, and validation with expectations, and how you and your child can navigate these troubled waters together.

CHAPTER 9

Effectively Managing Anxious Behaviors

As you know, many situations can provoke your child's fear and anxiety. Some of these may involve the sudden and unexpected: a barking dog appears without warning or there is an unanticipated change in plans. Other situations appear to challenge a child's fragile and developing sense of security and independence: being separated from a parent or managing an unfamiliar situation (with peers at a birthday party, for example) on one's own. I have described the processes by which your child's fear and anxiety engage you in the struggle to avoid, escape, or control anxious thoughts and feelings.

In this chapter, I want to accomplish two objectives. First, I want to return to the process involving you and your child when he is having anxious thoughts and feelings and why I think being responsive in these situations can be so difficult to do. Second, I want to introduce you to phase 4, strategies for effectively managing anxiety-provoking situations. Much of this discussion revolves around the unpleasant and unavoidable fact that your child's reactions to his anxiety, and your own reactions to his reactions, can create conflict.

CONFLICT AND ANXIETY

When we try to manage our child's anxiety, we are often actually trying to manage conflict. The problems defined by an anxiety disorder and the notion of a psychological disorder itself arise when your anxious child is *not* doing what he needs to do: greet people in the expected manner, go to school, go to another part of the house by himself, or focus on age-appropriate activities and expectations instead of spending so much time on avoidance and control tactics.

And because your child is not doing the things he should, or he is doing all these extra "coping" tactics such as hand washing twenty times a day or never letting you out of his sight, he is in conflict with life and its expectations. Because your job as a parent is to help your child engage life and meet its expectations, you are drawn into the problem and now there is conflict between the two of you. Or, if you simply enable your child's avoidance and control, there is conflict within you because you know that dance isn't going to help him in the long run.

Finally, when parents talk to me about the behaviors they don't want when their child is anxious, they frequently describe defiance or passive resistance, rude or provocative behaviors, and flat-out tantrums or aggression. I find it remarkable that this issue of conflict and anxiety is not more commonly addressed in the parent-child anxiety literature. On the other hand, books for parents of defiant children do cite anxiety as something to consider and address in those parent-child dances (for example, Barkley and Benton 1998).

Sadly, anxious children can become resistant and even defiant children. After all, as I've described, the hallmarks of anxious behavior are avoidance and control. Attempts to avoid and control anxiety and fear often result in parent-child conflicts over the many things a child needs to do, such as being polite and socially engaged (Abby), tolerating disappointment and frustration (Sterling), or engaging in day-to-day activities with an age-appropriate level of independence and a minimum of fussing (Beth and Joshua).

The strategies I've described in the preceding chapters will help you and your child avoid falling into and getting stuck in the old dance moves that are often marked by upset and conflict. But certainly in the early phases of this change process, and likely long afterward, there will be times when you and your child will lock horns over some expectation and you will need to assert your parental authority and command of the situation. And obviously *how* you do this matters; that too is a part of the dance. The new dance, even in the face of conflict, will rely on the same strategies we've covered in the first three phases: awareness, validation, and promoting skillful managing of self and others.

In this chapter I will talk about those everyday situations and processes that are potential minefields for anxiety and related feelings, such as frustration and anger. I will give you some strategies and things to think about so that you can cut down on the number of anxious upsets and conflicts you have to deal with, as well as some tools for dealing effectively with the upsets and conflicts that will inevitably come up.

Not all conflicts can or should be avoided. There are many times when you simply have to care more than your child does about a certain goal—dental hygiene, for example. You will then bear the burden of seeing that the teeth get flossed even if it generates a certain amount of unhappiness and resistance in your child. It's your job as the parent to see these big-picture or long-term goals even when your child can't. However, you don't want or need to be fighting over everything. Continuing to get in touch with and articulate your values and goals, and to find common ground with your child in these areas, will help you navigate this course.

UNCERTAINTY AND ANXIETY

One of the easiest ways to make your child anxious is to create situations that are ambiguous or uncertain. Think about your first day on some job you once had or the job you now have. Were you a bit confused about what to do? All around you people rushed by, intent on their work. They knew what to do, while you moved in awkward, self-conscious slow motion as you tried to figure out exactly what your work was. At some point, you figured out your job. Now you can likely do many aspects of it quite automatically. You've learned the choreography. You can do that dance. As such, you're more relaxed, confident, and far less self-conscious. One reason our many dances become established is that they make life predictable, even if they don't make life pleasant.

Predictability is extremely important to a child. Life can't always be predictable, but you can take steps to make your child's world somewhat more predictable while also teaching him to roll with the surprises.

As a parent, you try to set up your family life so that it runs according to a reasonable schedule, with routines and expectations that make life predictable. Another way of saying that is that you try to make life manageable and secure. Control is possible also, but perhaps not as much as we would like. And control, like avoidance, can be costly in terms preventing your child from developing age-expected coping and autonomy skills; if you controlled everything in your child's life, he would never become self-reliant.

We certainly can't always have control over our lives. When a person can't have control, prediction becomes even more important. If something bad is going to happen, I would like to be able to anticipate it and start coping. Knowing what's coming—there's a test tomorrow in math—can be a source of anxiety, it's true. But in terms of coping and being effective in life, it is better to know than to not know; I can study for that test and be ready for it, even if anticipating the test generates a certain amount of anxious thoughts and feelings. You know from experience that giving a five-minute warning can help a transition go more smoothly.

Similarly, ambiguity can be anxiety provoking. Again our human minds tend to grasp for the interpretation of events that we think will keep us safe by being forewarned. That is usually the worst-case scenario, if there are several to choose from.

So, one way we can reduce the overall level of anxiety in our child's life is by doing our best to make family expectations clear, specific, and objective to reduce ambiguity and unnecessary surprises. Not that we need to have a hundred-page manual covering all aspects of family life, but we can think about what it is we want our child to do and then articulate and encourage that. This is why I insist that the important social skills are clear, simple, and uniformly expected by all the important adults in a child's life. Problems arise when it is not clear what we want from our children or when what we from them want keeps changing (as we shall see below), based on how we are feeling at the time.

Many of us lead very busy lives with little control over events and often no ability to predict what's coming down the pike: "Oh, Mom, I forgot to tell you, we have play rehearsal this afternoon after school and I need a scarecrow costume and I'm supposed to bring three dozen cookies" or "Sorry, unexpected trip to Denver. Back in two days." Yet, to the best of your abilities, it will serve your child well if there can be schedules and routines that he can rely on and use to organize his activities and allow some anticipation of events in the service of preparation, as well as a store of experiences that tell you and your child you've been there, done that, and made it through okay: "Mom's off to rescue the company again. Two days of pizza and then madly cleaning up the house just before she gets back."

Good supple (strong yet flexible) routines and schedules can be thought of as a process that can organize children's behavior and guide them toward an outcome goal in the face of anxiety. Think of professionals who work in crisis situations, such as emergency-room personnel or firefighters: they have trained and practiced routines that allow them to effectively do their jobs in the midst of chaos and fear. Not that your household has to run like an emergency room. But taking the time to work out a good scheme for getting through the morning expectations, one with few chances to double back and get distracted by or retreat to some comforting activity can help you manage the mornings better and move your child toward the door in spite of what he may be thinking and feeling.

PHASE 4: STRATEGIES FOR MANAGING ANXIOUS SITUATIONS

In addition to being proactive and creating predictability, there are a number of strategies for managing anxiety-prone situations before, during, and after anxiety actually shows up. This is the focus of phase 4 of your behavior change campaign.

You know what your own anxiety-prone situations tend to be: Monday morning getting ready for school, bedtime, social occasions, and so on. In the next pages, I will describe ways in which the dance can be choreographed to cut down on conflict and get you to the goals of the first three phases of your behavior change campaign: awareness and understanding, skills, and validation.

One way to think about the dances you and your child do in these anxiety-rich situations is in terms of your child's (and your own) natural style of self-protection based on his (and your) temperament, which we discussed in chapter 2. Temperament, as you'll recall, is our inborn style of reacting to events in the world: withdrawing versus approaching, mild versus wild, and so on. Over time these traits develop into characteristic ways of dealing with challenging situations. We sometimes think of these self-protection behaviors as defenses.

Working With—Not Against— Your Child's Defenses

We all have defenses that protect us from being overwhelmed by life. For example, every time I fly on an airplane, I'm in total denial that this plane could possibly crash. In other situations, I may repress the memory of a distressing event, use humor to take the sting out of a painful situation, or rationalize my less-than-ideal behavior ("I've been under a lot of pressure lately"). These defenses—denial, repression, humor, rationalization— are just a few of the many ways we protect ourselves from feeling bad or feeling worse.

However, if my defenses are too rigid or dense, I may not be able to take in information I need to have. Your constructive criticism may be rejected without consideration or perhaps not heard at all. I may react defensively and try to turn the problem back on you. Your child will do all these things too if his defenses are too rigid when you need to address some issue with him. For example, Beth has had a difficult day. Some of the girls at school have begun to tease her about her germ worries. She comes home and starts to head into the bathroom. Peggy, her mother, follows her down the hall, telling Beth that if she can't get herself out of the bathroom, she will just have to wait because she, Peggy, needs to run something over to the neighbor's house. Beth erupts: "You're making me anxious by talking about it!"

On the other hand, a person's defenses can be too relaxed; he might be totally unprepared for or lacking experience with a potentially disturbing event. Being caught off guard, he might be overwhelmed by information or criticism you would like him to hear. This too can lead to a spasm of defensiveness and little communication or problem solving. For example, Sterling maintains some very strong expectations for how things are going to go. In his mind, he has the afternoon after school all set out: Mom will pick me up from after-school care, then we'll stop at the store and I will get a candy bar, then we'll go by the video store, and then we'll go home and I'll watch my video. When Angela comes to get him, Sterling is very excited to see her. He knows what's coming next. When he mentions stopping at the store, Angela says, "Oh, we can't do that. We have to go home right away because I have to call someone from work to follow up on something. I'm sorry." Sterling erupts: "This always happens. I never get to do what I want!"

So, before you deliver some challenging information or ask a provocative question, you may want to take a moment to "tune" your child's defenses. Tuning your child's defenses means providing a little information to start, often in the form of a validation, before giving the rest of the information. The idea is that this process can shift the child's self-protection system a bit so that it is neither too rigid nor too relaxed. The goal is to create a context in which your child won't be so overwhelmed by or react negatively to commands or information that typically provoke anxious arousal and conflict. For example, we often say, "I have good news and I have bad news." This is a setup. When someone says this to you, it alerts you that something is coming that may not be pleasant to hear, but it's unlikely to be truly awful. You're ready for what's coming next. In psychology, we think of this kind of setup or warning as an *inoculation*, a little bit of something that helps you deal with the bigger event that's coming—in this case, bad news or upsetting information. The following section will describe this process in more detail.

The First Arrow–Second Arrow Technique for Managing Anxious Situations

One form of inoculation is a technique I call "first arrow–second arrow," which I picked up from a karate class I once took. One day I was in class, listening to the karate master describe sparring techniques. He said that one might begin an attack with the first arrow, a feint or false move to draw the opponent's guard away from the intended target. The second arrow, the second strike, would then be directed toward the actual target. I thought, "This is what we do as parents"—that is, in a positive way, I give my child a bit of warning, a heads-up, before delivering the actual message.

For example, you might say, "I have something to tell you that's probably going to make you a little nervous" (first arrow). You pause and then say, "There will be some new kids at the party you haven't met before" (second arrow). Sterling's mother might have said, "Oh, you want to go to the store now [validation]. Well, I'm sorry, but I'm going to have to tell you something that will disappoint you [first arrow]. We have to go straight home today [second arrow]." Beth's mother might have said, "I know it annoys you when I mention the bathroom problems [first arrow]. But I just need you to know that I'm running next door for a few minutes, so I won't be here if you need me [second arrow]."

By doing this, you give your child some warning that information is coming his way that may generate some anxiety (for example, new kids at the party). But you've alerted him to that possibility and given him some appropriate vocabulary ("a little nervous") to describe what he's likely to feel. Now this news may actually terrify him. But you want to lowball these first-arrow warnings; you don't want to say, "I've got something to tell you that will probably scare the living daylights out of you!" Similarly, in a different situation, you would want to say, "I've got something to tell you that may make you a little frustrated"—or "annoyed" in Beth's case—as opposed to "I've got something to tell you that may enrage you!"

You can also pose important questions using the first arrow–second arrow approach. For example, you might say, "I'm going to ask you a question and I need you to tell me the truth" (or "…to think about your answer"). This can get your child to pause and consider before responding. By using this approach, you may be able to reduce his tendency to impulsively throw out an answer as children sometimes do. This type of impulsive response often results in his vigorously defending his response even if he knows that you know that he knows it's not correct.

Framing to Create a Bigger Picture

In the previous chapter, I introduced framing—the idea of putting events, thoughts, and feelings into a context to validate and increase awareness. Here I want to suggest that you can use framing as a way of managing situations that are ripe for anxiety and conflict. It's almost like giving a reason but not quite, because you can use this strategy to articulate a process or other temporary state and its relationship to an outcome goal. An example will make this clearer.

Recall when Sterling expected to get a snack and a video after his mother picked him up from after-school care. When he expressed his expectation to his mother, Angela might have said something along the lines of "Ah, you were thinking we would go to the market for a snack and then get a video [specific validation, shows she got the full message]. That sounds like it would be fun [a little bit of space or possibility]. But you know what? [There's another way to think about this, which will be my way.] We need to think about something [what I'm thinking]. I have something I need to do at home. It's an important call for my work [larger context against which decisions have to be made]. So I know you're going to be disappointed [first arrow], but we will have to go straight home from here [second arrow]. I'm sorry."

Angela's framed her decision within a larger context. The hope is that it will allow Sterling to see a bigger picture than the one he had in his mind as he entered that situation. This attempt at helping him see the big picture may not prevent Sterling from being unhappy or even from having a meltdown. But it does let him know what the deal is and why. It may help him to learn that there are more ways to think about a situation than just his own way at that moment, even if he's not happy about it.

Angela would want to be pretty matter-of-fact with this and keep it brief. She would not want to get into apologizing any more than necessary, or describing the work situation that necessitates this inconvenience or the dire ramification for her job if she doesn't make the call, nor would she mention that she could have had time to do it from work if she hadn't had to pick up Sterling up before the late charges started being assessed. It's not his fault; it's no one's fault. We don't have to be happy about it. It's the big picture.

Framing can also be used to put your inconsistency into a reasonable context. For example, you likely have the all-purpose "It's a special occasion" frame in your parenting tool kit. You can help yourself and your child respond well to unexpected or mitigating circumstances by declaring a "special occasion" of some kind and creating a context that puts everyone in touch with your values and goals. It can help make connections between events, possible thoughts and feelings, goals, and choices. For example, "We all feel a little lost and sad when your mom is on one of her business trips. And we're proud of her too, aren't we? So, let's all be extra responsible, keep our promises, and be extra kind to each other. I'll order the pizza."

MANAGING CONFLICT BY MANAGING THE DANCE

As I stated at the beginning of this chapter, there are two types of situations (which slightly overlap) that typically invite you or your child to have anxious thoughts and feelings. The first type of situation involves the unexpected: Sterling was not expecting to have his dream afternoon wrenched away from him. The second type of situation is when a child's capacity for self-reliance is overwhelmed: on certain days, Beth just can't manage without rescue from a parent. To this, I would add a third type of situation, which again overlaps somewhat with the other two. This type might be described as involving expectations, demands, and other transactions where you have a goal (getting out of the house in the morning) and your child has some other agenda—for example, getting you to let him stay home because his stomach hurts. The following strategies can improve the parent-child dance by helping reduce the amount of both uncertainty and surprise in a given situation, as well as providing structure and expectation for what needs to happen next, that is, the goal.

Doing the Do

You want to take some of the guesswork out of your child's day-to-day life, especially in situations that are at high risk for anxiety and conflict. These situations include directions you have to give that may be met with anxious thoughts and feelings or anger and resistance. One of the best parenting strategies I know is what I call "doing the do." When you must give a command, state it in terms of what you want your child to *do*, not what you don't want him to do. For example, it is a school-day morning and Angela sees that Sterling is sitting on the coach, mostly dressed, but barefoot and staring into space. She will want to say, "I need you to put on your socks and shoes now" rather than "Don't just sit there." Sterling may not start following Angela's direction right away, or at all, but she is working a basic component of her behavior change campaign: being clear and direct.

Studies have shown that children are much more likely to comply with "do" commands than they are with "don't" commands—for example, don't pull the cat's tail (Vigilante and Wahler 2005). There are two reasons for this. First, being told not to do something generates a certain amount of negative emotion or thinking in the child: shame, resentment, and so on. These thoughts and feelings are not conducive to compliance with your command. Second, if you tell the child to not do something, he must come up with the alternative. He may not come up with the alternative you'd be happy with. Instead of "just sitting there," Sterling might get up and turn on the TV or go to his bedroom. Telling your child what to do takes the guesswork out of compliance. That is why the sample social skills I gave you, to the extent possible, are described in terms of what we expect the child to do: "Use a pleasant face and voice and keep a calm body" instead of "Don't whine and jump up and down."

Now there are times when, as a parent, you simply have to say, "Stop!" But when possible, you should give "do" commands. This requires some thought on your part. What do you want your child to do? What does the situation actually call for? This could be an outcome goal, such as "Go upstairs and get your shoes." Or the goal at the moment could be to get to a better process: "You need to use your words and tell me what you want right now."

Reduce the Overall Number of Commands

Studies have shown that the probability of compliance with any one command is inversely related to the total number of commands given in a situation (Vigilante and Wahler 2005). Simply put, the more commands you give, the less compliant your child is going to be. If you want fewer conflicts, you can encourage more compliance by giving fewer commands. This doesn't mean letting the kids get away with murder or ruling the roost. It simply means that you pick your battles carefully; don't unnecessarily provoke conflict and anxiety with commands that could be avoided for the sake of more important victories.

Don't Ask Questions if You Are Actually Giving a Command

Parents sometimes think they avoid conflict by substituting questions for commands. For example, "Do you want to clean up now?" This works fine as long as the answer is a reliable, "Yes, Mother." However, often these questions are simply ignored or met with protest since the child knows full well what you are really getting at. In my opinion, you might as well get at what you really mean: "Please start putting the toys away now." In a similar vein, only present a choice to your child if it is in fact a real choice. If Catherine asks Abby if she wants to leave the party, she'll have to accept whatever answer Abby gives.

Don't Ask a Question if You Already Know the Answer

Trial lawyers know never to ask a witness a question to which they don't already know the answer. They want no surprises in court. If the witness lies, the lawyer has contradictory evidence ready. Parenting, however, is not cross-examination, and you can get yourself into real and difficult conflicts by asking questions when you already know the answer. For example, when "Did you bush your teeth?" is met with "Yes," you leap on the lie: "No, you didn't. I submit exhibit A—the bone-dry toothbrush!" Now you and your child struggle over both the lie and the transgression of not having brushed his teeth. This seems so unnecessary to me. It's both a waste of goodwill and an unpleasant dance you don't need to be practicing. Reduce conflicts by avoiding asking questions for which you already know the answer. If your child has not brushed his teeth, remind him to do so, guide him into the bathroom if necessary, and ignore the protests.

Tolerance: Creating Enough Space

If you look up the word "tolerance" in the dictionary, you find several definitions. The first definition is likely to be something along the lines of "enduring hardship." Another definition might be "building up resistance to a parasitic organism." In most dictionaries, further down in the list of definitions, you will find a description of tolerance that comes from engineering. Tolerance in this context is the maximum or optimal allowable distance between moving parts in a machine. The moving parts within your car's engine or your wristwatch were designed and manufactured to slide past each other with just the right amount of clearance or tolerance. If there is too little clearance between moving parts, they will rub together causing friction, heat, and possibly damage. If there is too much space or distance between moving parts, they may bang around and not work well together.

It is this last definition of tolerance that I find most applicable. Very often responsive parenting involves knowing how to create the right distance between you and your child in any given moment. Throughout this book I have talked about *leaning into* life; mindfully engaging the present situation in order to be effective. On the other hand, there may be times when as a parent the situation calls for you to *lean back*, giving your child some space both physically and psychologically. This is a dance move that can convey patience, grant autonomy, and allow a child to find his own way.

However, at times strong feelings such as anxiety, impatience, frustration, anger invite you to lean into a situation in the service of controlling or eliminating these feelings in your child or in yourself. This kind of engaging is not likely to be helpful and in fact describes so much of what is problematic about your current anxiety dance. Similarly, at other times you may be tempted to avoid dealing with a situation; instead of engaging you lean back or disengage. This kind of leaning back can be unhelpful if it is done simply to avoid difficult thoughts and feelings or if it comes across as invalidating or rejecting your child. Thus good *tolerance*, responsive leaning in or leaning back in the moment, is a matter of staying focused on your goals while keeping an eye on your thoughts and feelings in that situation. Let's look at an everyday example.

There may be times when your child is fumbling with a zipper or having difficulty tying his shoes. Now imagine that you're on your way somewhere and time is tight. The tendency will be to lean in, zip up the jacket yourself, and say, "We're in a hurry. Let me do that." Under more relaxed circumstances, you might hang back and let him fumble with the zipper in the service of his learning how to do it. In fact, as a parent, it would be so much easier for you to do it all for your child: zipping his coat, dressing him in the morning, cleaning up after him, and so on. For that matter, it would be much easier just to do his homework for him and be done with the struggles involved in that too. However, you recognize that your child needs to be able to learn to do these things himself. For you, that is both a value and a goal. And achieving the goals of self-care and autonomy requires a certain amount of fumbling, frustration, and impatience for everyone.

What Drives Tolerance—How Do We Decide?

So, your decision in those moments, while you stand there impatiently waiting for your child to figure out the zipper, is whether to lean in and deal with it or to lean back and allow your child to deal with it. There's no right or wrong answer here. It will depend on the circumstances and on your overall goals. There may be days when you are in fact in a hurry and leaning in to zip your child's coat is the thing to do.

The dilemma of whether to lean in or back is framed by this question: when your child is anxious and behaving in ways that aren't helping the situation, on what basis do you make that decision to lean in or lean back? It has been my experience, both as a psychologist and as a parent, that what drives a lot of tolerance—leaning in versus leaning back—is what *we* the parents happen to be thinking and feeling at that moment.

Angela becomes frantic and impatient when Sterling won't get going in the morning and they're both going to be late. Catherine becomes angry and frustrated when Abby won't acknowledge someone who is talking to her. Sid becomes annoyed and fed up when Joshua refuses to stay in bed. Al becomes discouraged and sad when Beth becomes stuck in the bathroom. So some mornings Angela leans in and dresses Sterling in spite of his protests. Some mornings she leans back and gives him his space, all the while frustrated that they're going to be late again. Catherine may lean in by getting down at Abby's level and sharply telling her to look at the person and say hello, now. When this doesn't work, Catherine leans way back by walking away or pulling Abby out of the situation, and she feels angry and resentful because she has to do that. Sid may lean way in by blowing up at Joshua, or he may lean way out by going into his study and playing a computer game while Nancy is left to deal with their son. With Beth, Al has a quick-in, quick-back out style that offers some tepid reassurance about her perceived threat, and then he changes the subject.

All this leaning in and leaning back, this shifting tolerance, is in the service of avoidance or control of the adult's thoughts and feelings. All of them will tell you that they are trying to manage their child and the situation, but they in fact are, God bless them, trying to get rid of their own upset in the moment. The goal of this kind of tolerance is the avoidance and control of parental thoughts and feelings. It is at the very heart of the old anxiety dance.

Changing the old automatic dance steps is largely a matter of shifting the tolerance: changing the leaning in and the leaning back such that you give your child what he really needs when he needs it. That might not be adhering closely to the agenda of the moment—for example, getting those shoes from upstairs. You may instead opt for an immediate goal that is more process oriented, such as getting some communication going or taking a moment to teach your child something about his emotions. Knowing what to address in that moment will come with increased mindfulness, the ability to register all that is going on without unnecessarily cherry-picking what's "okay" or "important" or even "acceptable." As B. H. Gunaratana put it, "Mindfulness reminds you of what you are supposed to be doing" (2002, p. 142).

One Type of Tolerance: Don't Just Do Something, Stand There

I once worked in an intensive child psychiatric hospital. There was often a lot to react to. A psychiatrist I knew there, Dr. Dea Eisner, taught me the "don't just do something, stand there" response. Often our best move is to not move at all. Unless the house is on fire or your child is dashing out in front of traffic, you can afford to pause for a few seconds or longer to take a deep breath, collect your thoughts, and come up with what you need to say and do—if anything. Tolerance in parenting can involve a wide range of responses that can be categorized as leaning in, leaning back, or holding steady. Notice when your urge is to do one of these. Notice if that urge is being driven by a frantic attempt to change your own or your child's thoughts or feelings, pressure to check yet another thing off your to-do list, or an orientation to what is real at that moment and what support and direction you may offer your child at that moment.

EXERCISE: Tolerance—Leaning In or Leaning Back

Consider the table below. This is a view of a typical interaction between Beth and her father. It describes a common situation, some typical thoughts and feelings Al experiences in that situation, and two possible responses: leaning in or leaning out or back.

Situation	Your Thoughts and Feelings	Leaning In	Leaning Back
Beth in the bathroom. Wants me to open the door for her.	Ambivalent. Feeling irritated and impatient but sad too. "How long will we have to do this?"	Validate Beth's wish for me to open the door. Choose to do that for her.	Say nothing and walk away.

Now I'm not saying that Beth's father should have done one response or the other. He had many other choices in the way of leaning in or leaning back. Al could have leaned in by telling Beth angrily that he wasn't going to continue to be manipulated by her. He could have leaned back, by validating her wish, and then gently encouraging her to do it herself.

Now I'd like you to list, in the far-left column, two or three common and upsetting events or situations that invite you to engage or disengage from your child. Note in the next column what shows up for you in the way of thoughts and feelings. In the third and fourth columns, describe what your leaning in or leaning back would look like in response to that situation.

Situation	Your Thoughts and Feelings	Leaning In	Leaning Back

Do the thoughts and feelings that come up for you tend to push you toward leaning in or leaning back? Think about the situations you've listed above and ask yourself these questions:

- In keeping with my values, process goals, and outcome goals, what would be in the best interest of my child's growth?

- What do I need to do—lean in or lean back—to make that happen, even when I experience my own unpleasant thoughts and feelings?

Write your answers here:

Process Goals	Outcome Goals	Leaning In	Leaning Back

MANAGING ANXIOUS BEHAVIORS WHEN THEY SHOW UP

Anxiety and conflict happen. Parents and children will be upset and power struggles will ensue. These upsetting situations can come upon you with lightning speed, or you may watch them approach like a storm moving across the land toward you, powerless to avoid it. In a perfect world, you would deftly avoid all these conflicts and crises. You and your child would never be anxious, frustrated, or discouraged. All communication would be clear and respectful. All problems would be solved. However, as a friend of mine says, "We're not in heaven yet."

So, given that our world isn't perfect, that we can't completely avoid anxiety and upset, what do we do when the inevitable happens? When I see parents in my clinical practice, I sometimes talk about what I call "big reactions." Big reactions are any kind of intense upset: a tantrum, acute anxiety, deep sadness, whatever our mind might be putting out at the moment, only *big*.

I will go to the whiteboard on my office wall and draw the arc of a typical big reaction: There you are (or there your child is), going along nicely (a horizontal line) when "Bam!" some emotion, such as anxiety, shows up. I draw a steep upward line, the waveform of the roller-coaster ride I referred to in chapter 4. From that initial burst of emotion, distressing in itself, we often see the emotion remain high, bouncing along, starting to come down, then shooting back up again, like a seismograph tracing the rumblings of an earthquake. We think the upset is over, and then the slightest thing will set it off again with new energy. I call these renewed upsets "aftershocks." Finally, gradually or abruptly, the reaction decays and emotions are back to baseline. Repeat as necessary.

All the emotion, represented by the seismograph-like waveforms on my whiteboard, corresponds to events in the world and inside your child's mind: something unexpected happens, a scary thought appears, a sibling makes that noise again. You want to change this pattern, to keep the reaction from happening at all, to make it less intense, to get it over with more quickly, to have it happen less frequently—all noble goals, and doable to some degree.

In twenty-plus years of talking with children and their parents about big reactions, I have learned that changing this pattern is possible. But how it changes and what changes first is interesting and perhaps contrary to what you might think.

First of all, I can tell you that when real, positive change occurs, the first thing that you will notice is that the duration of the big reaction gets shorter. The forty-minute pantrum or tantrum is now thirty minutes, now ten (holding there for a while), and now five minutes. That's still a long five minutes, but it is a positive change. In a moment, I will explain why this is and how you can exploit this phenomenon. The first thing to change in your child's upset behavior pattern will be the duration of those events.

The next thing to change will be how frequently the big reactions occur. You will notice that the events, the big reactions, occur less often: once a week instead of once a day, once a month instead of once a week, and so on.

The very last thing to change about a big reaction, however, is its intensity. This is very important to remember. If the big reactions are getting briefer and further apart in time, your efforts are paying off. Also remember, there's likely to be an intense big reaction waiting to happen at some point in the future. If it's still relatively brief and it's been a while since the last one, there's no need to panic. It may be distressing, but it's still a good trend. No need to abandon your campaign. Trust me on this.

The reason I think the intensity is the last thing to change is that the intensity is driven by biology; the immediate reaction is not under your child's control, neither in terms of whether or not it happens, nor in terms of how intense it will be. You may get a small one, you may get a big one. In time, it's true; the intensity of your child's reactions will diminish. This will be helped along by brain maturation and his own self-regulation skills. But in the initial phases of your behavior change campaign, be prepared for some wild rides.

Big reactions will become less frequent because you and your child will be gaining new skills for managing situations well. This will increase his sense of security and help lower the "trigger point" of his fight-or-flight reaction so that he can be more resilient in the face of situations that might ordinarily provoke anxiety. Confidence, based on his experiences with competence, eventually will make it so that he, and you, needn't be anxious about being anxious.

The decrease in duration, the first thing that reliably changes, will come from your targeting the back end of big reactions rather than trying to avoid them altogether. By "back end" I mean the point *after* your child's big-reaction emotions and behavior have shown up; this is the critical point when you need to decide very quickly how you're going to respond. What you will practice doing is catching yourself falling into your reactions, your old unhelpful dance, however that looks for you and your child. You will practice making the choice to alter what you're doing and take things in a more effective direction. Instead of moving into the escape-avoidance dance, you'll work toward learning a new dance routine, the effectiveness dance, where you assess the situation—activator, behavior, consequence—and then respond rather than react. Responding effectively draws on the various strategies, skills, and techniques we've discussed—simple awareness and validation, encouraging a social skill that is needed in that moment, framing or otherwise creating a bigger context—whatever the situation calls for that is in keeping with your values and goals. In this way, you will see the big reactions, the anxious upsets, become briefer and eventually less frequent and less intense. When your child is deep in anxiety, the best you can sometimes hope for is to emphasize basic process goals such as communication and cooperation. The dance doesn't even have to go well as long as you and your child make the effort to be aware of what you're thinking, feeling, and choosing. Hopefully what you both choose is to make the dance just a little more effective than last time; everyone is heard, everyone is respected, everyone takes responsibility for their actions, everyone works together.

Your job in that moment of high emotion is not to be perfectly calm and rational and only say and do the right things. Your job is to have your own reaction, notice that you're having it, and then do something obvious to change it for the better. For example, Abby's mother, Catherine, becomes very angry that Abby clings to her leg and refuses to join the other girls at the party. Because she is a sensitive child and they have done this dance before, Abby surely knows that her mother is upset even if Abby cannot articulate that in her own mind. It's just mutual distress. Catherine will notice that she becomes physically tense and starts to push Abby away even before that thought is formed in her mind. Catherine notices she is thinking about pulling Abby out of that situation. Catherine takes a few breaths.

Thinking Out Loud: Three Steps for Parenting Your Anxious Child

Catherine's second move, after noticing what's she doing and remembering to breathe, is to start thinking out loud. She will use clear and age-appropriate words and phrases to describe what is going on as she sees it and how Abby may see it: "Here we are at a birthday party. All these kids are so excited. They're running around having a good time and making *a lot of noise* [puts some intensity into her voice; whole-body validation]. I'm feeling all the *excitement* too [less threatening experience than fear]. I'm wondering if you're feeling a little scared along with all the excitement [validation]. Do you think we can sit over there on the couch and just watch for a little while before you join the kids? [Suggests an alternative coping response and an outcome goal, "joining the kids."]

Thinking out loud gives your child a window into how these situations work out. Here are the steps to remember:

1. Step back.

2. Consider the situation and what's going on inside you and your child.

3. Come up with ideas about how to cope or solve the problem.

The process is often not pretty, and it can be confusing and distressing. But by thinking out loud, you help both you and your child get the message that dealing with situations like this is not about never feeling bad; it's about recognizing what the situation calls for and doing your best in spite of what you think and feel at the moment. It's about communicating effectively with others and even with yourself. It's about using supple language, your relationship with your child, and social skills to forge ahead toward your goals—both yours and your child's.

SUMMARY AND A LOOK AHEAD

In this chapter, I have described strategies for managing the more challenging situations you may face as the parent of an anxious child. Implementing these strategies is hard work. It requires near-constant awareness of what is going on out in the world as well as inside you and your child. It means managing tolerance by creating an appropriate amount of psychological space between you and your child—leaning in or leaning back depending on the needs of the situation and of your child. It also requires letting your child experience some of what is going on with you so that he can learn that effectiveness in life does not come from never having problems or challenges but from prevailing in the face of them.

Many of the parenting strategies I have covered in this book, especially in this chapter, seem quite general and may seem only somewhat related to dealing with anxiety. The fact is that the overall quality of functioning in the home, the overall tone of transactions among family members (especially between parenting partners), greatly impacts the security and emotional development of all the members of the family (especially the children). Overall anxiety levels tend to be lower in homes in which family members are treated well and feel heard, where communication is effective, where life is reasonably predictable, and where people can roll with it when it's not.

The key to parenting an anxious child lies in balancing the many and sometimes competing goals you have as a parent: your child's security, growth, and needs for your involvement, management, support, and love—as well as your own needs for love, growth, and restoration when you become drained. Having a good sense of what you value, and making these values an explicit part of your goal setting and decision making, will help you and your child sort through the possibilities when a complex and emotionally charged situation appears.

As this book comes to a close, you may have noticed that we haven't exactly "cured" Abby, Joshua, Sterling, or Beth. It's likely they, and their parents with them, will continue to struggle with anxious situations for some time to come because life, especially life lived fully, can be a frightening and worrisome place. These children may benefit from individual psychotherapy now or when they are a little older. Their parents might seek out coaching from a psychologist or other mental health professional. Medications may be helpful at some point. The central goal of any treatment campaign should be living a vital and effective life and creating mutually supportive and loving relationships with those around them, and not merely the reduction of anxious thoughts and feelings. As they grow and look back on how far they've come, what we hope each of them will remember is not that life was without worries or troubles, but that they were understood, that problems could be worked through, and that others will help them if they treat others well.

What you can hope for is that the hard work of awareness, acceptance, validation, communication, patience, tolerance, and cooperation will relieve your future anxious situations of much of their tension, frustration, and conflict. You and your child will find you no longer have to be anxious about being anxious when you experience your various anxious, frustrated, and impatient thoughts and feelings in a new context, one that recognizes thoughts and feelings as transient phenomena that have some imperfect relationship with reality. Your child will find that much possibility lies outside the confines of his habitual ways of thinking and behaving. Your child will find that experience, his own or a trusted other's, can be relied on and used to guide his choices and help him keep to his commitments.

I hope that I have given you some new ways of thinking about your child's anxiety and how the "problem" of anxiety can seen in a new light, one that honors and dignifies the hard work you and your child engage in every day. I hope I have given you some tools to make that work more vital, effective, and rewarding. It has been my privilege to do so.

References

American Psychiatric Association. 1994. *Diagnostic and Statistical Manual of Mental Disorders*, 4th ed. Washington, DC: American Psychiatric Association.

Barkley, R. A., and C. M. Benton. 1998. *Your Defiant Child.* New York: Guilford Press.

Camus, A. 1956. *The Rebel.* New York: Vintage Books.

Cohn, J. F., and E. Z. Tronick. 1988. Mother-infant face-to-face interaction: Influence is bidirectional and unrelated to periodic cycles in either partner's behavior. *Developmental Psychology* 24(3):386–392.

Connolly, S. D., G. A. Bernstein, and the Work Group on Quality Issues. 2007. Practice parameters for the assessment and treatment of children and adolescents with anxiety disorders. *Journal of the American Academy of Child & Adolescent Psychiatry* 46(2):267–283.

Curtis, S. E. 2008. *Understanding Your Child's Puzzling Behavior.* Bainbridge Island, WA: Lifespan Press.

Dacey, J. S., and L. B. Fiore. 2000. *Your Anxious Child: How Parents and Teachers Can Relieve Anxiety in Children.* San Francisco: Jossey-Bass.

Diamond, G., and A. Josephson. 2005. Family-based treatment research: A 10-year update. *Journal of Child and Adolescent Psychiatry* 44(9):872–887.

Dumas, J. E. 2005. Mindfulness-based parent training: Strategies to lessen the grip of automaticity in families with disruptive children. *Journal of Clinical Child and Adolescent Psychiatry* 34(4):779–791.

Eifert, G. H., and J. P. Forsyth. 2005. *Acceptance and Commitment Therapy for Anxiety Disorders*. Oakland, CA: New Harbinger Publications.

Fonagy, P., M. Steele, H. Steele, T. Leigh, R. Kennedy, G. Mattoon, and M. Target. 1995. Attachment, the reflective self, and borderline states: The predictive specificity of the Adult Attachment Interview and pathological emotional development. In S. Goldberg, R. Muir, and J. Kerr (eds.), *Attachment Theory: Social, Developmental and Clinical Perspectives*. New York: Analytic Press.

Fonagy, P., and M. Target. 2000. Playing with reality: III. The persistence of dual psychic reality in borderline patients. *International Journal of Psychoanalysis* 81:53–873.

Ginsburg, G. S., and M. C. Schlossberg. 2002. Family-based treatment of childhood anxiety disorders. *International Review of Psychiatry* 14:143–154.

Gottman, J. 1997. *Raising an Emotionally Intelligent Child*. New York: Fireside.

Gross, J. J., and R. W. Levenson. 1997. Hiding feelings: The acute effects of inhibiting negative and positive emotion. *Journal of Abnormal Psychology* 106(1):95–103.

Gunaratana, B. H. 2002. *Mindfulness in Plain English*. Boston: Wisdom Publications.

Hayes, S. C., K. Strosahl, and K. G. Wilson. 1999. *Acceptance and Commitment Therapy: An Experiential Approach to Behavior Change*. New York: Guilford Press.

Hayes, S. C., K. G. Wilson, K. Strosahl, E. V. Gifford, and V. M. Follette. 1996. Experiential avoidance and behavioral disorders: A functional dimensional approach to diagnosis and treatment. *Journal of Consulting and Clinical Psychology* 64:1152–1168.

Hildebrandt, M. J., L. B. Fletcher, and S. C. Hayes. 2007. Climbing anxiety mountain: Generating metaphors in acceptance and commitment therapy. In G. W. Burns (ed.), *Healing with Stories: Your Casebook Collection for Using Therapeutic Metaphors*. Hoboken, NJ: Wiley.

Jackson, N. F., D. A. Jackson, and C. Monroe. 1993. *Getting Along with Others: Teaching Social Effectiveness to Children*. Champaign, IL: Research Press.

Kabat-Zinn, J. 1994. *Wherever You Go, There You Are: Mindfulness Meditation in Everyday Life*. New York: Hyperion.

Kessler, R. C., P. Berglund, O. Demler, R. Jin, K. R. Merikangas, and E. E. Walters. 2005. Lifetime prevalence and age-of-onset distributions of *DSM-IV* disorders in the National Comorbidity Survey Replication. *Archives of General Psychiatry* 62(6):593–602.

Merriam-Webster. 2003. *Merriam-Webster's Collegiate Dictionary*. Springfield, MA: Merriam-Webster.

Minuchin, S. 1981. *Family Therapy Techniques*. Cambridge, MA: Harvard University Press.

Mogel, W. 2001. *The Blessing of a Skinned Knee*. New York: Scribner.

Muris, P., H. Merckelbach, B. Gadet, and V. Moulaert. 2000. Fears, worries, and scary dreams in 4- to 12-year-old children: Their content, developmental pattern, and origins. *Journal of Clinical Child Psychology* 29(1):43–52.

Oxford Dictionaries. 2008. *Oxford's Pocket American Dictionary of Current English*. New York: Oxford University Press, USA.

Rapee, R. M., S. H. Spence, V. Cobham, and A. Wignall. 2000. *Helping Your Anxious Child*. Oakland, CA: New Harbinger Publications.

Rizzolatti, G., and L. Craighero. 2004. The mirror neuron system. *Annual Review of Neuroscience* 2:169–192.

Scotti, J. R., T. L. Morris, C. B. McNeil, and R. P. Hawkins. 1996. *DSM–IV* and disorders of childhood and adolescence: Can structural criteria be functional? *Journal of Consulting and Clinical Psychology* 64:1177–1191.

Shafran, R., D. Thordarson, and S. Rachman. 1996. Thought-action fusion in obsessive compulsive disorder. *Journal of Anxiety Disorders* 5:379–391.

Siegel, D. J., and M. Hartzell. 2003. *Parenting from the Inside Out*. New York: Jeremy P. Tarcher/Penguin.

Turecki, S. 1985. *The Difficult Child*. New York: Bantam Books.

Turner, S. M., D. C. Beidel, and L. H. Epstein. 1991. Vulnerability and risk for anxiety disorders. *Journal of Anxiety Disorders* 5:151–166.

United States Census Bureau. *United States Census 2000*. Retrieved October 24, 2008, from http://www.census.gov/main/www/cen2000.html.

Vigilante, V. A., and R. G. Wahler. 2005. Covariations between mothers' responsiveness and their use of "do" and "don't" instructions: Implications for child behavior therapy. *Behavior Therapy* 36:207–212.

Wahler, R. G., and K. L. Meginnis. 1997. Strengthening child compliance through positive parenting practices: What works? *Journal of Clinical Child Psychology* 26(4):433–440.

Wilson, K. G., and T. DuFrene. 2009. *Mindfulness for Two*. Oakland, CA: New Harbinger Publications.

The Valued Living Questionnaire. Unpublished manuscript. Available from the first author at Department of Psychology, University of Mississippi, Oxford, MS.

Winner, M. G. 2002. *Thinking About You Thinking About Me*. San Jose, CA: Social Thinking Publishing.

Winnicott, D. W. 1965. *The Maturational Processes and the Facilitating Environment*. New York: International Universities Press.

Woods, S., J. Krystal, C. D'Amico, G. Heninger, and D. Charney. 1988. A review of behavioral and pharmacologic studies relevant to the application of CO_2 as a human subject model of anxiety. *Psychopharmacology Bulletin* 24:149–153.

Christopher McCurry, Ph.D., is a clinical child psychologist in private practice specializing in the treatment of childhood anxiety. He is a clinical assistant professor in the departments of psychology and psychiatry at the University of Washington in Seattle, WA.

Foreword writer **Steven C. Hayes, Ph.D.,** is University of Nevada Foundation Professor of Psychology at the University of Nevada, Reno. He is among the most influential figures in contemporary behaviorism and clinical psychology. He is the author of innumerable books and scientific articles, including the successful ACT workbook *Get Out of Your Mind and Into Your Life.*

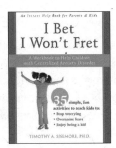

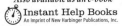